QUINOA

INTERPRETATIONS OF CULTURE IN THE NEW MILLENNIUM

Norman E. Whitten Jr., General Editor

A list of books in the series appears at the end of the book.

QUINOA

FOOD POLITICS and AGRARIAN LIFE
in the ANDEAN HIGHLANDS

LINDA J. SELIGMANN

UNIVERSITY OF
ILLINOIS PRESS
Urbana, Chicago, and Springfield

Publication of this book was supported in part by the
University of Illinois Press Fund for Anthropology.

Photos courtesy of the author unless otherwise noted.

© 2023 by the Board of Trustees
of the University of Illinois
All rights reserved
1 2 3 4 5 C P 5 4 3 2 1
♾ This book is printed on acid-free paper.

Cataloging data available from the Library of Congress
ISBN 9780252044793 (hardcover)
ISBN 9780252086885 (paperback)
ISBN 9780252053849 (ebook)

This book is dedicated to the memory of my father,
Albert L. Seligmann, to my mother, Barbara B. Seligmann,
as always to John and Mina,
and to my companions, teachers, and friends in Huanoquite.
Allinlla kawsakuychis *(May you live well)*.

Contents

Acknowledgments   ix

List of Acronyms and Initialisms   xiii

Introduction: Quinoa Prospects   1

PART ONE. BACKSTORIES: LAND STRUGGLES, THE ALLURE OF INFRASTRUCTURE, AND DEVELOPMENT DESIRES IN HUANOQUITE

1   Agrarian Reform, Revolution, and Reversals   31

2   The Power and Seduction of Infrastructure   43

3   Contesting Development, Alternative Paths   56

PART TWO. SOUP AND SUPERFOOD: THE POLITICS OF QUINOA PRODUCTION AND CONSUMPTION

4   The Expansion of Quinoa Production   77

5   Food Sovereignty, Food Security, and Sustainability   103

6   To Be Strong and Healthy   117

7   Voracious Consumption   144

Conclusion: Pragmatic Spirituality and Quinoa Desires   159

Notes 165

References 179

Index 193

Acknowledgments

The inspiration for this book emerged while I was working on a project documenting changes in the livelihoods of market women in Cusco, Peru. Tourism was booming, and businesses everywhere were celebrating Indigenous Quechua music, dress, and foods. Assorted snacks made from quinoa could be found in grocery stores and myriad window displays. And in the United States, quinoa was being heralded as a great food for all sorts of reasons. I began to wonder how Quechua cultivators of quinoa were experiencing this celebration of a crop they had grown for thousands of years that was now being promoted as an export commodity and a significant dimension of culinary tourism. A little to my surprise, when I returned for a visit to Huanoquite, where I had done many prior years of field research, a major quinoa-promotion project was underway. It led me to get to work puzzling out the hidden story that underpinned this transformative moment when a modest cultigen was being redefined as a major driver of future well-being. I could never have completed this project without the unwavering support, kindness, insights, and generosity of so many individuals and institutions. I am immensely grateful to the counsel of Michael Muse and the funding for this research provided by the Wenner-Gren Foundation for Anthropological Research. The people of Huanoquite have taught me, over many years, more than I can put into words, and I do not take their trust in me or my research lightly. When this book is translated into Spanish, I hope that it will serve as a source they can turn to as they determine which paths to take in order

Acknowledgments

to nurture their families and their livelihoods, and to protect their territory and water sources. In particular, I would like to thank Demetrio, Victoria, Deyvic, María Elena, and Rómulo for always making me feel welcome, no matter what, and the community and district authorities of Huanoquite for permitting me to undertake this research. The members of the Quinoa Cultivators Association as well as many nonmembers went out of their way to share with me their perspectives and practices. I expect they will recognize who they are, but for their own protection, I provide here only their first names: Agripino, Aleja, Andrés, Balbino, Demetrio, Domingo, Emilio, Erasmo, Ermenegildo, Ernesto, Felicia, Florencio, Francisco C., Francisco P., Fredi, Jidión, Guillermo, Hector, Hugo, Irene, Isabel, José Antonio, Juana, Julia, Julián, Julio, Justo, Juvenal, Lastenia, Leonardo, Leoncio, Lorenzo, Lucio, María, Margarita, Mario Eduardo, Martha, Miguel, Nilton, Paulina, Paulo, Pedro, Renato, Ricardo, Richard, Rolando, Rudolfo, Rufino, Sadith, Sara, Teodoro, Tomás, Valentín, Victor, and Zenovio. My thanks to engineer Rigoberto Estrada, director of the National Institute of Agricultural Innovation (INIA), and engineer Adrian Wendell Olivera Ayme, director of the Cusco Region Project for the Improvement of the Competitiveness of Organic Andean Quinoa and Cañehua, for permitting me to interview them and for their forthrightness in sharing with me their experiences working with the Cusco region quinoa project.

The hospitality of friends and colleagues in Cusco made a big difference to me. Jean-Jacques Decoster was amazing in his willingness to help others despite everything on his own plate, and he and Sara and Kori made me feel like I had a home away from home—delicious food, good company, and introductions to many others whom I never would have had a chance to meet otherwise. Bruce Mannheim and I have crossed paths many a time in Cusco, creating our own kind of ritual *tinku* and shared history—conversations and food and drink late into the night, and reflections on life, in general, and academia, in particular. Daniel Guevarra was my research assistant for my earlier work on markets and is now with the Sub-directorate of Interculturality, which is part of the Ministry of Culture in Cusco. Guevarra, his wife, Carla, and his mother, Julia Rodríguez Tamay, have always helped open doors for me in Cusco that I did not even know existed, and just as importantly, made me laugh and feel part of a family, again and again. Thanks also to Cecilia and Adriana Peralta, who offered me a comfortable place to stay while I was in Cusco; to Rosalía Puma Escalante, who assisted in providing me with quick and precise translations into Spanish of exchanges in Quechua that were recorded under challenging conditions, to say the least; and to Eliana Rivera, whose legal expertise on a domestic abuse case was invaluable.

Acknowledgments

The ups and downs of academic publishing are a challenge. Norman E. Whitten Jr. began the University of Illinois series Interpretations of Culture in the New Millennium, and he has sustained a lifelong commitment to scholarship on the Andes that has benefitted anthropologists across the world, including me. My book *Peruvian Street Lives* was the first one accepted for the series. This book on quinoa is being published as the series comes to an end. The close reading and constructive suggestions of the anonymous reviewers of this book have been of great help in making it more coherent and nuanced. Daniel Nasset was very excited about the initial project and helped shepherd my book through the review process and changes at the press with respect and responsiveness; Jennifer Argo and Mariah Mendes Schaefer did an excellent job of overseeing the editorial process and attending to my many questions; Ellen Hurst did a fine and meticulous job of copyediting my book; and Angela Burton, Jennifer Fisher, Emerald Oaks, and Roberta Sparenberg each made significant contributions to the publication process of this book. I owe Scott White a special thanks for his cartography skills and for bearing with me as he sought to produce accurate maps that relied on far fewer data sources than one would like for such a purpose. Many people took great interest in this book project. Special thanks are due to Sydney Silverstein for sharing her quinoa experiences with me and to Kevin Kinsella for taking the time to find his documents related to his early efforts to promote quinoa for domestic consumption in Peru.

While I was doing this *longue durée* fieldwork, our daughter Mina grew up. Always curious, always passionate about language, she has been a model for me of how to write lucidly and craft arguments carefully, and of never forgetting independence of thought and creativity. My husband John eagerly and bravely accompanied me to Huanoquite even though he does not speak Spanish or Quechua. A few of his fabulous photos grace this book, and he helped to prepare all the book's photos for publication. His observations and analytical bent challenged me to think harder about some of my own assumptions, and his companionship and presence helped make sure I stayed well on my first trip back to Huanoquite after five years. As I write these words, my mother, who is ninety-five years old, remains engaged and is eagerly awaiting the opportunity to read this book to satisfy her own intellectual thirst for understanding the world better; she is a great role model! Especially as the COVID-19 pandemic roared around the world, I felt lucky to be fortified, despite grieving the loss of friends and colleagues, by my family, including my sisters, Susan Seligmann-Moreno, Ann Lyons, and Wendy Seligmann.

I would like to extend my profound gratitude to Kathleen S. Fine-Dare. In facing our respective challenges, we became closer and have stuck with each

Acknowledgments

other through thick and thin. I have benefitted from our intellectual companionship and our personal friendship, which have endured and matured in good ways. I would also like to thank Ralph Bolton, who first introduced me to the Andean region when I was an undergraduate, and the students at George Mason University who were so enthusiastic when I taught my "Food and Culture" class. Many of them were refugees or immigrants, and the essays they wrote about food and family powerfully revealed their experiences of the entanglement of violence, loss, love, and food. Last but hardly least, Florence Babb, Ana Mariella Bacigalupo, Christine Harris Charest, Alma Gottlieb, Steve and Sally Herman, the "Lunch Bunch," Deborah Poole, and Susan Trencher are among the many people whose guidance and friendship I have benefitted from, and who have made life better for others.

List of Acronyms and Initialisms

AIQ	International Year of Quinoa (Año Internacional de Quinoa)
APEGA	Peruvian Society of Gastronomy (Sociedad Peruana de Gastronomía)
CBD	Convention on Biological Diversity
CDO	Certification of Denomination of Origin
CVR	Truth and Reconciliation Commission of Peru (La Comisión de la Verdad y Reconciliación del Perú)
FAO	Food and Agriculture Organization
FISE	Social Energy Inclusion Fund (Fondo de Inclusión Social Energético)
ILO	International Labor Organization
INDECOPI	National Consumer Protection Authority of Peru (Autoridad Nacional de Protección del Consumidor)
INIA	National Institute of Agricultural Innovation (Instituto Nacional de Innovación Agraria)
MIDIS	Ministry of Development and Social Inclusion (Ministerio de Desarrollo e Inclusión Social)
MINAGRI	Ministry of Agriculture and Irrigation (Ministerio de Agricultura y Riego)
MINCETUR	Ministry of Foreign Trade and Tourism (Ministerio de Comercio Exterior y Turismo)

List of Acronyms and Initialisms

OCM	Observatory of Mining Conflicts in Peru (Observatorio de Conflictos Mineros en el Perú)
PROMPERÚ	Commission for the Promotion of Peru for Export and Tourism (Comisión de Promoción del Perú para la Exportación y el Turismo)
QCA	Quinoa Cultivators Association
UNSAAC	National University of San Antonio Abad of Cusco (Universidad Nacional de San Antonio Abad del Cusco)

QUINOA

Introduction

Quinoa Prospects

In 2018, I returned to Huanoquite in the southern Andean highlands of Peru after a five-year hiatus, grateful that my journey, which had once taken eight to nine hours to make from Cusco, had only taken two. I had hardly caught my breath when my friend and *compadre* (fictive kin)[1] Lorenzo, who was also a well-respected farmer, strode up the road, exclaiming *"Comadre, biénvenido!"* ("Co-mother, welcome!"). After we embraced each other, he announced that we would go to harvest his quinoa (pronounced *keen-wa*) fields the next day in a place called Salvidayuq. I was exhausted, but Lorenzo asked if I wanted to take a look at the field that afternoon, so I went with him. His wife, Margarita, fragile and a little unsteady on her feet, met us there a little later. I had been told that she had been feeling unwell. We sat at the edge of the fields where Margarita shared thirst-quenching fruit with us. Marco, their grandson and my godchild, periodically set off bottle rockets to scare away the birds from the quinoa. Lorenzo walked the fields and confirmed that tomorrow was the day and that I should be at the house at 7:30 a.m. sharp.

The next day, along with eating, drinking, and working hard to harvest the quinoa with rarely a break, I listened as a lively discussion—most of it in Quechua—unfolded among the ten workers that Lorenzo had persuaded to help him out for a modest daily wage. Some of the conversation was about quinoa itself—complaints about the engineer who was supposed to teach them how to use a new piece of machinery but who had not shown up, the quality of the

Introduction

FIGURE 0.1. Lorenzo, member of the Quinoa Cultivators Association and my *compadre* (Photo taken by John R. Cooper)

harvest, and the effects of soil and weather on the quinoa—but most of the talk concerned the incursion of mines of all sorts (copper, gold, and iron) to the Huanoquite region. Some of the workers insisted that this incursion was a good thing because the Cusco Regional Government supported and invested in the mines and there was lots of work available in them. Others quietly commented that the mines would destroy their way of life because mercury and other poisons would leach into the soil and wreck the environment and the water on which Huanoquiteños depended. Still others conjectured that the mines would increase the population of Huanoquite as a result. Gold was on everyone's mind, it seemed. One man confided to the group that when he was younger, he had come across what he thought was sand. But when he picked it up and ran it through his fingers, it sparkled like gold. It turned out that it was gold, but when he went back to the same spot, it was gone, as was the sand. Another chimed in that gold nuggets would periodically appear in a nearby spring in Llaspay, one of Huanoquite's communities. And yet another soberly observed that along with the benefit of jobs at the mines, workers suffered terrible injuries from the machines they used. As we wended our way back to Huanoquite at dusk, one man whispered to me that most people in Huanoquite were opposed to the mines and were holding demonstrations and blockades against them. And several workers remarked that the fields were "cold" because after growing quinoa, other crops such as barley would not grow in them.

2

FIGURE 0.2. Sharing a meal at noon break by edge of quinoa fields

Lorenzo's quinoa harvest piqued my curiosity because it seemed to be about so much more than sowing and harvesting a food crop for purposes of consumption and exchange on the market. It quickly become apparent to me that the cultivation of quinoa (*Chenopodium quinoa* Willd.) was part of a panoply of initiatives and projects unfolding in the district that had a long history. Quinoa entered the vocabulary of Westerners and their dietary palate as a superfood in the twenty-first century, long after its incorporation into the diet of Andean highland peoples, around seven thousand years ago. A native seed, it has been celebrated as "an exquisite grain" that, tiny as it is, contains a remarkably high percentage of protein, important amino acids, minerals, and vitamins. It has surged in popularity, hand in hand with a passionate preoccupation among many westerners with the properties of foods they ingest and how they affect their personal physical and mental health and contribute to environmental sustainability.

To give readers an idea of quinoa's growing popularity, Peru's quinoa exports went from approximately 18.67 million kilograms of quinoa with an export value of $79.5 million in 2013, rising to almost 49.5 million kilograms with an export value of almost $137 million in 2019. It is the world's largest exporter of quinoa, and in 2019, nearly 37 percent of its production was bound for the United States, followed by the European Union. Bolivia was the second largest exporter of quinoa, following close behind Peru. In 2019 Peru accounted for over 55 percent (89,775 metric tons) of the global production volume of quinoa, which was approximately 161,000 metric tons.[2]

FIGURE 0.3. Quinoa plants growing (Photo taken by John R. Cooper)

The Peruvian government and nongovernmental organizations (NGOs) have worked hard to promote quinoa as a nontraditional export since as early as 2006, and with heightened enthusiasm in 2013 when the Food and Agriculture Organization of the United Nations named Peru's then first lady Nadine Heredia and Bolivia's then president Evo Morales as Special Ambassadors for the International Year of Quinoa. In Huanoquite, where I did my research, quinoa had always been grown as a minor yet cherished cultigen, but global demand for it had led state agencies and NGOs to herald it as future "gold" for those living in the countryside. The Peruvian government began encouraging the establishment of quinoa cultivator associations in many highland communities, targeting both men and women. For the farmers of Huanoquite, quinoa constituted their first experience cultivating a nontraditional export crop, and like many Quechua inhabitants of the Andean highlands, they welcomed the prospect of expanding its cultivation for the global market. Yet the story turned out to be far more complicated, with many challenges.

I began this book project to understand what happened when quinoa went from being a minor crop to a major export commodity in Huanoquite, but I soon found myself asking bigger questions that I address in this book: What ways are Indigenous inhabitants living in Andean highland communities confronting the consequences of the relentless demands of neoliberal globalization? How have they adapted to these demands?[3] Not surprisingly, the answers to these questions are neither wholly negative nor wholly positive. The mechanisms of adaptation that Huanoquiteños have pursued to perpetuate their agrarian livelihoods have included a wide range of new initiatives to supplement and complement their agricultural production while pushing back against development projects that show little or no understanding of the dynamics of their economic, cultural, and political lives and values. They have taken advantage of the benefits of becoming folkloric icons, especially for tourists, while trying not to ignore the mountain, water, and earth entities that they must vigorously attend to, to provide balance in their world. They have turned to exhausting and unstable transnational migration while funneling back into the district new kinds of knowledge and experiences they can use for their own purposes, including as weapons to confront state and bureaucratic machinations. They have organized, from time to time, into complex, heterogeneous, and dispersed social movements, and they have elaborated innovative kinship ties for purposes of expanding their communities beyond a diminishing agrarian land base and/or Indigenous territory. I posit that these adaptive mechanisms "work" for them but have also taken tolls on their well-being that are not just economic but also affective. There is an extractive dimension to them that has resulted in a more precarious livelihood than Huanoquiteños openly articulate. The most sobering prospect looming over Huanoquiteños has been the establishment of mining concessions and mining near them that would permanently create an unhealthy state of being for them and their world and whose effects go far beyond their ability to cultivate quinoa for a global market.

The pages that follow shed light on how food politics, development initiatives, and Huanoquiteños' agrarian history have intervened in the expansion of their quinoa production and how the expansion of quinoa production has affected the place and power of men and women in Huanoquite's households and communities, including those of brokers who have mediated quinoa's promotion and marketing. Ingesting food is about more than satisfying hunger. The meanings and feelings people associate with quinoa's production and consumption diverge, partly in accordance with assumptions that structure how they view their place in the world and in the cosmos. The interactions and intersubjectivities that have emerged among cultivators and consumers of quinoa, some of whom are Indigenous, others of whom are not, illuminate important differences in how people are situated in the cosmos and the economic and political forces that structure that cosmos. These differences bear on deeper and more fraught questions, such as the best ways to achieve well-being in the universe.

A final subject of this volume—the establishment of mining concessions near Huanoquite—might seem, at first glance, somewhat removed from the topic of quinoa in the Andes but is on everyone's mind because the ability of Huanoquiteños to perpetuate their agrarian livelihoods stands in the balance, given the potential environmental destructiveness of the mines. Hence, this is a story not only about quinoa but also about the broader ramifications of activities that constitute the economic and political regimes of our lives today, including the interactions among productive and extractive undertakings and the point at which a productive activity becomes extractive.

The District of Huanoquite: A Brief Overview and History

I began my first fieldwork in the southern Andean highland district of Huano-quite in 1984. Located in the Cusco region of Peru in the province of Paruro, it was renowned for its agriculture. At the time, I was interested in learning about farmers who had come to be recognized and respected by fellow villagers as knowledge brokers and how they acquired and disseminated their knowledge and practices related to agrarian activities. Most of the district's inhabitants spoke Quechua and considered themselves Indigenous. Over the years, I periodically returned there to do follow-up work on other topics and to visit people, many of whom had become good friends and some, compadres.

Located at 3,402 msl. (meters above sea level), Huanoquite is the second-largest district in the province of Paruro, comprised of nineteen communities and two annexes, with a total estimated population of 5,775 (see Maps 1 and 2).[4] Home mainly to Quechua-speaking farmers for centuries, it attracted many Spanish-speaking landed estate owners (*hacendados*) from the inception of the arrival of the Spanish conquistadors in the late 1500s onward. Most of its inhabitants speak and understand Spanish, but the preference, even among younger people, is to talk among themselves in Quechua.[5] The district is blessed with plentiful irrigation and a wide range of microecological zones in terms of altitude, light, soil, and slope, making it optimal for growing multiple varieties of quinoa and permitting households to diversify their crop production across the annual growing cycle. It has long been considered a major breadbasket for the entire Cusco region, and Huanoquiteños fondly refer to their home as "Cusco's little food dispensary."

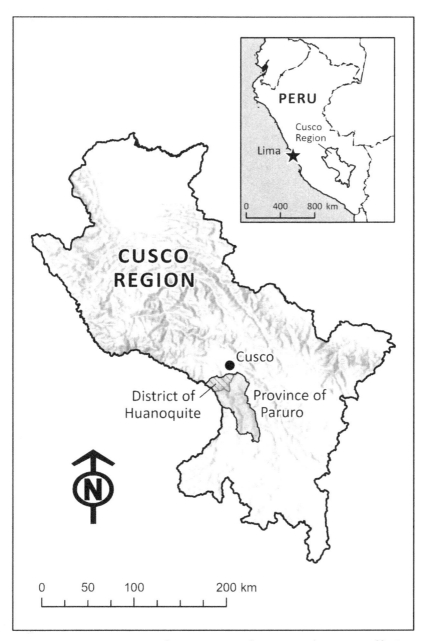

MAP 1. Cusco Region, Province of Paruro, District of Huanoquite (Map prepared by Scott White). Data sources: Esri, Inc., UNOCHA HDX, Instituto Geográfico Nacional (IGN).

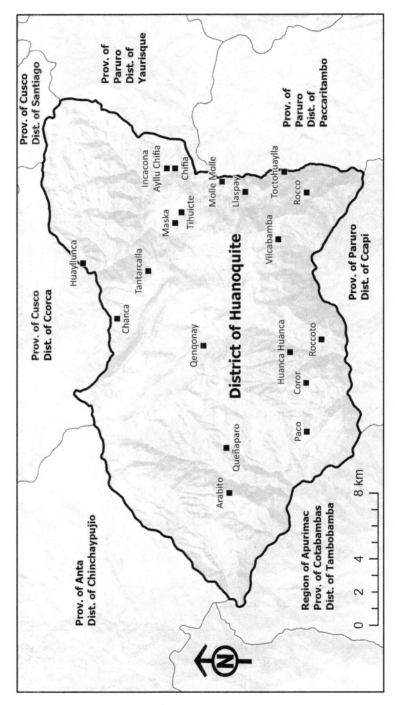

MAP 2. Communities of Huanoquite and neighboring provinces and regions (Map prepared by Scott White). Data sources: Esri, Inc, UNOOCHA HDX, Instituto Geográfico Nacional (IGN), Latlong.net, Seligmann 1995.

These qualities have made it an ideal site for experimenting with expanding quinoa cultivation, and it has now become the main quinoa-producing district in Paruro. Most households market part of their produce and purchase goods from the market to supplement what they cultivate. Cusco is a major marketing nexus and easily accessible from Huanoquite. In addition, wholesalers traveled from Arequipa and Cusco to Huanoquite to buy up quinoa and other agricultural products. Huanoquiteños also traveled extensively nationally and internationally, especially to Arequipa, Lima, Juliaca, Puno, Quillabamba, Maldonado, and Tingo María, and to Spain, Italy, Chile, Brazil, Bolivia, and Argentina.

At the outset, I want to say a few words about the terms that I use to refer to the main subjects of this account. The process of deciding on an appropriate system of terminology with which to refer to Huanoquite's inhabitants reveals the multifaceted ways that past, present, and future collide and inflect one another in a fluid and entangled fashion. Terms like *Indigenous* and *non-Indigenous* are problematic because they suggest dichotomies that are hardly clear-cut and certainly not apparent from the physical appearance of inhabitants alone. From the early days of the Spanish invasion onward, mixing took place between Indigenous Quechua inhabitants of the Andes and the Spanish, so distinguishing clearly between them rapidly became impossible. Here I have decided to use *Indigenous* and *non-Indigenous* in a sociocultural and political fashion to distinguish those who embrace Indigenous practices, values, and

FIGURE 0.4. Center of the District of Huanoquite

Introduction

FIGURE 0.5. Diverse production zones of Huanoquite

beliefs, even as they incorporate non-Indigenous ones and make them into their own, on the one hand, and those who not only embrace non-Indigenous practices, values, and beliefs but also frequently denigrate Indigenous inhabitants, on the other hand. That is, the expression and exercise of racial discrimination is, to a large extent, built into the distinction. Even so, there is no easy way to avoid the pitfalls of essentialism. In order to take advantage of tourists' desires to interact with Indigenous culture, for example, a wide range of people may perform Indigeneity for economic gain; some of these people have roots in Indigenous communities, and others have none and, in fact, may have no affinity for Indigenous culture or lifeways. Or Indigenous people may enact an idealized Indigeneity for purposes of mobilizing politically and gaining the attention of the international community to defend their resources and territory; that idealized projection of Indigeneity may become incorporated into their sense of who they are and their history.[6] In a somewhat contrasting vein, some Indigenous inhabitants may be far from fluent speakers of Quechua but embrace their Indigenous heritage. Regardless of the terms used, differences exist among Huanoquite's inhabitants. Indigenous people are not monolithic, and in the case of Huanoquiteños, they themselves deploy these terms and personas for their own purposes. There is a fluidity to identity that uneasily coexists with categorical labels. Given these complexities, throughout the book, I will use the terms *Huanoquiteños* or *Indigenous Quechua inhabitants* to refer to those who consider themselves Indigenous, either within Huanoquite or, more generally, in the Andean highlands. Similarly, I will use *non-Indigenous Huanoquiteños* or *non-Indigenous inhabitants* to refer to those who do not consider themselves Indigenous. The terminology is intended to draw attention to individuals who embrace the kinds of distinctions I have specified above. Among the most useful discussions of ethnic and racial relationships in the Andes are those of Bourricaud (1970), Cotler (2013), De la Cadena (2000), Larson and Harris (1995), Quijano (1980), Seligmann (1989), and Wade (2010). It is also important to understand that most, but not all, Huanoquiteños are also peasants (*campesinos*). Their relatively small landholdings provide for their household's needs, and the majority sell a part of what they produce on the market.

A second conundrum for me as an ethnographer has been the question of whether or not to identify my interlocutors. All of them gave me permission to interview them and take photos of them. Some of them—mostly non-Indigenous Huanoquiteños or organizational representatives in Cusco—were also public figures. In addition, a General Assembly of elected community authorities from throughout the district voted to permit me to pursue this research and the district's mayor signed a formal document to that effect. Nevertheless, I know that communities are fractious and politics can be dangerous. Hence, I have used pseudonyms for my interlocutors, although I have identified well-known public officials who consented to interviews with me.

Development and the Projection of Development

The story of quinoa raises questions about what development means for Huanoquiteños and for agents of the state and NGO personnel. It illuminates why particular projects and policies are initiated, who catalyzes them, who benefits from them and why, and what values are at stake. Many quinoa-growing communities of the Andean highland have encountered conditions like those I found in Huanoquite. Agrarian reform; subsequent measures to reprivatize land; infrastructural modernization and construction projects of roads, health posts, and educational centers; the entrenchment of neoliberalism; and the promotion of extractive economies as an engine of national growth were among the most important general forces and events that had contributed to the form and content that development projects and policies had taken in Huanoquite. The assumptions that catalyzed development projects in Huanoquite had embedded within them attitudes about food, hunger, race, gender, and progress. Many of these projects showed little understanding of the livelihoods and values of

Indigenous people of the Andean highlands; at their worst, they represented a distressing continuity with prior racist and gender-biased projects in which Quechua people's lives were expendable even when their images might be valued commodities for consumption. All these attitudes made their appearance in Huanoquite, alongside some genuine efforts of NGOs to adapt their projects and expectations to the reality of Huanoquiteños' lives. Huanoquiteños also undertook their own projects that often unfolded with more success.

Edward Fischer and Peter Benson (2006), in their ethnography of the global export of broccoli grown by Maya farmers in Guatemala, discuss the ambivalence of desire and moral projects among them. My own understanding of how development dynamics colored life in Huanoquite conforms to Fischer and Benson's argument that contradictions within the spheres of economic production and consumption are mediated by moral discourses—those of development agents, Huanoquiteños themselves across generation, gender, and class divides, and by ethnographers with their own research agendas (like me). While researchers—through their moral projects—may seek to discern and explain the dangers of globalized economies, for example, they may inadvertently ignore the experiences that structure the daily lives, desires, and profound concerns of the people with whom they work (Fischer and Benson 2006, 17). Huanoquiteños simultaneously held out hope and desire that infrastructural and development projects introduced to their communities would improve their lives while recognizing that their past experiences with such projects had been negative, or at least less than satisfactory, in achieving constructive transformations for themselves and their communities. In documenting the long history of development initiatives in Huanoquite—including the most recent efforts to expand quinoa cultivation for the global market—I try to show the kinds of contradictory desires and aspirations embedded in development projects and what their moral implications might be. I also try to hold at arm's length some of my own more pejorative perceptions of prior development initiatives with which I was familiar, in order to better listen to, observe, and convey what my interlocutors felt.

Nourishment, Knowledge, and the Food Politics of Quinoa

Over the centuries, Huanoquite has regularly attracted interest from outsiders because of its remarkable diversity of ecological zones and its proximity to the city of Cusco, ancient capital of the Incas and tourist mecca. In learning about quinoa's physical characteristics, hearing about farmers' experiences growing it, and talking with women about how they processed, cooked, and marketed it, I realized that, in addition to taking account of the long history of development projects in the district, I needed to better grasp the ways quinoa was understood and embraced as both a soup and superfood. The relationships between food and culture have long intrigued anthropologists who recognize that food nourishes the body, and simultaneously expresses, reflects, and sometimes challenges class, ethnic, and gender ideologies. Contradictory historical and cultural experiences and imaginaries are expressed through food in particular contexts. Quechua women have long overseen quinoa foodways, including its arduous processing prior to use, and they have helped to select quinoa varietals that are best suited for the purpose to which they will be put, whether for food, ritual meals, flour, beer, medicinal remedies, barter, retail exchanges, or regional market transactions. Although quinoa has rarely been a central component of Indigenous meals but rather a complement—in contrast to potatoes, for example, which are a staple of Andean highland communities (and Huanoquite is famous for its potatoes)—it is regarded as quintessentially Quechua and a gauge of women's contributions to the well-being of their households, especially when it is consumed as a soup or beverage. Too often there has been a disregard for the power and knowledge of women and relationships of gender, even when women exert political agency and are "central to rural life and the production and consumption of foods" (Andrée et al. 2014b, 28). Thus, in addition to learning what the agricultural and economic effects of the rise in quinoa cultivation were, I look at the place quinoa occupied in meals, nourishment, and reciprocal labor exchanges in the Andes. I talked to Indigenous women about their views of quinoa as a food, sat in the kitchen with them as they prepared and served it, and compared their relationships to quinoa with those of nonproducers of quinoa inside and outside of Peru.

What is quinoa as a food? Scholars in the field of critical food studies have looked at the effects that the growing demand for Indigenous and "healthy" food products from across the globe, such as quinoa, have wrought on producers and consumers alike. Debates revolve around whether the demand for foods produced from native crops such as quinoa have resulted in the improvement of the standard of living of those who grow them; who controls the marketing of these products; how value is added to them across commodity chains; and what happens when national governments and private corporations invoke, manipulate, and encourage the circulation of images of Indigeneity, whether for purposes of encouraging consumption of Indigenous food products or for promoting tourism in general.[7] Even as the state, often in tandem with international and transnational entities such as the International Monetary Fund (IMF) and the World Bank, as well as corporations have implemented

Introduction

neoliberal globalization measures which encourage export-based economies, a move away from food production for domestic consumption, and mono-cultivation, these policies take place in the context of local knowledge, needs, interests, and pressures—what Peter Andrée et al. call "localized globalism." We therefore need to document the concrete ways that these policies are "adopted, adapted, or resisted in multiple ways, and with what kinds of impacts" since they are almost always "contested processes, and small-scale or subsistence farmers are far from disappearing" (Andrée et al. 2014a, 4).

These studies also raise important concerns about satisfying international demand for "miracle" foods like quinoa, which are described in scientific and biomedical terms, and simultaneously encouraging their domestic consumption in the interest of improving local health and nutrition (McDonell 2015). Development initiatives pay lip service to improving the health of Indigenous communities and may, at times, move beyond rhetoric, instituting instructional seminars or food programs, but their health improvement projects, rather than addressing deeper causes of hunger and undernourishment, frequently focus most of their attention on women, whom they expect to learn to prepare and serve foods with specific micronutrients. In turn, this creates an additional burden on women, holding them responsible for the health and nutrition of their families.

Aya Hirata Kimura (2013) has persuasively argued that the emphasis on "charismatic nutrients" as a stimulus to create demand and encourage the marketing and consumption of specific foods is one aspect of global economic neoliberalism. This kind of focus on healthful nutrients breaks down food products into distinct components and assumes that the onus of not providing proper nutritional elements rests on households and, more narrowly, on mothers, rather than on causes of inequality that prevent robust health. Kimura found that these kinds of assumptions have caused international donors to focus on the dyad of mother-child "as a scientific necessity" to reduce hunger and supply children with proper nutrition, and to increase the surveillance of mothers and their bodies and hold them responsible for meeting their children's nutritional needs. Women are often held responsible for "the lack" of iron, protein, or calcium in their children's diet. Viewing hunger in this way is easier as a policy than recognizing and arriving at ways to deal with the many other variables that intervene in the nutritional status of households (Kimura 2013, 32). Kimura puts it well when she contrasts the satisfaction of viewing lack of food as something that can be rectified through simply providing the right nutrients and the much thornier problem of dealing with questions of access to land, environmental degradation, patriarchy, systemic racism and marginalization, and the pressures to pursue monocropping, for example. In her words, while the image of hunger "as a matter of missing nutrients can be institutionally and culturally appealing because of its simplicity, that very simplicity belies the much messier reality of the global food problem. Falling outside the aura of charisma are less glamorous actors and multiple layers of problems that pervade the world food system" (2013, 21).

The attention to quinoa as a "healthy" food because of its micronutrients has also raised concerns among political activists and scholars who argue that the surge in demand for quinoa internationally has made it unaffordable to those who grow it and as has been true of many other export crops, led to a reduction in the varieties of quinoa that farmers are growing. These effects could bode ill for Quechua inhabitants who have, through experimentation in different microenvironmental conditions over the centuries, introduced at least three thousand landraces of quinoa and about one hundred cultivars (Gamwell and Howland 2017). Rojas et al. (2015) document that, according to the FAO, there are globally more than 16,263 *ex situ* accessions of the genus *Chenopodium*, including quinoa, its wild variants, and related species, in fifty-nine genebanks across thirty-nine countries (56). This is one reason why it is so important to connect the dots between the global celebration of Indigenous foods and the agrarian world and lives that have produced them over millennia.[8]

Whether we have at our disposal exact numbers or not, it is the case that Indigenous inhabitants of the Andes have adapted quinoa, a remarkably versatile cultigen, to a dizzying number of water, soil, altitudinal, and weather conditions, as well as taste preferences (See, for example, Andrews 2017; Bazile 2015; Gamwell and Howland 2017; and Urdanivia 2014). There has always been confusion about the difference between crop *varieties* and *landraces*. Deborah Andrews offers some clarity on this, explaining that a landrace is a local variety of a domesticated plant species that has developed largely through adaptation to the natural and cultural environment in which it lives. It differs from a cultivar, which has been selectively bred to conform to a particular standard of characteristics as a variety. Landrace populations are often variable in appearance, but they can be identified by their appearance and have a certain genetic similarity. Landraces have a continuity with improved varieties. The relatively high level of genetic variation of landraces is one of the advantages that these can have over improved varieties. Although yields may not be as high, the stability of landraces in the face of adverse conditions is typically high. As a result, new pests or diseases may affect some but not all the individuals in the population (Andrews 2017, 19). This matters as, increasingly, quinoa is promoted for export and more emphasis placed on quinoa cultivators to produce improved varieties rather than landrace populations for the international market.

Production and Extraction

The promotion of quinoa and the expansion of its production must take account of the complicated ways in which Huanoquiteños' livelihood activities involve at one and the same time productive and extractive dimensions. The willingness of the Peruvian government to grant mining concessions to transnational corporations in regions proximate to Huanoquite has meant that the very foundation of agrarian life in Huanoquite is being threatened due to the pollution of water sources and the destruction to roads and fields because of mining traffic. Further, as Eric Hirsch (2022) eloquently describes, based on his research in the Arequipa region of Peru, many governmental or parastatal-NGO development initiatives proposed for purposes of production or tourism—activities that on the surface seemed constructive—turned out to catalyze the excessive extraction of Indigenous inhabitants' time, labor, and even their identities. This could readily be seen among Huanoquiteños who participated in the Quinoa Cultivators Association (QCA) and a number of other top-down development projects. I found that their capacity to adapt to conditions of late capitalism, neoliberalism, and tourism prospects—often celebrated—resulted too often in sacrifices and negative consequences for them. These consequences included the exacerbation of gender and income inequalities, exploitative labor practices, the narrowing of landraces they cultivated because of pressures to satisfy export demands, and the exhaustive burden of taking on excessive risks that led to anxiety and struggles to recover from failure.

Pragmatic Spirituality: Living and Engaging in Cosmopolitics

In telling the story of quinoa in Huanoquite, I wanted to better understand how Huanoquiteños saw themselves in the world, and more broadly, how they conceptualized the universe and their place(s) in it. These are questions of ontology that have received renewed attention from scholars doing research on Indigenous Quechua political thinking and mobilization.[9] In her research, Marisol de la Cadena (2010, 2015) found, as have others (e.g., Allen 2002), that Indigenous Quechua people considered themselves part of a universe inhabited by sentient beings, whether the beings had a tangible materiality in the form of earth, rock outcroppings, mountains, plants, or springs or a more intangible presence, as deceased ancestors or light, for example. These power beings, places, and objects are called *wacas* in Quechua. For many Huanoquiteños, their well-being depended on their capacity to operate within, tap into, and engage in reciprocal relationships with the powers of the universe, which included human sentient beings and so many other beings. Huanoquiteños were alert to the vitality of their environment and its destructive and beneficent potentialities. They channeled or harnessed the power of these beings in the present for purposes of modulating deleterious events of the past, nurturing multiple other species and elements and ensuring their future well-being in the form of good harvests, health, and safety. Their multitemporal worlds overlapped and inflected each other. Their named mountains (*apus*) and rocks (*wacas*), which had different qualities that they recognized when they made blessings to them (*samincha*), required their attention, especially at times of sowing and harvesting their crops, illnesses, taking long journeys, or in general, at important transformative moments or occasions. For example, they were always careful to bless Yachikauri and Huanakauri, two prominent *wacas* in the form of rock outcroppings, located on either side of Huanoquite, because "they shelter the village, protecting it like doors," and they were also like "a wall of defense." They viewed San Miguel, a massive and extensive mountain, as both "an apu and an angel," the most ferocious and angry of their mountain spirits," and therefore "in need of appeasement."

At the same time, pragmatism, a vibrant dimension of Quechua ontology, has been remarked on by scholars but has nevertheless gotten muffled by a tendency to characterize Andean people's ontology in a romanticized way that overemphasizes its spiritual nature. Huanoquiteños' understanding of the universe, their place in it, and the resources they drew upon for their social reproduction was intensely pragmatic. They were open to using the power of literacy, law, bureaucracies, and western scientific knowledge if it served their needs, along with mountain spirits, earth beings, and water and coca transmitters and mediators. De la Cadena (2010, 2015) discusses Quechua Indigenous cosmology as "cosmopolitics" and writes dramatically and vividly about the clash of Quechua ontology and that of western bureaucrats in her life history of a Quechua political leader who sought to retain and regain control over his community's lands, which had been taken by landed estate owners. Whereas Quechua leaders and shamans were open to tapping into and channeling whatever power and knowledge weapons were at their disposal that they thought they could use constructively—sentient beings, their observational powers, writing, and legal documents alike—non-Indigenous politicians and bureaucrats generally disdained and denigrated the reality of sentient beings *and* the capacity of Indigenous people to skillfully wield documents, knowledge, and demeanors that constituted the legitimacy of audit culture.

As I show in the pages that follow, in order to protect or enhance their livelihoods, Huanoquiteños drew on their pragmatism as a critical resource that was integral to their characterization of the sentient beings of their universe and the relationships among them. Sophie Chao, in her research among the Marind, an Indigenous people of West Papua, discusses their relationship to oil palm as hunters, gatherers, and fishermen, and how the establishment of oil palm plantations had caused them to experience systemic and disturbing changes in their multispecies interactions. From reciprocal relationships with more "wild and free plants" they were now experiencing "violent care" as plant lives had become imposed, domesticated, and harnessed for a world market, leading to cosmological imbalances that they expressed in dreams and nightmares (Chao 2018, 629). In a similar fashion, the shift among Huanoquiteños from their modest cultivation of myriad and dispersed landraces and varietals of quinoa—which entailed subtle interrelationships with all manner of species, both plant and animal (including humans)—to large-scale production of only a few types of quinoa, incentivized by the Peruvian state for the global market, had perturbed and intrigued them as they scrambled to acquire as much knowledge as possible about how to handle the consequences of these shifts for themselves and the networks of the multispecies universe in which they lived. At the same time, as Chao found in her work, Huanoquiteños encountering and participating in these changes felt considerable ambivalence because they were operating with partial knowledge, and some of these changes and their consequences were neither visible nor tangible, and it could take time for their effects to be felt (Chao 2018, 640). Using everything they had at their disposal—including their imaginations—they sought to diminish and control disruptions to their ontological positioning, and one of the main resources they relied on in this process was their down-to-earth pragmatism. That pragmatism was honed from knowledge they had accumulated over centuries as peasant farmers who had studied the physical environment, worked the land, and traded and sold their surplus. Their pragmatic spirituality had also very much emerged from their embeddedness in regimes of colonialism, capitalism, and neoliberal globalization, and from their interactions with non-Indigenous inhabitants whose reach into their lives entailed navigating an infuriating maze of bureaucracies that constituted the Peruvian state. Bringing together the power of pragmatism with the powers of a universe of sentient beings provided them with negotiating weapons and tools of persuasion they could sometimes use effectively with agents and organizations. It served as a bastion of a resilient and distinctive Indigenous Quechua praxis. At the same time, their labyrinthine maneuvering of the contradictory powers in the world exposed them to vulnerability, a double-edged sword in their efforts to figure out the best course of action they could take when encountering dangers, needs, opportunities, and obstacles. The very spiritual-pragmatic fusion of these dimensions of their ontology meant that, unlike so many development experts or agents of the state, they were skeptical of any single "silver bullet" that would solve all their problems.

Present and Past Lives:
The Anthropology of Long-Term Fieldwork

A final strand that informs this book is my experience as an anthropologist who has done long-term field research in the Andean highlands. I returned to Huanoquite to do this research because I felt that context and historical depth would permit me to better understand the relationship between quinoa and Andean livelihoods in general. Many excellent studies of quinoa have taken place at the macro-level but few tell us about more nuanced ways that the drive to export quinoa is shaping people's lives on the ground in Andean highland agricultural communities.[10] I had done extensive field research over a forty-five-year period in the southern Andean highlands in rural and urban settings, including four highland agrarian and herding communities, and my doctoral research on agrarian reform and its consequences had taken place over more than a year's time in the district of Huanoquite between 1984 and 1985. My returns there for shorter periods of time over the following thirty-five years provided me with a wealth of longitudinal data I could draw on to grasp how agrarian practices, including crop diversity and arrays, land tenure arrangements, labor regimes, and political organization had changed over the years; in what ways the expansion of quinoa cultivation might be contributing to those changes; and how Huanoquiteños themselves experienced and felt about these changes. In short, I could take a longer view in documenting and analyzing changes in agrarian lives in the district.

Before the 1980s, ethnographic research among Indigenous Quechua communities in Peru had flourished. That research diminished dramatically because of a civil war in Peru that took place between 1980 and 1992, leading fewer anthropologists to return to fieldwork in the countryside afterwards, even when the violence of the war subsided.[11] The magnitude of urban migration that took place in Peru and the recognition among anthropologists that even though people might live in one place, such as a rural community, they were very much embedded in far-flung social, economic, political, and informational flows, led to a decline in research in Peru's highland regions, some of which were located at great distances from cities, and an increase in research in urban areas or on the nature of the flows themselves (Gose 2011, i-ii). For these reasons, it seemed even more urgent to me to return to Huanoquite and learn what people were doing in a substantially changed agrarian landscape.

Because of the many years I had spent doing research in Huanoquite and the changes in my own life, I found myself reflecting more and more on my relationships with people in Huanoquite whom I had known for a long time, especially during the course of my research trips there in the summers of 2018 and 2019. I realized with a sense of profound sadness and excitement that it might be the last time I had the chance to interact with Huanoquiteños whom I had known across three generations. The very young children I had met so long ago were now full-fledged authorities of communities in some instances, and many of them remembered my presence from the 1980s, mirrored in tattered black and white photographs of their families that I had given them when they had so graciously permitted me to visit them in their homes, accompany them to their fields, and interview them.[12] Community leaders and young adults who had been generous enough to take risks talking to me, especially during the throes of Peru's civil war, and who had opened local archives to me so that I could learn more about the details of the history of Huanoquite, were now elders and more dependent than ever on the labor of their children and grandchildren—in Huanoquite and other places—to keep their lands and livestock intact. More than a few older Huanoquiteños I had known had died, although some remained, and a new generation had made its appearance. Many of them trusted me enough to share with me their ideas about what direction Huanoquite's future should take, and their opinions and desires about particular practices, material culture, organizations, and not least, about me as the visiting anthropologist. Because of this, I was much better poised to reflect on continuities and disjunctures that were circulating among Huanoquiteños in the district and beyond.

From where I stood, Huanoquiteños, in general, and younger ones, especially, seemed far less interested in knowledge per se and far more interested in how they could pragmatically convert that knowledge into fulfilling needs or desires that they or their communities had. This was partly because they no longer acquiesced to power relationships that had prevailed in the past between themselves and outsiders, such as anthropologists and government bureaucrats, and also because they were better able to exercise their own agency as citizens. While welcoming this shift and recognizing how I might have been partly complicit in perpetuating inequalities, most of the time I was in Huanoquite, I was acutely aware of how my own nostalgia colored the ways I saw and talked about things, even as I was documenting and taking account of all that was ongoing, had changed markedly, or in some cases, had vanished.

Sentiments not dissimilar to my own sense of nostalgia prevailed among Huanoquiteños in their attitudes toward me. Many Huanoquiteños had frozen me in time from decades earlier when I had spent over a year in the district, younger, energetic, capable of traveling up and down the mountains by foot in a way that I could no longer do. They, too, entertained a sentimentalism about who I had been, and it was hard for them to understand my aging process and the changes in my own thinking and behavior. Taking account of generational perspectives and reassessing my prior analyses of life in Huanoquite has definitely colored my interpretations of Huanoquiteños' concerns in the twenty-first century.[13] Quite frankly, I harbored my own nostalgia, wishing that I had the energy to keep up with the younger generation of Huanoquiteños to better understand how they were managing to knit together the multiple strands of their lives that spanned worlds and territories in ways that built on what their forebears had done but were infused with intriguing innovations to meet the challenges that faced them. They carried both the burden and possibilities of interculturality.

The Plan of the Book

This book is divided into two parts. The first lays out the history of past political regimes and the overwhelming racialized topography that has characterized daily life for Indigenous inhabitants of the Andean highlands of Peru. It analyzes key moments and policies that have shaped efforts of Indigenous Quechua inhabitants both to maintain and regain control of their agrarian land base, and the conflicts that have ensued as a result. It also reviews the history of the establishment of infrastructure between and within Huanoquite and the nature of the promotion of development in Huanoquite. The trajectories roads take, the technologies that are introduced and predominate, and the assumptions underlying development projects tell us a great deal about Huanoquite's relationships with the state and private capital, and about the desires of Huanoquiteños themselves. These backstories underpin why Huanoquite and other similar regions have become sites for expanding the cultivation and export of quinoa for a global market. They also help to explain what is at stake for Huanoquiteños in prioritizing a nontraditional agricultural export at the same time that the Peruvian state has been granting mining concessions to foreign corporations without paying greater attention to their deleterious impact on highland agrarian and herding communities.

Chapter 1 summarizes the impact that a far-reaching and radical agrarian reform, implemented in Peru in 1969, had on Huanoquite and then turns to a discussion of what the consequences were when the state subsequently turned back the agrarian reform and promoted the privatization and individual titling of lands in the countryside. These changes in land tenure regimes help to explain how the demand for quinoa has affected the lives of Huanoquiteños. Community household rights to land had become more tenuous than ever before because of the rise of private holdings. The ability of communities to act in a unified fashion existed in tension with growing inequality among households and their individualized efforts to find ways to sustain themselves, albeit in often innovative ways. While some of these projects and plans at first glance seemed to be noteworthy creative success stories, they were also often high-risk. They revealed specific ideologies of the state and its bureaucrats (and sometimes their absence) and showed how Huanoquiteños' options were structured by expectations and value systems that they themselves often regarded ambivalently. The paths Huanoquiteños had pursued to make a living in Huanoquite were hardly Manichean choices, but rather complex and contradictory.

Chapter 2 looks at the power of infrastructure as it has intervened in the choices Huanoquiteños face. Changes in infrastructure that have taken place over the last half-century have been as important as agrarian policies in transforming the livelihoods of Huanoquiteños. In 1984, the journey to Cusco from Huanoquite took between eight and nine hours and had been fraught with landslides, accidents, and the whims of truck drivers who might simply decide to have a break and drink well into the night at a rickety roadside bar, making subsequent travel even more hazardous. A beautiful Inca road, paved with stone, had been far more reliable and a straight shot (almost) to Cusco, taking four to five hours walking. However, it was generally not an option for anyone carrying heavy loads, unless they had a burro or llama. In 2016, the vehicular road from Cusco to the district was redesigned and paved until it reached Yaurisque, a notorious truck stop for drivers because of its bars and restaurants. From there, the road split into three arteries. A paved road continued eventually to the open-pit copper mines of Las Bambas; another paved road went to the district of Paccaritambo; and an unpaved road continued the rest of the way to Huanoquite. Because the road has been paved partway between Cusco and Huanoquite, the journey now only takes one to two hours. The impact of this has been explosive, permitting far more connections among people, places, and goods and more entrepreneurial opportunities. In 2013, no one had a cell phone. By 2018, almost everyone did. At the same time, people were well aware that the only reason the road had been paved a good part of the way to Huanoquite was because of the state's support of mining concessions. This overshadowed many of the positive changes that were underway.

When I returned in 2018, the district had become the site for all sorts of innovative economic activities, many of which had not been foisted on villagers by state or development agencies. The more far-flung travels of villagers, their keen observational powers, and the knowledge they had tapped into via the internet had led them to try out these ventures. One man had established a trout farm; a group of women had formed a textile association; several families had become beekeepers; the municipality was gathering up milk for cheese and making yoghurt; a chauffers' association, fifty-two young men strong, had appeared; large greenhouses were thrown up where strawberries and flowers were being grown under irrigation; and the first internet café was coming into being.

Chapter 3 asks why, at this point in time, so many Huanoquiteños were exploring a wide range of entrepreneurial ventures and how they differed from state- and NGO-sponsored initiatives. The voices of elders and youth challenged the assumption that there was a unidirectional arrow that relentlessly led to migration from countryside to city. These ventures should not simply be viewed as celebratory products of ingenuity and entrepreneurial verve. They were partly catalyzed by the needs of households that were being squeezed to find complementary economic activities that would permit them to remain in Huanoquite and farm their lands. Huanoquiteños also wanted to explore new avenues of economic mobility while retaining control over their livelihoods, as well as over where they chose to live and with whom. They had a deep appreciation of the beauty of their home's landscape, history, and culture, and that appreciation has grown over the last twenty years, partly due to social media, tourism, and a celebration by Peruvians of Indigeneity, and this, too, is part of the story behind agrarian livelihoods of the twenty-first century in the Andes. Huanoquiteños are bent on imagining new ways of living in a very old place.

Part 2 of the book is dedicated to unpacking the assumptions that have guided how Huanoquiteños are cultivating their lands as they encounter and participate in globalization, the pressures to migrate, and state policies that support mining and agroindustry. It discusses the long- and short-term strategies and the cultural resources that Huanoquiteños are drawing on to perpetuate their communities and territorial bonds and to resist the incursion of corporations and state policies that threaten their livelihoods.

Chapter 4 provides readers with an understanding of the stages of quinoa production and documents the efforts of state and non-state actors to expand quinoa production in Huanoquite. It shows what motivated some households and not others to cultivate quinoa in greater amounts and looks at the differences in the assumptions and expectations, with respect to quinoa cultivation

Introduction

and marketing, held by the Regional Government of Cusco and INIA, which was a branch of the Ministry of Agriculture (MINAGRI), on the one hand, and by Indigenous farmers on the other.

Chapter 5 delves into food politics. Food security and food sovereignty are both of concern to Huanoquiteños. Food security—ensuring that people do not go hungry and are able to gain access to basic nutrients that permit them to thrive—is highly politicized. Peru's government paid far more attention to incentivizing its rural inhabitants to produce healthy foods for the rest of the world than to ameliorating the conditions that contributed to malnutrition or hunger among those same inhabitants. Increasing quinoa cultivation for global consumption has not necessarily improved the livelihoods of Huanoquiteños, though it sometimes made a big difference to some of them. Racial discrimination and stigmatization of Indigenous foodstuffs, inequitable land tenure regimes, and the need to encourage the development of accessible regional markets and robust infrastructure all intervened in questions of food security among Indigenous agrarian households. Food security was also only one side of the coin. The other was food sovereignty. Food sovereignty concerned control, autonomy, democratic participation, and agency, but different parties understood these criteria in markedly different ways. The chapter highlights some of the tensions surrounding quinoa, ranging from control over the knowledge that made quinoa so attractive to the rest of the world as food, to questions of individual or community control over food resources and consumption. Important questions persisted with respect to whether the promotion of quinoa worldwide was wreaking havoc with Indigenous control over biogenetic resources in Peru, local seed selection and crop diversity, marketing practices, and domestic consumption patterns.

The chapter also addresses the stress and conflicts that ensued in Huanoquite, including among farmers themselves, as a consequence of their motivations to scale up their production of quinoa for export and their desires to cultivate crops that would ensure the well-being of their communities and households. In the introduction to their edited volume, *Nature and Culture*, Sarah Pilgrim and Jules Pretty suggest that a complex of "knowledge-belief-practice" mediates nature and culture and that "ecoliteracy" or "local ecological knowledge" is packed with observations, understandings, and social memories that societies use "to guide their actions towards the natural world." Huanoquiteños (and Indigenous Quechua people, in general) have a very long history of inhabiting a world that *is* nature-culture, and as such, they do not view culture as existing apart from nature. Yet development agents and experts tended to discount the incredible value of their local knowledge because, usually, it

24

was not generalizable and "it tend[ed] to be locally distinct, place-based, set within a cultural context, and inclusive all of the inter-related components of the human-environment complex in that area" (Pilgrim and Petty 2010, 6). It is exactly the specificity of local knowledge—too often ignored—that has guided Indigenous Andeans for millennia to survive and thrive in their environment despite the challenges it has presented. As Peter Andrée et al. (2014b, 43) succinctly note, contestations over knowledge and expertise, whether formal or informal, are driven by the questions of "Whose knowledge counts? Whose knowledge is seen? and What counts as knowledge?"

Chapter 6 brings the voices, aesthetics, and activities of women in Huanoquite to the foreground. Government and nongovernmental entities had begun to view women as better candidates than men for introducing new farming practices and experimental development projects, and for implementing them. The women themselves held views somewhat at odds with respect to these undertakings, though they did not necessarily advertise them. In fact, their views were often ignored despite a greater awareness today of the many kinds of labor activities that women took on to care for their households. Sitting in a dusky kitchen, sipping an herbal tea or slurping a soup while quinoa sizzled away, roasting in a cast-iron skillet, the picture would shift, and so many of the women I visited would begin to discuss with enthusiasm and detail what they thought about quinoa, how it contributed to the quality of their lives, and some of what they found problematic about the overwhelming emphasis on markets and on supply and demand. Women were canny about the intricate calculations that went into buying and selling, and they too looked forward to profitable returns on their quinoa (and other crops they grew), but one result of the division of labor in most Quechua households in the countryside was that, while women were responsible for seed selection; for processing, preparing, and serving food and drink, including for labor parties; and for selling small amounts of quinoa on a retail basis, men were responsible for finding wholesale or bulk buyers for their market share of production. Women cared greatly about expanding opportunities for their children, and they held passionate views about what tasted good and which food was good for what purpose. These dual concerns intervened in how they thought about quinoa (as well as other foodstuffs).

Women in Huanoquite talked about and prepared quinoa in different ways than did people in the United States. The second part of this chapter reviews the reasons for these differences. PROMPERÚ (Commission for the Promotion of Peru for Export and Tourism), along with INIA and MINAGRI, was the main government agency charged with promoting quinoa internationally and branding Peruvian quinoa. An analysis of the many brochures, documents, and advertisements PROMPERÚ has produced over close to a decade offers insight into why, internationally, certain properties of quinoa and quinoa preparation have gained in popularity. It is important to understand that "differences" in how people viewed and prepared quinoa—whether they were Indigenous or not, Peruvian or not, did not exist in realms that were closed off to one another. Instead, crosscurrents and curiosity fostered new ways of thinking about and preparing quinoa. How people interacted with food was underpinned by what they viewed as healthy, good for the body and being, and by their need and desire (and the needs and desires of other entities of the universe) for a particular food. Tourism and Peru's acclaim as a culinary destination of gastronomical delights with Indigenous roots also colored how quinoa and other Indigenous foodstuffs were regarded in ways that were quite different from how Indigenous inhabitants viewed them. In short, these valorizations of food were embedded in highly politicized ideologies.

The final chapter funnels outward again to consider the preoccupations that the workers who had helped to harvest my compadre Lorenzo's quinoa voiced to me about mining activities near Huanoquite. A grave concern of Huanoquiteños has been the current and prospective environmental damage caused by mining. Whatever the immediate successes or failures of the quinoa project in Huanoquite, Huanoquiteños knew that the mines were not minor harbingers of collateral damage. Rather, Huanoquiteños were confronting the prospect that their entire district might become uninhabitable due to mining concessions the state had granted to multinational companies. The mining would pollute the waters of five lakes located high above Huanoquite, lakes that Huanoquiteños considered sacred. The waters of the lakes fed the hydraulic system of rivers, underground springs, and irrigation canals which gave life to Huanoquiteños' fields. As they had done so many times in the past when facing dire life conditions, Huanoquiteños were drawing on storytelling, organizing, and political resistance to challenge the development of the mines. They were also selectively using what I call *borderlands knowledge* to fight back against some of the most powerful and sobering kinds of destructive forces that humanity has encountered, many of which were silently and relentlessly establishing themselves within proximity to Huanoquite itself.

Life has hardly been easy for Huanoquiteños but they have succeeded in persevering because of their pragmatic spirituality and their capacity to knit together knowledge drawn from their experiences as border dwellers. As such, they negotiate between city and countryside, state and community (and intra-community tensions), between their quotidian lives as Quechua farmers and the images of Indigeneity celebrated by tourists, and between the deep memory of prior topological regional socioeconomic arrangements, land struggles, and racism, on the one hand, and the erasure of history on the global horizon on the other hand. Over the last fifty years, they have had to wrestle with the reversals of agrarian reform, the brutality of civil war, and the embrace of a neoliberal economic and political agenda, all of which have fractured a sense of community solidarity and political organization. Youth regularly migrate, but many have returned with new skills. Women have gradually become more empowered, and children are receiving a better education in Huanoquite as well as in Cusco. Community assemblies continue to take place in which the rhetoric of acknowledging "fellow comrades and companions" has become a central discursive strategy, calling attention to its very fragility.

During the 1990s, anthropologists began to describe processes of globalization and their history. Now, more than two decades later, ethnographers have become far more immersed in understanding what it has meant for people to live across boundaries, on various scales at once, and among multiple and differing regimes of power. Here, I try to convey through an ethnographic lens the relationships and knowledge that Huanoquiteños draw on to live in such complex assemblages of contradictory, multidimensional spatiotemporal worlds, whether for purposes of experimenting with growing quinoa for the global market or for battling the power of transnational mining companies and the state.

Amid the rampant expansion of mining, deforestation, and exploitation of natural resources, Andean nations remained preoccupied with questions directly relevant to land and labor conditions in the countryside, sometimes very much *because* of the desires of the state to control rural populations. Those who till the soil are, and have been, major actors in Latin America, whether we choose to call them peasants or laborers on the land, "Indians," Indigenous, migrants, or community members (Edelman and Haugerud 2005; Collins 1988; Edelman 2014). They may provide remittances that allow for domestic agriculture to continue or, alternatively, their food production may heavily subsidize industry and their participation in nonagricultural work. The food they produce; the exchange relationships they forge; the entrepreneurial activities they interweave among extended family members; the innovations they arrive at, as well as their deep understanding of place and practice and the interconnections among them in their environment; the political ideas they develop; the social movements they build; and the aesthetic expressions they create are just a few of their cultural, political, and economic contributions as participants who are increasingly savvy about the challenges they face in forging a livable future on the world stage.

PART ONE

BACKSTORIES

Land Struggles, the Allure of Infrastructure,
and Development Desires in Huanoquite

CHAPTER 1

Agrarian Reform, Revolution, and Reversals

A radical national agrarian reform took place in 1969 in Peru. The reform and subsequent reversals to it form a critical backdrop to understanding the tumultuous changes that Huanoquiteños have since participated in and to explaining why the district has become a key site for agricultural experimentation, including the cultivation and marketing of quinoa. The 1969 reform bolstered the political, economic, and cultural rights of citizenship in some measure for Peru's Indigenous inhabitants, but reversals to it diminished many of those rights by means of policies that promoted a market in private land and weakened the economic and political clout of communities. This chapter covers principal aspects of these policies and their bearing on the structuring of Huanoquiteños' current agrarian activities.

The 1969 Agrarian Reform

As was the case with most agricultural regions in Peru, Huanoquite experienced the uneven and mixed implementation of the 1969 Agrarian Reform. There are many excellent accounts of this unique reform (see Cant 2021; Mayer 2009; Seligmann 1995; Caballero 1981; Caballero and Alvarez 1980; Matos Mar and Mejía 1980), which sought to return land to those who actually tilled it and who, in many cases, had controlled the land since long before the early sixteenth-century Spanish invasion and conquest. By the twentieth century, many lands of Indigenous Quechua inhabitants had been taken over by hacendados (large landed estate owners).[1] The latter were less concerned about the productivity of their estates than about maintaining their status as a feudal elite. Men and women suffered in these conditions, experiencing sexual abuse, brutal racial discrimination, debt peonage, and exploitative labor regimes.

A long history of uprisings against and resistance to landed estate owners by campesinos as well as workers preceded the 1969 reform and hastened its passage, but perhaps the key force that catalyzed the reform was a desire among politicians to modernize Peru's economy, including its agricultural sector, for purposes of supplying cheap food to stimulate an industrial, urban economy. The reform was implemented by a military junta headed by General Juan Velasco Alvarado. It was based on a Yugoslav model in a misconceived effort to create economies of scale by establishing agrarian cooperatives on the coast and in the highlands. With its assumptions of collective, socialist economic and political praxis, the model hardly conformed to land tenure or labor regimes among Quechua highlanders that had come into being as a palimpsest, the result of pre-Inca, Inca, colonial, and post-Independence social and political forces. Even geographically, the model made little sense. On the coast, one could find extensive stretches of relatively flat agricultural land; in the highlands, land was carved up by intermontane valleys; it had originally been held by communities in parcels that went from lower to higher altitudes and to which members had use rights. These lands had been usurped by hacendados whose estates often cut across lands that had belonged to multiple communities.

Before the reform, one could find Huanoquiteños working full-time on landed estates, while others sharecropped lands, worked part-time on estates, exercised their use rights to lands that their communities had held "since time immemorial," or cobbled together some subset of these modes of tenure and labor. The reform, however, focused most of its attention on expropriating hacienda lands and turning them over to farmers who had worked full-time on the estates. The estates were restructured into cooperatives with the assumption that their members would then work and market their harvest together and collectively make decisions about their enterprise and how to run it. They were viewed, first and foremost, not as Indigenous but rather as peasants (See Seligmann 1993 for how these conflicting labor and legal regimes affected Huanoquiteños).

The reform successfully expropriated most of the lands that had belonged to hacendados—of which there were many in Huanoquite—and diminished substantially their political clout. However, the hacendados, before they departed,

1. Agrarian Reform, Revolution, and Reversals

decapitalized their properties, and a handful managed to remain embedded in communities with smaller pieces of their land that nevertheless often had the most fertile soil and best access to irrigation waters. Huanoquite was unusual among highland communities because one significant stretch of land that was expropriated was a high, relatively flat, pampa that was converted into a cooperative of eight hundred hectares called Tihuicte. Many Indigenous households that were members of communities that comprised Huanoquite had also worked on what became Tihuicte, and on other estates, but very few of them received much in the way of land from the agrarian reform because they had only worked part-time on the estates. This quickly created resentment and fissures between community members and cooperative members because community members were not beneficiaries of land to the same extent as cooperative members even though hacendados had also taken portions of their lands. At the same time, once most of the landed estate owners left, communities were able to gain more access to lands at multiple ecological levels than cooperative members; they were less dependent on the Peruvian state than cooperatives; and they continued to farm their lands as they had in the past, but with greater time and freedom of action.

Among community members, the predominant form of land tenure was that of usufruct. That is, community members had rights to land which they farmed as households, so long as they fulfilled their labor obligations to their community, which included cleaning and maintaining its irrigation canals and laboring on lands that were considered "communal," dedicated to the economic and ritual needs of the community itself. The amount of land households held in usufruct only changed if the size of respective households changed or if community members did not fulfill their labor obligations to their community. Members of newly formed cooperatives, in contrast, were expected to farm collectively—a very alien practice for them. Furthermore, communities were able to rely on an extant political mode of organization, "the community" (more on this below), whereas cooperative members had to build from scratch the administrative and political structure of the cooperative.

Despite the reform's flaws, it was incontrovertible that Huanoquiteños acquired legal rights as citizens that they could exercise. They now had the right to use the law to defend and demand lands that had been unjustly seized from them. With the abolition of slave labor, they had no reason to follow the orders of landed estate owners and could exercise greater autonomy over their labor. Most important of all, communities pursued official recognition as "Comunidades Campesinas" (Peasant Communities) with legal title to their land and with the capacity to litigate and negotiate as legal entities. Legal recognition required recognizing and registering with the state the landholdings (and other resources) of the community and obtaining title deeds for their lands. Official recognition also facilitated the ability of communities to obtain benefits—loans, assistance, and public services—from state entities. Formal education became a reality, although it remained saturated by racist ideas and practices and it was difficult to find teachers who would endure the hardships of life in the countryside.

Reversals of Reform

Before Peru's civil war officially began in 1980 with the bombing of ballot boxes in a village called Chuschi in the central Andean highland region of Ayacucho, the momentum the agrarian reform had set in motion in the highlands to re-distribute land and political power to farmers had already been arrested. In 1975, General Francisco Morales Bermúdez deposed the junta led by Velasco in a bloodless coup, and in 1980, he then relinquished presidential power to Fernando Belaúnde Terry (1980–85), a civilian president from whom Velasco had seized power in 1968. Morales had already begun the process of privatizing some industries and had attempted, unsuccessfully, to revive the floundering Peruvian economy. It was only after Belaúnde won the 1980 Presidential election that more dramatic and cataclysmic changes to the Reform took place. As Nuñez Palomino (1995, 41) explains, Belaúnde was intent on stimulating the national economy by relying on neoliberal economic principles and promoting agrarian development through the intensive participation of private capital. In 1980, he passed an executive decree, DL 002, known as the "Law of Agrarian Development," which permitted collective lands to be reprivatized and formally removed most constraints that prevented agricultural land from being bought and sold on the market by individuals, especially those that had belonged to the cooperatives. Most of the cooperative lands were broken up into *minifundios*, small parcels, and allocated to individual households.

A decade later, President Alberto Fujimori (1990–2000) announced "the reform of the agrarian reform" (Legislative Decree 653), officially overturning the 1969 agrarian reform measures, and passed the 1991 "Law to Promote Investments in the Agrarian Sector." In 1993, the new constitution erased references to the concept of agrarian reform altogether (Klarén 2017, 30). The new laws raised limits on the amount of land that owners could hold privately in the countryside, jungle, and coast; permitted Indigenous community members to rent out community lands to noncommunity members, including foreigners, for up to thirty years; and declared that land that appeared not to be under

1. Agrarian Reform, Revolution, and Reversals

cultivation could be seized by the state unless communities retained title to those lands (Egurén 2004). This decree, in turn, would later play an outsized role in permitting the state to grant mining companies concessions without prior consultation. A final law incorporated into the 1993 constitution allowed communities to transfer land rights to third parties and simultaneously gave them the autonomy to dispose of their lands as they saw fit (Egurén 2004, 46).

In the countryside, the fissures between community members and cooperative members, the general discontent among Indigenous inhabitants who had received less than others from the reform than they had expected, and the growing insecurity of tenure arrangements were exploited by the Shining Path movement (*Sendero Luminoso*), whose members began a civil war in 1980. They partly justified the need for civil war by arguing that the agrarian reform had failed and that overthrowing the state through revolution was the only path left to take.[2] In Huanoquite, the Shining Path became active in the early 1980s, and one cell targeted the tractor that Tihuicte cooperative members had invested in at huge cost to farm the flat pampa. Members of the Shining Path cell blew up the tractor with dynamite before fleeing. The district was occupied by special forces (*sinchis*), and eventually civil defense patrols formed, composed of Huanoquiteños themselves, to keep order in the district (See also Starn 1999 on the state's reliance on civil defense patrols).

The civil war officially lasted from 1980 to 1992, when Abimael Guzmán, who had been a philosophy professor at the University of Huamanga in Ayacucho and had become the leader of the Shining Path, was finally arrested. The war resulted in more than sixty-nine thousand deaths (including massacres and disappearances), most of which were of people from Quechua-speaking regions of Peru. Both members of the Shining Path movement and military and paramilitary forces viewed Quechua rural populations as a significant target and threat, and many villagers were caught in the brutal crossfire of demands for allegiance and loyalty, even among neighbors who might not share the same sympathies.[3]

Privatization, Neoliberalism, and the Free Market

The reversals of the agrarian reform must be placed in the context of global and national, economic, and political changes taking place within and beyond Peru. Privatization went hand in hand with the inception of the neoliberal restructuring of the economy, the embrace of free market principles and deregulation, and the increasing decentralization of the Peruvian state in the 1980s. How did this play out for households in Huanoquite? In the case of the Tihuicte cooperative, much of the land that had been farmed was converted into residences for prior cooperative members. Instead of potato, maize, and barley fields, and the sight of livestock grazing, small adobe compounds, some of two stories, soon dotted the landscape of the relatively flat pampa. Former cooperative members had to obtain title to their houses and pay for them. They redefined themselves as the "urban" residential neighborhood of Tiwinki, registering their properties and declaring themselves part of the "community" of Maska in Huanoquite. Any remaining agricultural lands of the cooperative were now considered within the political jurisdiction of the community. At the same time, members of the nineteen communities belonging to the district of Huanoquite, especially nearer to the district capital, also began the process of gaining individual title to their lands. Cooperatives established by the Reform were dissolved, and a mosaic of political and tenure regimes took their place. In some cases, households divvied up cooperative lands and then obtained private title to them; others announced themselves as "associations"; and still others merged their lands with those of neighboring communities, which then also determined how they allocated their lands.

Especially in high-altitude production zones, community members had always rotated crops over a five- to seven-year cycle in order not to exhaust the soil. In addition to planting different kinds of crops from year to year, some of which would replenish the nitrogen in the soil, farmers would then leave a whole sector (*raymi*) of community fields fallow for a period of time or permit them to be used for grazing livestock. Raymis were not viewed as individual property but as property of the community even though parcels of raymis, in accordance with use rights, were distributed to community households, and parcels were also allocated for communal funds and the needs of community authorities. Allocation of lands to households depended on the total amount of land available and the capacity of each community member to work it. All parcels within a raymi were worked in the same crop. In the high-altitude puna, the crop rotation of raymi parcels was called *t'iqray*. A typical five-year cycle might be potatoes; broad beans if the soil still had plenty of nutrients, or barley and other tubers if it did not; wheat; lupines; and potatoes again, if the soil could tolerate them. Otherwise, the field was left to rest. There was flexibility to the rotation, with farmers taking account of climate and soil conditions and consulting each other as they decided what to plant the following year. Because of the new regulations following the reversals of the agrarian reform, if it appeared that land was not being cultivated (e.g., lying fallow), then it was vulnerable to "taking" by the state. This threat, in the long run, has been deleterious, even to the state's interests of increasing agricultural productivity.

1. Agrarian Reform, Revolution, and Reversals

Within communities, intense debate began to occur about the status of raymis. Growers—including of raymi land that they were renting from community members—began to establish their own patterns of rotation or sometimes did not rotate crops at all. For example, members of the QCA began to grow quinoa—which quickly exhausts the soil—on raymi lands. By not allowing the raymi land to lie fallow, the soil became more exhausted and produced less each year since it was constantly in use. Some households felt they should have sole discretion with respect to how they could use their raymi land. Others suggested that raymi land should be permanently parceled out, that individual title should be granted to younger people with little land, and that community authorities should not intervene at all in how raymi lands could be used. This proposal was rejected in 2018 by community members with a decision that raymis should remain collective, but no doubt the issue will once again arise, and some households with private title to community raymi lands will not necessarily comply with the community's decision (Maska Community Meeting, October 1, 2018).

Egurén (2004, 72), reviewing the available data and evaluating the effects of the government's policy of opening the doors to a supposedly "more efficient" land market that would incentivize agricultural productivity in the countryside, concluded that

> it has not benefited small farmers and peasants. The liberalization of the market, rather, has benefited intermediaries. Associations of small producers may help to overcome a series of disadvantages linked to their lack of individual negotiating power and on occasion—apparently very few—entrepreneurial initiatives may be stimulated to satisfy the needs of small farmers if they succeed in organizing themselves.

Egurén goes on to explain that, especially in the highland regions, small producers did not have a sufficient cushion to weather the vagaries of the market; they did not have access to credit; and while they might seek to sell a portion of the products they cultivated, they also used part of what they grew to feed themselves and their family. Hence, the market had either not worked to the advantage of—or it had completely excluded—smaller farmers. And the majority of Indigenous farmers in Huanoquite *were* smallholders. It is difficult to obtain accurate statistics with respect to current household land tenure in Huanoquite, but available data shows that the majority were small holders (73.5 percent) who cultivated an average of less than 2 hectares of land, with a range, according to one assessment, from close to 3 hectares per household to less than 0.4 hectares (Censo Agrario, 2012)

In Huanoquite, because of their inability to take advantage of the market, smaller farming households began to turn in greater numbers to nonagricultural activities to meet their household needs. They also relied on intermediaries (who took a markup) to sell what they had. Rather than incentivizing greater agricultural productivity through an efficient land market, neoliberal economic measures—such as the encouragement of the privatization of landholdings—created greater inequity among agrarian households. For Huanoquiteños, while gaining title to their land seemed to offer them a measure of security and more control over their decision-making, individual title rather than use rights within the jurisdiction of the community benefitted those with more land and access to market mechanisms and credit, and it made it more difficult for households to fall back on the community as a safety net for all sorts of assistance, including labor and loans of one sort or another. As I discuss below, informally, Huanoquite's communities did continue to offer some support to their members despite the weakness of the legal authority they had.

Legal Authority, Political Authority

One of the most conflictive and contradictory dimensions of "the reform of the agrarian reform" was that communities were authorized to decide who had the right of access to community lands at the same time that they confronted community members seeking individual title to their lands, which the latter then had the right to sell or rent to noncommunity members. To be clear, for communities to retain control over their lands, all of it had to be properly titled. However, title rested in the individual/household community member, with some lands titled as belonging to the community itself as a unit. María Luisa Burneo (2012, 29) explains this paradox, pointing out how it resulted in a proliferation of conflicts within communities as well as between them, and between communities and state entities:

> It was paradoxical that communities had the function, recognized as legitimate by community members themselves and the Law of Peasant Communities, to decide who had access to community lands at the same time that when the community, as an entity, allocated lands to community members without deploying a formal process, they became vulnerable to the dismembering of those same lands as part of the community's territory.

In Huanoquite, most communities had continued to retain a degree of political authority over the allocation of lands for purposes of privatization. That is, households were expected to obtain permission from the community in question to pursue title to their land and to their residence. However, a single norm did not exist with respect to how communities went about allocating lands. Some communities demanded that even when members gained individual title to their lands, they only rent or sell them to other community members. In other cases, communities imposed no such restriction. Huanoquite dedicated assembly after assembly to attempting to ensure that community lands were not bought, sold, or rented to noncommunity members without the express permission of the community as a whole, represented by its authorities and the consensus of community members. Nevertheless, a land rental market persisted, especially among better-off households.

The privatization of land encouraged an entrepreneurial spirit and greater engagement with free-market forces. This made itself apparent in Huanoquite in various ways. For example, members of the QCA were all farming quinoa on lands to which they had title, and most of it had once been part of the community. As would be expected, they tended to be the better-off households within Huanoquite. The privatization of land had also made communities more vulnerable. Authorities representing their community sought to retain its clout as a collective entity. However, the possibilities for corruption were great among authorities, individual community members, and lawyers, surveyors, and engineers hired by households and the community itself to obtain legal title to particular pieces of land and ensure that prior established boundaries of parcels were honored in transactions. A battle of archival records, falsified documents, and sales transactions ensued that presented maps and descriptions of the same piece of land but with differing boundaries and ownership history. Without going into the details here, these titles had to be filed in the public property registrar and if they were for agricultural use, required a labyrinthine bureaucratic process. When I interviewed Hugo Herrera Catari (Interview, July 30, 2018), the mayor of Huanoquite, I asked him what he thought were the biggest and most serious problems facing the district. He commented that I might be surprised by his answer, but he was quick to respond: "Land boundaries—between communities, between households, and between those from Huanoquite and property owners from outside."[4]

Market Aspirations, Social Inequalities, and Development

Decentralization and neoliberal market dynamics diminished the security and strength of Indigenous Quechua communities even as households acquired more freedom to pursue new kinds of economic activities. The privatization of land brought about greater inequality among households. It also fostered a desire among both wealthier and poorer households—for somewhat different reasons—to experiment with agricultural and entrepreneurial undertakings, some of which have been fostered and encouraged by state agents; others of which have been the result of their own observations, travels, educational training, and conversations.

The tension between the security of obtaining title to land and property and the capacity of wealthier households to accumulate more land has been accompanied by a critical shortage of labor with which to perform agricultural tasks—sowing, weeding, hoeing, harvesting, and threshing. (Table 1 is a generalized template of the staggering agricultural labor tasks that had to be scheduled over the calendar year for crops in the high puna and in the lower valley in Huanoquite.) This, too, demonstrates the limits to generating efficiency by means of encouraging a free land market: Households with more resources were more able to pay wages to poorer workers. At the same time, the lack of reliable access to labor was a constant preoccupation for wealthier farmers because poorer farmers, while wanting to earn cash by working for wealthier farmers, also relied on traditional reciprocal labor practices in which they worked on one another's fields. For them, time was at a premium and they not infrequently rejected the pleas of wealthier farmers to work on their fields in exchange for cash. In addition, whereas households used to be able to rely on multiple sons and daughters for purposes of providing labor and labor exchanges, because of younger people's desire to pursue alternatives to agricultural labor, not infrequently only one son or daughter remained in Huanoquite who was fully committed to an agricultural livelihood, though the others participated from time to time.

For Huanoquiteños, land and the energy they invested to cultivate it carried more than economic meaning. They were both tillers of the soil and Indigenous Quechua inhabitants of the land. Their land and what had become incorporated into it served as carriers of memory, of history. Yet that history could sometimes vanish without a trace once changes to the land transpired and one kind of economic and political logic was substituted by another. How Huanoquiteños viewed themselves was also transformed in the context of their relationships to land and labor: Did they grant primacy to their behavior and demeanor as individuals or as community members? How could they protect their land rights except, perhaps, by joining in solidarity with other community members, especially when they confronted entities with far greater political and economic power? I myself experienced a sense of disorientation—almost shock—at the transformation of the topography of Huanoquite and the fields I remembered when I returned to them after five years away. In addition to

Table 1. Schedule of Monthly Agricultural Labor Tasks

	CROPS GROWN IN HIGH ALTITUDE PUNA											
Month	Oct.	Nov.	Dec.	Jan.	Feb.	Mar.	Apr.	May	June	July	Aug.	Sept.
Broad Beans		Hoe	Hoe			Weed		Harvest				Sow
Quinoa						Weed		Harvest	Harvest	Thresh		Sow
Wheat	Sow					Weed				Harvest	Harvest/Thresh	
Barley	Sow	Sow				Weed			Harvest	Harvest/Thresh		
Potatoes	Sow		Hoe	Hoe		Weed	Harvest	Harvest				
Other Tubers	Sow		Hoe			Weed						
Tarwi		Hoe				Hoe/Weed		Harvest	Harvest		Sow	Sow
	CROPS GROWN IN VALLEY											
Maize	Sow		Hoe	Hoe		Weed		Harvest			Irrigate	Sow
Early Potatoes	Hoe			Harvest	Harvest	Weed				Irrigate	Sow	Hoe
Wheat					Weed				Harvest	Har/Thr	Sow	
Quinoa		Sow	Sow		Weed			Harvest	Har/Thr	Thr		

Note: This table is adapted and modified from Guillet 1979. Quinoa and wheat are both grown at higher and lower altitudes.

houses proliferating on what had been agricultural and grazing lands, a building boom was underway; fewer and fewer households were herding livestock; an elementary school, a middle school, and a high school now occupied some of those lands along with two playing fields; and two stadiums had been constructed; people who were not from the community were promoting all sorts of new land uses; dirt roads that had not previously existed snaked into the high puna and lower valley areas, traveled by motorcycles, pickup trucks, and an occasional lorry rather than horses, burros, or llamas. During my time in Huanoquite, I was haunted by a simultaneous sense of excitement and uneasiness, much like what Huanoquiteños themselves were experiencing.

CHAPTER 2

The Power and Seduction
of Infrastructure

The design and construction of roads, paths, and trails—in short, connectors—have had an enormous impact on the livelihood options and dreams of Huanoquiteños. To build the roads that snake through the Andean highlands, skirting sheer drops and crossing turbulent rivers over rickety bridges, is a monumental and expensive feat. Such feats structure space and identities and proclaim the presence or absence of the state, effects that are not lost on inhabitants of the region (Harvey and Knox 2015).

The history of Huanoquite's road systems is still partially visible today: in the form of ancient trails and footpaths made by herders in their daily treks to graze their animals; by farmers going to work on their fields, located up and down mountains and valleys; and by trade routes taken by villagers to exchange livestock, agricultural products, and other desired goods. The Inca road, a marvel of construction made of polished stone and the collective sweat and labor drafts of Indigenous inhabitants incorporated into the Inca empire in the fifteenth century, extends from Huanoquite to Cusco. There are also avalanche-prone dirt roads designed by bureaucrats, engineers, and landed estate owners with a poor understanding of the environment and territory they were traversing. Indigenous Quechua inhabitants also built these roads in slave labor conditions; more recently, wide asphalted roads have made their appearance as state public works.[1] The material trajectories roads take provoke memories and sentiments about places along the way that matter to particular sectors of the population. For example, bureaucrats and landed estate owners disrupted existing Indigenous social relationships built on patterns of trade and transport that had once radiated out in all directions from Huanoquite, bolstered by the existence of salt mines in Huanoquite proper. Huanoquite had once constituted a dynamic regional space but when the Spanish colonialists and landed estate owners gave primacy to constructing roads directly to the regional capital of Cusco (also the Inca capital) from multiple sites that had once been part of Huanoquite's regional space, Huanoquite itself became an end point rather than an entrepôt. Subsequently, the close ties among population centers that had created a vibrant regional space diminished in strength, though some of them remained and were activated for purposes of trade and political mobilization from time to time.

At a different scale, the Peruvian state's nationalist aspirations to celebrate modernity, integration (usually emulating western ideals), and dynamic economic growth and commerce led it to promulgate large-scale road building projects, such as the massive east-west Interoceanic Highway extending from the Pacific to the Amazon and linking Peru to Brazil. Penny Harvey and Hannah Knox (2015, 7), in their account of roads and infrastructure in Peru, summarize well how much these connectors matter economically, politically, and ideologically:

> In Peru, as in many developing countries, roads have meanings that go well beyond their physical functionality. Banks and governments view them favorably as technologies of social integration, economic development, and modernization. They are also relatively easy to sell to the wider public in places where poor communications systems exacerbate the physical and economic hardships of everyday life. Indeed, many Peruvians long for roads with a fervor that we found hard to fathom at first, given some of the more deleterious effects that roads are often held responsible for in more critical accounts. That said, it must be stated from the outset that people are not wrong in their understandings of the correlations between the presence of a road and the possibilities for economic growth that these smooth connective surfaces afford. Roads enable the networked flow of goods, labor, and services. They deliver the basic conditions of modern living, although, as all scholars of modernity are aware, the benefits are uneven and unpredictable.

Roads in the Andean highlands also make impressive statements about power and labor, statements engraved as memories among those who built and maintained so many of them with what amounted to forced labor overseen by landed estate owners and state agents. Benjamin Orlove, in an insightful article on the relationships between dirt and identity among Indigenous inhabitants of the Andes, points out how Indigenous inhabitants viewed dirt roads as part of their communities because of the investment of their own labor in building and using them and the historical knowledge of their territory embedded in the dirt itself. Non-Indigenous inhabitants, in contrast, viewed these same dirt roads as a gauge of racial distinction, contrasting them with well-built, state-sponsored asphalted roads while being oblivious to the Indigenous labor that had also gone into turning them into a productive resource. Orlove (1998, 212) notes,

> These roads appeared on government maps, and the national Ministry of Transport and Communications would occasionally lend a heavy truck to carry tools or gravel out to assist the villagers who repaired the roads, either by forming large communal work groups to carry out the task or by assigning shorter stretches of road to individual households. To the Indians, though, the labour that they performed confirmed the fact that the roads were as much part of their village territory as the fields, the pastures, the houses, the school buildings and chapels, all of which they maintained through their work. In the minds of the government officials, then, the vehicles were on government territory, rather than village lands, as long as they remained moving on the roads; in the minds of the villagers, they entered the village territory as soon as they crossed from the neighbouring village.

Confirming Harvey and Knox's observations, Huanoquiteños have not viewed these roads in a negative fashion. Though they may have been exploited to make the roads materialize, and all too frequently, communities were not adequately compensated for lands taken from them for the purpose of building roads, they hoped the roads might fulfill their aspirations. Almost all of them were eager for public works improvements that would allow them to travel between city and countryside without fearing for their lives. They dreamed of better jobs in the cities, educational opportunities for their children, health care that would make the difference between living and dying, being able to transport their agricultural products and livestock more easily and in greater volume to urban markets, and bringing services, resources, and tourism to their communities.

Their dreams, indeed, began to come true, but not exactly as they had imagined. Despite rhetoric issuing from the presidential palace in Lima and the various regional and departmental offices of the government in Cusco, nobody paid much attention to the dismal state of Huanoquite's principal road from Cusco to the district for decades.[2] The truckers, stalwart sailors of the road,

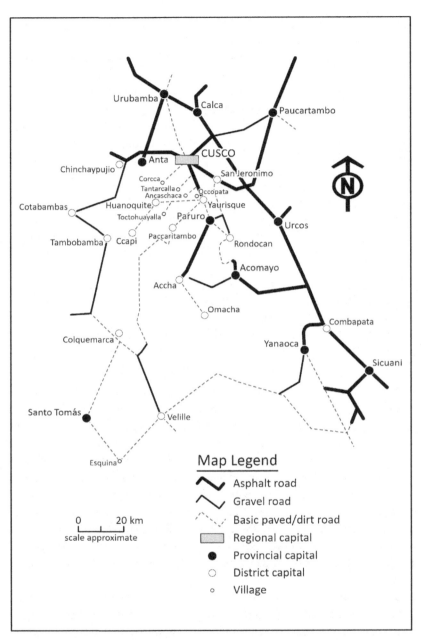

MAP 3. Cusco-Huanoquite regional road network (Map prepared by Scott White). Data sources: Seligmann 1995, Baca 1983, Ministerio de Transportes y Comunicaciones 2017.

full of bravado, determined if and when villagers would travel, and the road itself set its own limits, prone to landslides and impasses. Only between the late twentieth and early twenty-first century, during Alberto Fujimori's two-term presidency (1990–2000), after the civil war had begun to subside, did government officials take seriously the need to attend to infrastructure in the hinterlands. District municipalities like Huanoquite were allocated equipment and a budget to maintain roads in conjunction with the regional government in Cusco. Buses began to regularly traverse the road. Though still not paved, it was better maintained, thus shortening the journey. There were many reasons for this change of heart. At the national level, Peru had embraced neoliberal economic policies, political and economic decentralization, and the assumption that good roads would encourage the incorporation of Indigenous inhabitants into the market economy. Roads were necessary for the continuing expansion of Peru's export economy from coast, jungle, and highlands. The state and regional governments also sought to do what they could to attract the mining concessions they were quietly (and usually secretly) granting to multinational corporations (See Harvey and Knox 2015, 181; Salas 2017, 142–43). Not least, as well, the state viewed the improvement of roads as an important weapon in its arsenal to prevent the resurgence of a movement like the Shining Path.

Designed Roads and Prospects of Transformation

What did this mean for Huanoquite? The Cusco Regional Government made a momentous decision in 2006 to pave the road from Cusco to Yaurisque, a district capital in the province of Paruro that was on the way to Huanoquite. Three roads split from Yaurisque. One continued onto Huanoquite; a second went to Paruro; and a third went to Paccaritambo. The road was also reoriented so that as it left Cusco, it passed by Huancaro where an enormous agricultural market fair had been institutionalized and took place twice a week. However, once the road got to Yaurisque, only one road was asphalted, the one that continued to Paruro, while the road to Huanoquite remained unpaved, making a treacherous climb of multiple hairpin turns to its final destination. Huanoquiteños marveled at the first part of the road, and they hoped that, eventually, the last and most dangerous part would eventually be paved. By 2009, the road changed their lives dramatically and unexpectedly.

Huanoquiteños have always been "watchers," something that Catherine Allen (2002) documents beautifully in *The Hold Life Has*, her ethnography of the Quechua people of Sonqo in Peru's southern highlands. They acutely observe the places and people around them and the interactions among them.

They also listen closely. Several years after the road had been improved, they began to notice planes and helicopters flying overhead and enormous vehicles carrying equipment that traversed the same road they took from Cusco but then continued beyond Yaurisque. It did not take long for them to grasp that while they had thought they could try to use the road to their advantage, the decision to improve it had had little to do with them and everything to do with what was happening beyond and to the west of Yaurisque: the activities associated with Las Bambas, an open pit mine at four thousand msl. with mining concessions of gold, copper, silver, molybdenum, and other precious metals that had been staked out between multinational corporations and the Peruvian state.[3] The entanglement of infrastructural improvements—in this instance, road-building—and the proliferation of mining in the highlands reveals the Janus-faced power that the state wields: its absence deliberately creating marginalization, its presence creating both opportunities and devastating prospects (Harvey and Knox 2015, 39–40).

The road has catalyzed an explosion of entrepreneurial undertakings, such as Huanoquite's chauffers association. Formed of fifty-two young men, each of whom had managed to beg, borrow, and steal enough to drive a van or car that served as a taxi, they shuttled people, one trip a day, between Huanoquite and Cusco. The members all paid into the association, which operated with impressive order. They also offered "express" service to folks like me who wanted an entire taxi to secure their belongings and have the convenience of traveling right away instead of waiting for a cab or van to fill up. People were finally able to schedule appointments with doctors that they could keep; they could plan ahead to participate in the lottery to draw a coveted spot in the Huancaro market to sell their wares there and elsewhere; and bureaucratic personnel and teachers no longer needed to worry about getting to their destinations in a timely fashion. Admittedly, the vehicles the members used varied in quality, and although safety standards existed, they were rarely enforced. One of the most harrowing trips I survived took place when I was traveling from Huanoquite back to Cusco and there was a freak snowstorm. The defroster of the taxi did not work, so shivering, we drove through a blizzard with the windows rolled all the way down for the entire trip, and we narrowly avoided head-on collisions with oncoming traffic the driver could not see. Nevertheless, Huanoquite had its "taxi station" in Cusco; it was thriving, and it was, importantly, a way for young men to retain a foothold in both Huanoquite and Cusco.

When I traveled the road for the first time, I also noticed new, enormous signs announcing archaeological sites to visit along the way. This too was something the road had brought. Many Huanoquiteños hoped that tourists would

2. The Power and Seduction of Infrastructure

visit their "linda tierra" ("beautiful land"), as Huanoquite's Facebook page announced.[4] The use of cell phones among both young and old in Huanoquite complemented the extension and improvement of roads. Cell phones allowed for rapid communication about prices in various markets, coordinating with buyers, doing business, in general, and keeping in touch with friends and relatives who might be widely scattered. Huanoquiteños also used cell phones to access the World Wide Web and learn new things. It tied them into the market and allowed them to explore opportunities they might never had thought about before. Internet service was poorly developed in Huanoquite, although the municipality had its own fiercely protected server, which allowed it to also take care of any number of bureaucratic operations more easily without making repeated journeys to Cusco.

The ease of transport, the existence of multiple Inca archaeological sites in the area, and the possibility of adventure—hiking high into the mountains and white-water rafting—were among the reasons that Huanoquiteños imagined their home could become a magnet for tourists in ways that could be economically advantageous to them but would not damage their relationships with other beings that also inhabited their universe. Many other ventures were underway, which I will discuss at greater length in chapter 3. Huanoquiteños were eager to establish their own agricultural fair that they could hold regularly in their district capital, and they had entered into delicate negotiations among themselves in general assemblies with respect to exactly where, how often, and on which lands the fair should be held; where vehicles should park; and what should be charged to participants in the fair. In short order—after at least forty years of discussion, on and off—two stadiums, a health center, and a community center had been built, as well as a salon for the stunning colonial-era Catholic church where meetings could be held, no matter the faith of those gathering. Father Roy Wilson Aroni Peralta, the Catholic priest of Huanoquite, was more progressive and open-minded than those who had preceded him. For centuries, priests in Huanoquite had constituted a tightly knit triumvirate along with the landed estate owners and the police. Father Roy, as he was known, had pushed hard to obtain funds from the church hierarchy in Cusco to build the salon along with living quarters where visitors could spend the night. One highlight of the project was a first—a visit from Monsignor Richard Daniel Alarcón Urrutia, the archbishop of Cusco, to inaugurate the salon. It had also not gone unnoticed that at the mass prior to a feast and dancing at the salon itself, the archbishop began by first blessing specially selected ears of maize followed by the more typical communion wafers that devotees consumed for communion. Another first was that Father Roy, in his remarks, spoke of "common unity," emphasizing that the church was the people, that anyone was welcome to use the salon, not just Catholics, and that it was incumbent upon the "community" to bring its youth into the fold and not forget about the elderly. He concluded by complimenting Huanoquiteños on the beauty of their verdant home.[5]

Having seen what a good road could do, authorities mustered help from the district municipality to build secondary roads to fields and outlying communities. Gone were the donkeys, horses, and occasional llamas that had been a familiar sight to me in the past, and fewer were the giant lorries carrying passengers and freight in the back. As these modes of transport were replaced by pickup trucks and motorcycles, it became easier for people to see who was going where and what their business might be in Huanoquite. In 2018, I interviewed Hugo Herrera Catari, mayor of Huanoquite, just before his term ended (Interview, July 30, 2018). His father had been a teacher, and Hugo, too, had become a teacher. Passionately committed to making improvements that would benefit the children of Huanoquite, he was especially proud of two initiatives that he had taken during his time in office. Many of Huanoquite's communities and annexes were located far from the district capital where the elementary, middle, and high schools were. Herrera succeeded in making sure dirt roads from these communities were built and maintained (with the help of villagers and municipal funds and equipment), and the municipality purchased a school bus that made the rounds every morning and afternoon to bring school children to and from these distant communities and annexes. He had also established a scholarship so that at least one, and maybe two, of the very best of Huanoquite's high school students could pursue university in Cusco. Given that Huanoquite's population was well over five thousand, he wanted to transform the health post into a mini-hospital in Huanoquite, improve basic sanitation and potable water throughout the district, and ensure adequate nutrition for children by incentivizing the use of Indigenous foods such as quinoa as part of school breakfasts and lunches. He recognized the importance of the road but said, "Projects are not a question of cement. They are a question of education and health. Society doesn't see this, but yes, when one analyzes well, those are great successes, more than a house. Without education, we see the ugly corruption. Without education, we will never see equality." When I asked Herrera if he had encountered any issues while serving as Huanoquite's mayor, he commented, "You should never lose hope. Hope is all we can lose." Nevertheless, during his term in office, he sadly discovered that his idealism clashed brutally with the patron-client system of competing for budgetary allocations from the various regional government offices in Cusco, and he was not successful in much of what he wanted to achieve. In his words,

2. The Power and Seduction of Infrastructure

FIGURE 2.1. Teachers, authorities, and members of different district organizations carrying signs protesting government corruption on Peru's Independence Day. One sign reads, "The government cannot combat corruption because the government is corruption." Authorities also carried a constructed coffin and held up a sign declaring, "Corruption Should Be Buried."

The worst problem in Peru at the national level is the corruption. If you go to the Ministry of Housing, Education, Health, or Transport, if you don't give, if you don't get yourself godfathers, you won't get any projects going. This is clientelism, paternalism. And corruption. Even the janitorial staff. They ask, "how much?" This extends to the ministers themselves and they ask a lot from you, not a small amount. And they use bribery. To get loans, etc. A lot of mayors have suffered from this. This shocked me a lot. I would say to you that I learned a lot from my term as mayor and I can tell you corruption is the reality at the foundation of Peru's political system. It is deceptive.

Markets, Machines, and Roads

A close connection existed between roads and markets. The Huancaro Agricultural Fair in Cusco had been a resounding success, and Huanoquiteños were singled out at the market for the agricultural products they offered for sale there, especially their potatoes. They were able to sell to wholesalers as well as directly to small buyers at the fair. Wholesalers also made their way to Huanoquite to buy products in bulk, a relatively new development. A new position had been added to the municipality—machine operator—who maintained all the machines, including threshers, tractors, and all different kinds of vehicles, that the municipality now owned and rented to individuals and communities. The current machine operator had been one of the two principal truck drivers who, year after year, had made the dangerous and exhausting journey from Cusco to Huanoquite on the dirt road. Eventually, he had left Huanoquite altogether and migrated to Spain where he had lived for many years. In 2017, he returned to Huanoquite where he was then living and working.

The road was directly linked to the quinoa boom and had facilitated the ability of personnel from NGOs, the Ministry of Agriculture, and the Cusco Regional Government offices, as well as prospective quinoa wholesalers, to make the journey to Huanoquite. Huanoquiteños who were members of the QCA were more easily able to journey periodically to Cusco and Lima where periodic meetings of multiple cultivator associations were held. Huanoquiteños told me these meetings were critical because association members from different parts of the highlands exchanged valuable information among themselves with respect to their experiences growing, processing, preparing, and marketing quinoa to them. This kind of networking was relatively new to Indigenous inhabitants, and they were enthused about it.

Huanoquiteños, more than ever, were living as borderland dwellers, anchored to their communities while selectively drawing on all manner of ideas, material, and practices that flowed to and from the village from so many parts of the world. The improvement in transportation and communication infrastructure had enhanced the circulation of knowledge for these purposes. Many initiatives that the road had ushered in, either directly or indirectly, had given Huanoquiteños alternatives to consider pursuing.

Navigating Attachments to Place and Opportunity

Because of the road, it had become much easier to obtain building supplies and complete construction projects. A building boom in the district capital itself was underway. Some of these houses were being built by younger households that now had sufficient resources to build their own homes in Huanoquite; others were being built by villagers who had moved to the district capital from outlying communities because they wanted greater proximity to the road and because they were working in the mines near Huanoquite. These building ventures, partly made possible because of the private market in land, had created dissent and concern. Families who decided they no longer wanted to live in Huanoquite had sold their residential lands to newcomers, sometimes without permission from district or community authorities.

2. The Power and Seduction of Infrastructure

While few young Huanoquiteños wanted to spend their lives solely as agriculturalists, they did want to continue living in Huanoquite and farming part of the time. Huanoquite's Facebook site mentioned above, "Conociéndote Huanoquite Linda Tierra," was maintained by its municipal authorities, but many different Huanoquiteños contributed to it with gorgeous visual images and videos that they themselves shot. Some authorities used it as a platform for their political ambitions, but the page also offered a glimpse of the sentiments of pride, tenderness, and attachment that Huanoquiteños expressed about their territory and that bound them to it. They found their landscape to be stunning, and they viewed the road as a means to create "a field of action" for themselves, as one young man told me. To give readers a sense of the feelings that Huanoquiteños expressed about their home, below are three posts Huanoquiteños made to their Facebook page between 2019 and 2020.[6] One young man, commenting on several photos he took when he traveled from Huanoquite to an outlying community overlooking the Apurimac River, posted: "This is the forest of Loretuyuq, with its immense natural beauty, demonstrating the rich variety of trees, plants, and an abundance of crystalline water, located in the Apurimac Valley" (December 9, 2019). Another commented: "Perhaps I live in a humble dwelling but thanks to my hands and mother earth you have enough products to eat all year. I don't ask for your money. I only ask that you value me" (March 21, 2019). And a third, a young woman, wrote the following during the lockdown throughout Peru, due to the COVID-19 virus: "We have so many delicious plates of food to enjoy during these days with our family without needing to depend on industrial products" (March 20, 2020).[7]

Instead of moving to Cusco, young people were remaining in Huanoquite, building two-story houses for themselves of "noble construction material," rather than adobe, and because many of them did not yet have families, they could afford such investments as a means of "planning ahead." Mobility itself was a strategic variable in young people's calculus of their marriage prospects, and a house and a car, pickup, or motorcycle had come to substitute for the savings insurance that a cow or horse had represented at one time. While I was with a labor party of farmers threshing wheat one day, a woman from the community of Toctohuaylla in Huanoquite joked about how they called it "Tokyo," and they referred to another nearby village, Nayhua, as "Nueva York."

At the same time, the improvement of roads had catalyzed concerns with respect to divergent paths Huanoquiteños were taking, growing inequalities within the district between those with sufficient capital to take advantage of opportunities that the road offered, and a simmering anger that the roads were less about them, their futures, and their environment than about international capital flows, as they witnessed the machines and resources thundering to the mines above them and the spewing dust from trucks carrying minerals back to Cusco for eventual export.

Harvey and Knox (2015, 74, 181), elaborating on the contradictions that have accompanied Peru's roadbuilding, note that "although roads are powerful technologies for achieving state projects of territorial integration, they are also spaces within which people are forced to grapple with ongoing questions about what kind of future they are engaged in, who this future is for, and how it should be brought about. . . . In spite of the self-proclaimed transparency of public works projects, their organization produces the conditions within which ambiguity, secrecy, and inequality proliferate as a way of enabling private gain to accrue in the guise of public concern."

The reality was that even as Huanoquiteños were dreaming of and making their own futures in creative fashion, seizing on the advances that communications technology and roads and their arteries had to offer, they were increasingly aware of how enmeshed the public works they welcomed were with the desires of mining companies in collaboration with the state. Kregg Hetherington, in a longitudinal study of the development and expansion of soybean monocropping in Paraguay, writes about how different population sectors there perceived, understood, and intervened in a monumental and destructive transformation of a mixed agricultural economy and landscape to one of monocropping and environmental degradation. He documents how state functionaries and rural activists believed that, through regulatory actions, the state would regulate soy expansion and would defend people's "right to live well in a healthy environment." Instead, it turned out that regulators themselves "often found themselves protecting soy itself, enforcing laws that were meant to strengthen the crop and promote its expansion." He concludes that "[t]he problem perhaps was less state absence than regulatory capture or even more fundamentally that the entire regulatory apparatus had been built by the soy sector to service its own interests" (Hetherington 2020, 10).

A similar kind of dynamic colored the entire history of infrastructural expansion and top-down development projects in the Andean highlands, often cloaked in a discourse that suggested that the primary goal of these activities was to benefit the lives of Indigenous Huanoquiteños. In reality, the state's rhetoric and policies rarely conformed to reality. They were co-opted and intertwined with the interests of a multiplicity of actors whose goals, whether to assure the colonial expansion of landed estates, stimulate Indigenous agriculture for the development of industry, incorporate Huanoquite's farmers into the neoliberal global economy through the export of their quinoa, or lure foreign companies

2. The Power and Seduction of Infrastructure

to invest in extractive activities, like mining, created enormous tensions, misunderstandings, and deliberate confusion.

When inequalities are carved into the very fabric of society, as in the Andean highlands, the idea of a single "public," or civic, space for engagement and consultation is not generally borne out. Rather, as Nancy Fraser (1992) points out, the reality instead is the existence of "counter-publics" who are often completely excluded from decision-making due to questions of gender, class, ethnic, racial, or cultural discrimination, or some combination thereof. In this context, the *appearance* of protecting collective interests often meant consultation with community authorities who could be co-opted and coordination with private corporations rather than with those whose lives might be most impacted by the development of roads, a strategic practice in the spirit of progressive corporatism. Huanoquiteños were not consulted about many infrastructural projects that involved their fate, but as a counter-public they did debate issues from which they were excluded and tried to determine the best course of action to take.

The lack of consultation on the part of the state and regional government angered many Huanoquiteños who voiced their ambivalence, discontent, and anxiety in private. Some of their sentiments were apparent in the frustration of the mayor with the corrupt mechanisms of allocation of resources from the Cusco Regional Government. The Peruvian state decided what concessions to make and where roads should go. Hence, Huanoquiteños' fury that the significant stretch of road between Yaurisque and Huanoquite was not paved despite how much it mattered to them. They knew it was because there was no gold or copper or molybdenum in Huanoquite proper.[8] And an even more recent project that was being floated was to build yet another road, bypassing Yaurisque entirely. Instead, it would more or less follow the ancient trajectory of the Inca road in a straight shot from Cusco to Huanoquite. However, this was, again, not at all about the convenience or welfare of Huanoquiteños. The project would represent a significant shortcut to the mines that lay beyond Huanoquite in Ccapi and Chumbivilcas. Huanoquiteños welcomed improved infrastructure in the form of paved roads they could use for any number of reasons and activities, some of which I have outlined above, that would permit them to thrive as border dwellers in a complex web of networks. Nevertheless, the state, in conjunction with private corporations, too often had other less salubrious designs in mind when they invested in constructing and paving these same roads.

CHAPTER 3

Contesting Development, Alternative Paths

This chapter looks closely at projects that state and parastatal-NGO entities have introduced to Huanoquiteños and at those projects that Huanoquiteños have initiated themselves. Comparing and contrasting these projects offers a window onto how Huanoquiteños envisioned improvements in their well-being. Huanoquiteños have learned from top-down imposed development initiatives, many of which have tantalized them with false promises, but rather than reject them entirely, they have sometimes attempted to revamp them by tapping into resources in Huanoquite and the knowledge they have garnered and interpreted from an astonishing number of sources, experiences, and travels. While distinctions can be drawn among different kinds of projects, especially between those that have encouraged community sovereignty more than neoliberal entrepreneurialism, many projects that Huanoquiteños pursued drew on contradictory ideologies because they believed they would promote greater autonomy *and* offer a better fit with their existing economic activities, as well as their place in their communities and in the universe, writ large.

In the introduction to their edited volume, *Indigenous Life Projects and Extractivism: Ethnographies from South America,* Juan Javier Rivera Andía and Cecilie Ødegaard (2019, 39) comment on the danger of not recognizing that throughout the history of Indigenous people any number of entities have introduced and created "new kinds of values and new types of evaluating agents" which do not act in a cognitive or material vacuum. As Huanoquiteños sought

3. Contesting Development, Alternative Paths

to constitute or perpetuate their relationships with human and other-then-human entities that constituted their world, they assessed whether or not new kinds of values and evaluative agents and processes that filtered into their world would enhance livability for them, and in what ways. Along these lines, more generally, Rivera Andía and Ødegaard (2019, 21) argue that "Indigeneity . . . cannot be seen as referring to a pre-existing, static formation of identity but, rather, as informed by the complex politics and interdependencies of capitalism and state-building as well as by class, language, ethnicity, and racialised hierarchies in particular contexts." Citing García (2005, 6), they urge that the lives of Indigenous peoples be approached and described in nondualistic ways that do not resort to "the all-or-nothing terms of authenticity and invention, cultural survival and extinction" (Rivera Andía and Ødegaard 2019, 21). Looking at the evolution of these projects in Huanoquite over time was one way to uncover their nuances and complexities and to try to avoid dualistic and dichotomous portrayals of Huanoquiteños' lives and values; the history of these projects revealed important lessons for the more recent efforts to expand Huanoquite's quinoa cultivation.

Because of the privatization of agrarian land, even while many Huanoquiteños remained members of their communities, their ideas and practices about how they could best nurture their land so that it would feed them differed. These differing ideas were the product of the cultural, political, and economic worlds in which they were situated. They contributed actively to the creation of the fabric of the history on which agrarian life in the Andes was unfolding in the twenty-first century. And their opinions about whether to embrace one or another "project" made it clear that a static and reified understanding of *who* Indigenous Quechua inhabitants were, made no sense even though many non-Indigenous people viewed them in essentialist ways.

Although there was occasional convergence—even unanimity—concerning project benefits, more often, Huanoquiteños disagreed about whether or not a project would improve their lives. Their past experiences with projects that parastatal NGOs had proposed and implemented nevertheless colored their receptiveness to new ones that were introduced. They initially viewed them with skepticism, a bit of hope, and weariness, and they always entertained the possibility that something might usefully invigorate their livelihoods and that they would be able to channel it constructively. Almost inevitably, though, they became resentful of the failure of personnel to keep their promises and of their tendency to discriminate and stigmatize them; Huanoquiteños' sneaking suspicion (not infrequently garnered from their past experiences) that they were being used as tokens by NGO agents and bureaucrats to show that they were doing *something* rather than nothing was not unfounded. Participants came to view projects tactically, juggling who and what might make it possible to comply with the project demands without leading to the depletion and exhaustion of their own energy, which they needed for any number of other life activities. Below, I first begin by examining some of the concepts that state and para-statal NGOs enacted in their world-making as they sought to introduce and implement their ventures.

Social Welfare and Development: Projecting Indigenous Poverty and Need

Prior to Peru's civil war, parastatal and nongovernmental organization (NGO) initiatives proliferated. Many were well intentioned but were based on little information on the ground and infused with ideals that derived from western economic and philosophical frameworks. Admittedly, this is an overgeneralization, especially given the evolution of NGOs over time, their interface with state entities, their location, and the diversity among them. Some NGOs were provisioners of social services, others contributed directly to the construction of infrastructure that the state either did not or would not provide, and still others operated as organizations that were trying to influence national and international political actors with respect to best practices for alleviating poverty and inequality, and for promoting development (See Yanacopulos 2019, 153–64).

Even today, the staff of NGOs runs the gamut from those comprised primarily of nonnationals to others where the leadership is nonnational but those implementing projects on the ground are nationals. In many cases, the same model is used transnationally but collaborations on the ground are adjusted in the context of local conditions and politics. In short, both Indigenous initiatives and those promoted by NGOs had to be evaluated in light of the historical, economic, and cultural forces within which they were embedded.[1] Current and prior ethnographic research on NGOs operating in Huanoquite, especially those partnering with the equivalent of Cusco's Regional Government at the time, the Ministry of Agriculture, and the Ministry of Health and Human Service, espoused similar assumptions to those I mention here (See Seligmann 1995; 1997). This was also true of Dutch and German NGO efforts to resuscitate and extend Huanoquite's irrigation system (see Seligmann and Bunker 1994). Their assumptions led to serious flaws in their project design and implementation.

While projects succeeded from time to time in Huanoquite, more often they created a staggering duplication of monies invested in the project and a waste of resources; they were not enthusiastically welcomed by households;

58

3. Contesting Development, Alternative Paths

they overwhelmingly overlooked the contributions of women and their roles and agency; and conflicts among communities over participation, boundaries, and conflicting investments of labor ensued, some of which became volatile. NGO personnel disparaged and criticized inhabitants for their laziness and ignorance even when they themselves failed to comply with promises they had made, and all too often they allied themselves with Peruvian state officials, police, and members of the religious hierarchy. In short, the attitudes and assumptions underlying the projects were saturated by paternalism, ineptitude, and an uncritical embrace of western assumptions about modernization and development.[2]

For well over a decade during the civil war, NGOs disappeared from the landscape because many personnel associated with development projects became targets of the Shining Path movement, and conditions, especially in the countryside, were too dangerous. At the beginning of the twenty-first century, they made a reappearance—fewer in number—and today, villagers and their authorities emphasize that the goal of proposed projects is "mitad mitad" (half and half), with Huanoquiteños and their authorities asserting themselves far more in negotiating the terms of collaboration with NGOs and with government initiatives. In fact, it would be more apt to call these entities quasi-governmental rather than nongovernmental since many of them worked in partnership with the government, as well as with populations they had targeted for their projects (See also Edelman and Haugerud 2005, 27–28).

While I was in Huanoquite in 2018 and 2019, three such organizations were actively working with Huanoquiteños: CEDEP AYLLU (EU), Pachamama Raymi (Holland), and Caritas (Spain). In addition, the Peruvian government had sponsored numerous social welfare programs, among the most important of which were: Cuna Más (More than a Crib), FISE (Fondo de Inclusión Social Energético—Fund for Social Energy Inclusion), Vaso de Leche (A Glass of Milk), Comedor Popular (People's Kitchen), Qali Warma (Healthy Children), and Programa Juntos (Together).

Cuna Más was designed to support infant development and education and was operated by the Ministry of Development and Social Inclusion (MIDIS— Ministerio de Desarrollo e Inclusión Social).[3] Monies were also provided by MIDIS to the municipality for Comedor Popular and Programa Juntos. Comedor Popular and Qali Warma sought to reduce hunger and poverty and coordinated with "Club de Madres"—Mothers' Club—to prepare and offer food regularly, especially to children, in school cafeterias. They encouraged the use of local products and resources for school breakfasts and lunches. Programa Juntos was a conditional cash transfer program that operated in districts where

59

the poverty rate was more than 40 percent. It provided women who were heads of households that included a nursing mother and children up to the age of nineteen who had lived in the district for at least six months with a monthly lump sum every two months that went toward the basic subsistence of the household and toward furthering the education of the children in the household. That sum, depending on household composition and demographics, could be close to one hundred dollars every two months. The program relied on means testing to determine eligibility as well as household continuation in the program.

FISE, which operated out of the Ministry of Energy and Mining, attempted to reduce the use of solid fuels (especially wood and manure) for energy among rural households, replacing it with natural gas and other sources of electricity. Vaso de Leche consisted of monies allocated by the Ministry of Health to the municipality, and its objective was to provide at least three glasses of milk per day to children under the age of six who were suffering from malnutrition; it also sought to improve the nutrition of the elderly and often worked with Caritas.

Huanoquite was featured in national newspapers in 2019 because of the poor health and malnutrition of children in the district. Ministry of Health statistics stated that at least 20 percent of Huanoquite's population suffered from chronic malnutrition and more than 7 percent of children under the age of five suffered from anemia, almost double the national average. Approximately 56 percent of the population was considered poor, and 20 percent were considered extremely poor. It is difficult to ascertain the accuracy of these statistics.[4] Huanoquiteños tended to suffer from anemia because their diet was less based on animal-protein than might be found in what might be called a "traditional" western diet, but this did not mean that they were malnourished. For thousands of years, Quechua inhabitants of the Andes have lived without ingesting high amounts of animal protein. Instead, they have consumed protein from time to time, especially on ritual occasions, in the form of guinea pig, freeze-dried alpaca and llama meat (*ch'arki*), mutton, beef, pork, and increasingly, chicken, and they have consumed foods prepared from quinoa and related crops (*kañiwa* and *kiwicha*), which also provide high amounts of protein.

Rivera Andía (2019, 172) points out that "labels of being in need and poverty create visibility for Indigenous people" but also often stigmatize them and ignore the violation of Indigenous rights that are the historical product of systemic racism and the diminishing and fractured land base of Indigenous households. The uses and impacts of these labels have been well-documented in many world regions, as Kimura's (2013) volume makes clear. McDonell (2015, 75), discussing the tendency of parastatal NGOs to focus on "Miracle

3. Contesting Development, Alternative Paths

Food Narratives" (MFNs) as panaceas to poverty and malnutrition, puts it well: "MFNs locate the cause of the problem within the malnourished people themselves. Be it their poor agriculture techniques, 'superstition,' or high birth rates, the problem is the local people, sometimes national policies, but never global economic structures." By viewing Huanoquiteños through a filter of poverty, hunger, and malnutrition, NGOs embraced distorted ideas about why certain foodstuffs might not be available to households, for example, and too often assigned ignorance and blame to mothers for hunger and malnutrition. Nevertheless, mothers took advantage of these programs; authorities also did, bolstering their power by obtaining monies for communities and municipalities to provide these resources.

The Comedor Popular and Qali Warma programs were exceptions to the portrayal I have offered above because of their efforts to address deeper questions of sustainable nutrition in Huanoquite itself. Even they depended on the goodwill of households—especially women—whose labor was already overextended—to provide their household's potatoes, quinoa, or maize *gratis* and to help prepare children's school breakfasts and lunches. In July 2018, Qali Warma and the Regional Department of Agriculture in Cusco took note of the burden being placed on Indigenous Quechua women and held a workshop to encourage the identification of locally grown products with high nutritious value that could officially be made part of school lunches. Quinoa was identified as one such product. The next step planned was to identify local growers, the amount needed of each product, and what kind of assistance could be provided to growers to facilitate local supply of these products, all of which had high nutritious value (Carlos 2018). This policy constituted a noteworthy shift from assuming households would provide their quinoa and other homegrown foodstuffs free of charge as a kind of expected contribution to the school, but it remained a plan that had yet to be implemented.

Programa Juntos, according to evaluations of its programs—which have existed since 2005—in Amazonia and the Andean highlands has been modestly successful in improving health and educational performance among participating households. Most likely unintentionally, the program has encouraged the formation of joint and extended households across generations to qualify for eligibility. In Huanoquite, these households often consisted of younger migrant families who returned periodically to Huanoquite (six months at a time), thus allowing the entire household to claim Programa Juntos funds. In one case with which I was familiar, the son had married a woman who hailed from Bolivia. They lived in Los Altos, Bolivia, near her family for several years over the course of which they had three children, the youngest of whom was still nursing. The parents worked at a recycling plant but were trying to start up a sewing business at the same time so that they could be self-employed. After a catastrophe in which they were robbed of "everything they had," including their three sewing machines and their "good" clothes, the mother and her three children returned to Huanoquite to live with her in-laws while her husband worked in Lima with two relatives in a fast-food fried-chicken operation to pay back debts he owed. The situation was tense because of the sudden addition of four household members, their need for a place to live, and the challenges the daughter-in-law encountered taking care of her children, helping her mother-in-law, and trying to continue farming the small number of fields belonging to her husband. Programa Juntos was a great aid in boosting basic disposable household income and allowing households to determine how those funds should be spent.

Projecting Autonomy

Many government programs, even though they could be beneficial to households by providing a welcome safety net, had a scaffolding that was intended to assimilate Indigenous peoples into dominant western practices of child-rearing and diet.[5] The programs depended heavily on women and their resources to comply with their objectives. I talked with several women who felt great anxiety about what the programs expected of them, especially as they juggled carrying on with their daily responsibilities and standing in long lines to be counted to receive canned milk, for example, or contributing a quota from their household stores so that their children would receive meals at school. Women were not unfamiliar with these kinds of demands, which conformed to audit culture, but they calculated the value of their time and resources in the context of a multitude of other activities they *needed* to attend to, and these needs were invisible to state and parastatal agents, as a matter of course. It is not possible to quantify the balance between the investment of their labor and what they received from it, but the programs tended to extract women's labor more than they produced a mechanism for sustainable household reproduction.

Huanoquiteños also pursued their own initiatives similar to those promoted by parastatal-NGO organizations that focused on production and consumption, but they were qualitatively different in the assumptions they made and how they were structured. They were less subject to bureaucratic frameworks that assessed whether participants were "need-worthy," impoverished, "native," or "Indigenous," and they tended to build on existing knowledge and experiential practices that were already circulating in the community. One teacher from Huanoquite who was talking to me about different government-sponsored and NGO projects in the district exclaimed in some exasperation, "All of those

3. Contesting Development, Alternative Paths

programs are intended for *campesinos* (peasants). But what about the rest of us here? We are Huanoquiteños too. We are teachers and many of us here are making less than farmers!" Her point was that "peasants" hailing from Indigenous Quechua backgrounds had been the object and target of development programs for years, exceptionalized and victimized at the same time that others, including those who were poorly paid professionals but did not fit categories established by the government for social welfare programs, might also want to benefit from recognition and exercise of their skills in their communities.

Some NGOs had taken to heart the need to reevaluate the developmentalist assumptions they employed in their projects, but few if any of them seemed to be operating in Huanoquite.[6] Christopher Shepherd (2010) has documented how various actors, who included farmers and NGO project agents, valorized local knowledge and tradition, culturally, economically, aesthetically, and epistemologically, in different and unexpected ways in several agricultural biodiversity projects in the Cusco region. He found that what was considered "Andean" was selective and that farmers, while they had a great fount of "local" expertise, also drew on knowledge across time and space that was not bounded but rather constructed. That meant that what was "Andean" and what could be considered "local" had to be negotiated by NGO agents and farmers as they sought to decide what agrobiodiversity and its conservation meant and entailed. The result was that "non-pro-Andean actors," as Shepherd (2010, 639) calls them, were reevaluating their views and perceptions of agrodiversity as "a drag on development" or "inefficient," especially in the face of climate change and the need for food security. He also found that, for similar reasons, they were reconsidering their assumptions that poverty could be equated with lack of nutrition and food.

Huanoquiteños' recognition that they could take advantage of expertise that went far beyond "traditional" knowledge, as it has too often been stereotyped, was evident in one assembly I attended. Community members had decided that they wanted to build additional reservoirs to "harvest" their water from sources high above Huanoquite for purposes of irrigation. Instead of turning to outside engineers and construction workers, they decided that they should take advantage of their own youth, "the younger generation," as they put it, "who were now professionals" and who could "help design and build the reservoirs" (Community Meeting of Maska and Tihuicte, April 2, 2018). Huanoquiteños tried to make things work in both Huanoquite and "elsewhere," and as I note in chapter 2, many Huanoquiteños who had left their communities for long periods of time came back. Some returned because they had failed to gain a foothold outside of Huanoquite, but many others came back to help with sowing or the harvest, to inherit resources, to support their aging parents, or to apply their acquired skills to endeavors in Huanoquite, often for the improvement not only of their own households but also of the community. They might live on the margins in some people's eyes, yet they played the margins for everything they could.

The projects Huanoquiteños undertook were more likely to cross ethnic/racial categories and class and generational strata and involve Indigenous and non-Indigenous interactions and participants. Their general impulse to pursue these projects was *not* because they saw themselves (or other Huanoquiteños) as victimized and impoverished but because they thought the projects would directly benefit them and Huanoquite in a long-lasting way. Huanoquiteños who had acquired skills in small industries as carpenters, bakers, electricians, weavers, computer whizzes, machinists, mechanics, and plumbers also promoted ventures. Few intended the exercise of their vocational skills to serve as the mainstay of their household's livelihood but rather as complements to their agricultural activities, which made it possible for them to provide better for their households and, on occasion, to pursue their own hopes and dreams. Their skills contributed significantly to improving livelihood conditions, in general, for other Huanoquiteños. When I saw these mechanics or weavers in action, they never explicitly articulated their desire to contribute to community well-being, but they exhibited a pride in their skills, and I witnessed many instances where villagers openly praised them. The range of their projects was surprising and moved between individualized and community undertakings, which were often in tension with each other. At the same time, the efforts they undertook to foster or take advantage of activities that would provide them with greater economic autonomy and diminish systemic racism all too often ran the risk of exacerbating individualism and inequalities. Below, I offer a few examples of these grassroots initiatives, which were more mitad mitad and were the brainchild of individuals, households, and even communities.

What About the Cheese?

I was intrigued by the many motorcycles traveling the dirt roads of Huanoquite high into the mountains and down into the valleys. Sometimes it was clear that driver and passenger were young couples on an outing or headed to a destination. But after I saw a few of these motorcycles with metal cannisters securely tied on the back, I asked what was in the cannisters and was told milk. Milk to make cheese and milk to make yoghurt. Villagers, together with funds and support from the municipality, started this project. Huanoquiteños have always had their own Vaso de Leche program, but *this* milk did not come out of a Gloria Leche can. Instead, udders were the answer. The cows' productivity was not as high as participants might have wanted because, since the dissolution of the cooperative and the transformation of the flat pampa of Tihuicte into household residences, less grazing land was available, and households had become focused more on agricultural than herding activities. But the milk was "*rica, rica*" (rich, rich). It was collected in the morning, and then Huanoquite's own brand of cheese and yoghurt were made. The project started in 2018, and according to participants, they were making fifteen to twenty cheeses a day that were very popular and sold locally at twelve soles per kilo (about four US dollars). The woman recounting this to me added, "We've gotten prizes for Huanoquite cheese at the agricultural fairs in Paruro, even Lima. We hope we can continue to expand!"

The Fish Will Multiply

Ernesto was a little boy of eight when I first met him many years ago. I knew his father as well, a shrewd and curious man, blind in one eye, who had since died. Ernesto was now in his forties and lived just on the outskirts of Huanoquite proper. In 2018, I was walking by a compound where I noticed a series of three concrete reservoirs on a slope with water pouring down from one to the next, cascading through pipes. Some of Ernesto's fields, it turned out, were located at a site that had plentiful water coming from two springs. He had the idea that perhaps he could channel some of the water through pipes down to

FIGURE 3.1. Trout farm project

his patio and experiment with a trout farm. His son, who was studying at the university, worked with him, and they successfully created the structure, supplying it with tiny trout they had bought in Cusco. The trout were maturing, and he hoped that by the next year he would be able to sell them at the market. In 2019, when I returned and asked him how the trout farm was doing, he was thrilled because, so far, it had been successful, and he was able not only to sell fish in Cusco but also to other Huanoquiteños.

Paulina's Dreams

Paulina's grandparents had once owned the mill in Huanoquite that was used for grinding wheat into flour. It eventually shuttered in the late 1990s but for many years had served as a vibrant nexus of Huanoquite's social and economic life. Exuding energy, Paulina had a beautiful smile and a youthful face. She laughed frequently. She had no kin ties with hacienda families but her connection to the mill had given her substantial social power and an education. Her husband, Samuel, was a key quinoa cultivator, and people had enormous respect for his skills as a farmer. Paulina also farmed and was a founding member of the QCA. One day, Paulina invited me to harvest her maize with her and a labor party of ten. She asked me to be at her house at 6:00 a.m. I was feeling very ill—sick to my stomach—but dragged myself there. She spent another three hours whipping up a feast of rice, noodles mixed with carrots and onions, fish, and *mote* (hominy). On the way to the fields, carrying food for ten as if the cannisters and plastic tubs were light as a feather, she picked up a cheese, which she allowed me to carry, and when we arrived at the fields, she put together a delicious meal. Unlike so many of the labor parties I had observed, this one was based on *ayni* (a direct exchange of labor, accompanied by food, drink, and coca) rather than *jornal* (a daily wage accompanied by food, drink, and coca). The atmosphere was also different, characterized by a lack of hierarchy and an abundance of playful ribbing and joking.

Paulina had always had dreams. She had become a member of an association of women artisans that was established in Huanoquite in 2018. Initially consisting of thirty members, it had dropped to ten because many of the participants could not afford the primary materials for production. The association's goal was to produce weavings. A woman came from Spain every two months to buy up what they had produced in Huanoquite and resell it in Europe. The municipality decided to support the project by providing a weaving teacher, but the women had to purchase the raw materials and treadle looms. Paulina had yearned to be a weaver since the age of fifteen, so much so that she sold all her sheep to be able to purchase her loom and yarn. A carpenter in Cusco made the loom in parts, and the association members bought them. Paulina's first loom cost S./650 (650 soles), but she found another carpenter to make the same loom for half the price, which was much more affordable for association members. The women wove on their looms in the same municipal building where a machine called a *perladora* or *escarificadora* was housed. The machine, which no one knew how to use yet, was intended to rid quinoa of its bitter outer hull of saponin. Paulina's second loom was in a sunny room in her house. The women made scarves and carrying cloths with traditional designs, using synthetic yarn. Paulina and the other members of the association planned to renegotiate their original contract for the following year because they had determined that the price for their products should be higher, given the labor they invested in making them. At that time, the woman from Spain was buying up their scarves at thirty-five soles and the carrying cloths they wove at forty-five soles each. I visited the association one day. The women worked hard with great energy, and they shared with me the pride they felt in what they were making and their pleasure at the autonomy they experienced, including the welcome additional funds they could control. I was especially struck by the sense of peace that prevailed while they were working. I hesitate to make too much of it, but it was clear to me that this was a space, a refuge, for them, in which they were exchanging confidences, sometimes offering support to one another, and in which they had carved out a "place of their own" where they were exercising their rights as women.

FIGURE 3.2. Paulina, a member of the Women's Artisan Association and the QCA

These were just a few of the initiatives percolating in Huanoquite. There were others that were more complex whose design and implementation were arrived at by entire communities or even the district. Many households wanted to build extensive greenhouses for flowers and fruit to sell in Cusco's San Pedro Market and at the Huancaro Agricultural Fair; they were hoping to sell meals produced from their own harvests at the planned agricultural fair they were trying to establish; and two communities in the district were lobbying to expand their access to irrigation waters and were proceeding apace to ensure that their property rights were protected, despite enormous bureaucratic obstacles and corruption.

Women also continued what they had always done. They regularly diversified their household kitchen gardens, trying out new fruit trees, medicinal herbs, and vegetables, such as carrots, broccoli, and cauliflower. Margarita's kitchen garden, for example, was a tiny wonder, and she called it her orchard. The last time I visited it, it was abundant with specimens of pear, plum, lemon, avocado, peach, *sauco* (*Sambucus peruviana*), and *kapulí* (black cherry, or *Prunus capuli*) trees; she was also growing many apple trees, poppies, roses, medicinal herbs of all sorts, and even examples of barley, maize, quinoa, beans, squash, onions, cabbage, and wild tobacco plants. In the corner was a beehive, and a cobblestone path and irrigation canal wended their way through the little paradise.

Women, it was clear, were eager to explore new ideas and practices, but they had to be careful about selecting what they wanted to pursue over the long-term, and they resented the condescending oversight that many NGOs insisted on so that they could receive funding and legitimacy. Pachamama Raymi, which was focused on poverty alleviation, implemented many projects in Huanoquite, especially with women. These included improving the structure of residences and kitchens, teaching women to produce onions, lettuce, and carrots in their vegetable gardens, encouraging them to cultivate avocado trees and other kinds of trees whose fruit could be eventually sold on the market, raising guinea pigs for sale, and teaching women to gather mushrooms. Most of these initiatives did not catch on, but women selectively began to plant one or two avocado trees, one or two other fruit trees, and some of the vegetables in their house gardens. In fact, in all the kitchen gardens I visited, most women's efforts focused on cultivating and experimenting with medicinal herbs and condiments. Almost all of them had decided to stop the large-scale raising of guinea pigs, and although some of them had "improved" kitchens, they alternated between using their adobe stoves and their propane ranges—the latter mainly for frying things or for cooking food in a pressure cooker. In short, they exerted their agency assertively in these mitad mitad arrangements.

Although few Huanoquiteños had attempted to set up a tourism business, the son of a retired teacher had built a three-story hostel where he was promoting tourism homestays. He wanted to encourage volunteer tourism and ecotourism (read adventure tourism in the form of rafting wild rivers and hiking). He envisioned tourists staying in the hostel, having the experience of working on his land, taking them on a regional tourist circuit, and then performing cures for them.[7] I never saw any tourists during my research visits, but that did not mean that the imaginary fostered by the tourism boom in Peru had not sparked a desire among Huanoquiteños to participate in it.

One household was on the verge of opening an internet café. In another case, Inés, whose adult son had been badly handicapped since birth, had formed an informal association to lobby passionately and hard with the municipality to establish services for at least thirty-five villagers who were disabled or handicapped. She had succeeded in gaining some resources for the project and had been elected as president of the association. These *"obras"* (works)—such as constructing an archway that proudly announced that visitors were entering Huanoquite's territory—might seem superficial or modest to an outsider, but they were important to Huanoquiteños, and almost all of them were motivated by people who had a desire to stay in Huanoquite and do more than subsist.

Rhetoric and Action: The Meaning of Collectivity

Key entities that intervened in the ability of Huanoquiteños to discuss, design, fund, and evaluate collective projects of one sort or another were Huanoquite's communities. Huanoquite's assemblies involved communities belonging to the district as a whole and were the place where more collectively grounded projects were floated and debated. These debates became extremely heated from time to time because of people's desire to remain united as a community, a desire that clashed with the growing individualized control over property, resources, and decision-making in villages. And women, who constituted about one-third of attendees, continued to have to battle to be heard as full-fledged community members in these gatherings because of patriarchal ideas that persisted about who was permitted to speak in meetings. How did Huanoquiteños deal with these contradictions?

When such debates came to a head while I was there, authorities sought to arrive at compromises. They leveled veiled criticism at community members who did not regularly participate in meetings, primarily lived elsewhere, or who had failed to inform other community members of decisions they had made that had repercussions for the community as a whole. These criticisms circulated in the community as gossip and in whispers, but they were also explicitly voiced in community meetings. Youth who sought to become members of a community had to formally declare their commitment to live and work in Huanoquite for at least three years; they had to convey humility when they asked for permission to become community members in a meeting; and they had to be sponsored by at least two community members who also spoke frankly about their strengths and weaknesses before they were admitted on a probationary basis by means of a voice vote. Community members were not afraid to openly raise their concerns about a potential member—past acts of juvenile delinquency that the person may have engaged in, their failure to show respect, or their absence from a labor party they had promised to attend. These acts were seriously discussed, but in all the cases I witnessed, the person was eventually permitted to become a probationary member. In the past, when young people who were reaching adulthood wanted to be officially admitted to the community, they were referred to as *yanapakuq*, a Quechua term meaning "one who must help." A motion had recently passed that stated they should now be referred to simply as *assimilantes*, a term derived from Spanish (but not actually a Spanish word) meaning one who is absorbed or incorporated into the community. This subtle change in terminology may indicate a challenge to the more authoritarian relationship that has existed between elders and youth.

FIGURE 3.3. General Assembly of community members of the district of Huanoquite

3. Contesting Development, Alternative Paths

The criteria that continued to hold sway over people's views of their membership in a community were reflected in the content of a brochure prepared by community authorities to celebrate Huanoquite's fiftieth anniversary as a formal *Comunidad Campesina*. The brochure noted, "we are human beings and workers who work the land where solidarity, reciprocity, compromise, and constant respect for the improvement of agro-livestock productivity and the conditions of social, organizational, cultural, and political life are the priorities of our peasant community" (Renato Quispe Enríques, President of Maska, 2019).

Discourse served as a vital means in community meetings to encourage community awareness and action at the same time that it called attention to the undercurrent of individualization that could fragment whatever political potency remained of collective action. "*Compañero,*" or its plural form (its equivalent is not so much "companion" but rather "comrade"), was the preferred form of address that was used in meetings once the person speaking had recognized each community authority by name. After almost thirty years of attending these kinds of meetings, I was especially struck by the growing assertiveness of community members who were far less shy or submissive than they had been in the past about demanding their rights as campesinos, as community members, and as Peruvian citizens who deserved resources from the district municipality. They vehemently rejected any residual power remaining to hacendados, deriding them because they now often had to do their own work and they criticized community members who were still willing to work for hacienda families and their heirs. In one recent meeting, the president of Maska announced that "hacendados had never given anything to Huanoquite and that there was absolutely no reason that people who worked for them should share any information about what transpires in our assemblies" (Community Meeting, October 1, 2018).

A Note on Engaged Anthropology

Huanoquiteños also openly demanded in formal community meetings that I specify what the positive consequences of my anthropological research would be for them; they wanted my earlier book translated into Spanish; and they wanted me to contribute to an upcoming irrigation project by purchasing some of the cement for it, which I did. As had been true for my research undertakings in the past, they had authorized my research on quinoa prior to my arrival in a general assembly, but they asked me to make a public address about it in another community assembly after I arrived. I explained that although my work

PART ONE. BACKSTORIES

FIGURE 3.4. Community members at Assembly reviewing the maps of tenure and production zones I had prepared from my earlier research on agrarian reform

on quinoa was primarily research rather than directly applied, I hoped they could use it to help them decide if it made sense or not for them to continue to increase their cultivation of quinoa and under what kinds of conditions. I hoped that my research would permit people—Peruvians and *"extranjeros"* (strangers) to become more cognizant of Huanoquiteños' knowledge, skills, and organizational power. And I hoped my research would encourage Huanoquiteños themselves to be more aware of the ways that women had contributed to the vitality of their households, farms, and aesthetic traditions. Given the issues that the Huanoquiteños themselves had faced and surmounted over centuries and were continuing to encounter, my explanations did not seem terribly persuasive, but I also tried to be honest about my own limitations so that they could decide how they felt about my research—whether or not they wanted me to continue it and, also, how they might want me to modify it.

The last two decades have ushered in a growing interest in engaged and collaborative research among anthropologists (Fine-Dare 2020; Rappaport 2017; Goldstein 2012; Low and Merry 2010; Lassiter 2005; and Hale and Stephen 1995). The shift from a hierarchical program of research in which anthropologists would arrive at a field site, having pretty much already decided what they would focus their research on and in which they were often unaware of their

3. Contesting Development, Alternative Paths

power, to one in which anthropologists would decide in collaboration with people at a field site (sometimes along with other actors as well) how their field research topics should be shaped and the work they should (or should not) undertake, with the goal of benefiting inhabitants for specific purposes, is becoming much more common. This shift is not dissimilar to the demands of Huanoquiteños that development projects of one sort or another be, at least, mitad mitad. Along the same lines, my interactions and conversations with Huanoquiteños over the years, including in formal settings like community meetings, had helped me to recognize my own limitations. I could collaborate with them, but the contributions I could make were modest. I could provide knowledge and information they wanted and could use, including historical, legal, and archival data and maps, some of which were difficult for them to access; I could assist in analyzing and answering their questions about the content of documents; engage in productive conversation and debate, not only with Huanoquiteños but with many other actors as well; translate my work into Spanish and communicate it as best I could in Quechua, in which I was less fluent; and make sure I always left several copies of my books and articles in Spanish in the municipal archives. (They had regularly disappeared over the years, but I learned in 2021 that Huanoquiteños had decided to raise funds to establish a staffed municipal library, an excellent way to make all sorts of information more widely available to district inhabitants and to prevent it from disappearing). Huanoquite's Facebook page also gave me a chance to stay up to date with what was happening there, and if there was a way to contribute, I did. Beyond that, however much I wished it were otherwise, I did not have the economic or political power to assume a role as catalyst of major transformations. Dedicating myself to acts of accompaniment and to contributing funds to modest endeavors has made the most sense to me, as has using many different media—public talks, radio, podcasts, newspapers, and popular journals, as well as more academic venues—to communicate and support alternative ways of understanding issues or problems that Indigenous people have faced and situation they are attempting to resist.

Florence Babb (2018) offers an excellent longitudinal appraisal of multiple development projects in the Central Andes in conjunction with how her own positioning as a feminist anthropologist underwent changes as she became more cognizant of the position, needs, and demands of women themselves, a process that she views as a necessary decolonization of knowledge and of feminism. She retrospectively examined the research she and others had done on three different general anthropological topics in Peru: development, the informal economy, and tourism. She traced how the research record revealed that gendered and racial discrimination were often ignored in these works. She also recognized the great hurdles that remain to truly engage with Indigenous voices and scholars in ways that will revise and sometimes entirely overturn existing assumptions in anthropological research. More specifically, she showed how anthropologists participating in the famous Cornell Vicos Project did not even *see* that women were playing key roles economically, and she documented how her own contributions in this regard were ignored.[8] Later, when anthropologists began to recognize the vital roles of Indigenous women in all aspects of agrarian life, she realized that Peruvian and Indigenous scholars who were women had already been making great headway in their analyses of gender relationships but that she herself had not consulted them at the time. She concludes that we must consciously reconsider our practices as a first step to a more profound decolonization that will expose and transform the roots of inequality and racism.

Part of the process of decolonizing knowledge requires a reassessment of how Indigenous people themselves approach development and what criteria they consider important. This chapter has offered a brief history of the projects introduced in Huanoquite, some by non-Indigenous agents of state and parastatal organizations, others by Huanoquiteños themselves. One impact of the history of project-making in Huanoquite was that the very *existence* of prior projects with some measure of success (although many had failed), along with the improved infrastructure in the district, which I discussed in chapter 2, attracted further projects. Huanoquiteños drew extensively on centuries of experience and knowledge transmitted from generation to generation—from old to young, but also from young to old—that had provided them with resilience, toughness, and organizational skills, which they could activate for purposes of asserting themselves collectively. They also drew on local networks. Nongovernmental and state bureaucracies embraced an audit culture that demanded codification, standardization, uniformity, and simple commensurability, pegging products or activities to the value represented by the market and the unit of the individual, and they saw these qualities as significant benefits for those who participated in their projects. Some Huanoquiteños embraced these practices as well. Over time, a few parastatal NGOs had begun to design projects in which achieving sustainability was a key concern. These discordant knowledge assumptions and criteria explain the mixed reception and success of various initiatives in Huanoquite. The next three chapters document how many of these same assumptions and criteria—poised between neoliberal entrepreneurialism and community sovereignty—came into play in efforts to stimulate the cultivation of quinoa as a nontraditional export in Huanoquite.

PART TWO

SOUP AND SUPERFOOD

The Politics of Quinoa Production and Consumption

CHAPTER 4

The Expansion of Quinoa Production

Twenty-five years ago, few people in the United States and Europe had ever heard of quinoa. This was true of many other foods that had originated among Indigenous inhabitants across the world. Quinoa caught on, first slowly, and then became wildly popular—in restaurants as well as households where it was celebrated as a pseudo-grain that was remarkable for its healthful properties. A seed rather than a grain, it provides a high percentage of protein; it contains all nine amino acids that the body cannot make on its own; it can be prepared in many ways; and it has medicinal properties.[1] The geographic distribution of quinoa extends from southern Colombia all the way to Chile and can be grown at altitudes that range from sea level up to four thousand msl. (Jacobsen 2003, 167). I had first encountered quinoa in 1974 on a semester-long study abroad program in Peru. For the program, we collaborated with students at the Universidad Nacional de San Antonio Abad del Cusco (UNSAAC) on cultural ecology projects, comparing life in a Quechua herding village, Tucsa, with that in an agricultural village, Santa Barbara.[2]

Santa Barbara, the lower of the two villages, was located at more than 3,962 msl. in a very narrow valley and was not particularly hospitable to agriculture. Nevertheless, here and there I glimpsed fields of quinoa—an odd-looking plant resembling amaranth with a four- to five-foot yellowish hard stalk on which a heavily laden panicle of about five or six inches, comprised of bright magenta, yellow, pale pink, and ivory, and black tiny seeds, swayed at the top. From afar,

FIGURE 4.1. Cecilia rinsing quinoa to rid it of saponin in 1974. In Santa Barbara (Canchis), nestled in a high narrow valley, quinoa grew at between 3,600 and 4,000 msl.

the fields of quinoa shimmered with color. One day, I came back from a day of field research to find Cecilia, the elder woman of the household where I was living, rinsing quinoa seeds again and again. It was very hard work, and I asked her about why she needed to rinse it so frequently. She explained that the outer hull of the tiny seeds was bitter, almost poisonous. It was called saponin and the seed was inedible if it was not rinsed repeatedly, up to ten times, even twenty in some cases. Another day, I came home and Cecilia was washing her hair in the froth that constituted the residue after the quinoa had been rinsed, which I thought was ingenious. I didn't think much further about quinoa, but I did take some photographs of these activities.

Fast-forward almost forty years later. In Huanoquite, hardly ever viewed as a quinoa growing region, some of the best farmers in Huanoquite were intent on expanding their cultivation of quinoa. I remember my compadre Lorenzo shrewdly scrutinizing varieties of quinoa displayed at the annual agricultural fair of Huancaro and after some negotiation, deciding to take a chance on

4. The Expansion of Quinoa Production

purchasing black quinoa to experiment with growing it. No one in Huanoquite had grown black quinoa before. While quinoa was never wholly eliminated as a crop, non-Indigenous people had viewed it as a lowly crop because it was a native cultigen. Indigenous Quechua inhabitants, on the other hand, had never thought much about its market potential, but they embraced it as filling and delicious and appreciated that it could adapt to all sorts of environmental and climatic conditions. They were also aware of its resilience, and they knew of many ways they could put the entire quinoa plant to use.

In all the years I had done research in the Andes, I had never heard people speak with any particular reverence of quinoa but I loved the soups women made with it. Possibly because of the growing global embrace of quinoa and local incentives to encourage its cultivation, Indigenous Quechua and Aymara cultivators in the Bolivian *altiplano* had begun recounting to anthropologists a few origin narratives of mythical tone conveying the high regard they had for quinoa and its characteristics (see Ofstehage 2011).[3] I did not come across any of these in the southern Peruvian Andean highlands, but it is conceivable that they exist and, also, that new narratives may be appearing that celebrate quinoa's properties. Andrew Ofstehage (2011, 107) collected one such narrative from people in Los Lipez, a quinoa growing area in Bolivia that showed how, because of its ability to adapt to drought, quinoa prevented hunger among inhabitants of the high Andes. Here I paraphrase what he views as a foundational narrative: There was a time when a terrible drought affected the altiplano, causing famine and widespread disease. The people prayed to Mama Thunupa [Mother Thunder] to send rains and food. She sent Ñusta Huira [Princess Fat], another goddess, to end the suffering. Ñusta Huira walked throughout the southern altiplano, saying that she was sent by Mama Thunupa to end the drought and famine, but she was not received in the same way throughout the area. In the north, people doubted her provenance, and she was received coldly; further south, people received her warmly, but still with doubt. In the far south, in Los Lipez, she was received as a goddess and treated as such. People followed her and praised her. At the end of her journey, she gave them *quinua real* (real or true quinoa) and in the areas where she was coldly received, she left only a short plant that would be sufficient to feed the people.[4] In Los Lipez she left the largest and most nutritious grain to honor them. She explained, "For all the places I've walked, a plant very resistant to cold and frosts will be very tall and its fruit will have an extraordinary ability to combat hunger, cure sicknesses and will be resistant to droughts. You are all a strong and intelligent people" (Ofstehage 2011, 105).

Looking back in time, quinoa had been cultivated more extensively, even prior to the establishment of the Inca empire. It appears that the Incas, who viewed maize as a high-status crop and as the basis for preparing *chicha*, a home-brewed, fermented beverage like beer that they used in almost all their rituals and sacrifices, had already begun to encourage the cultivation of more maize and less quinoa. After the Spanish invasion in 1532, quinoa was markedly marginalized. It was relegated to the status of "food for Indians," and the conquistadors viewed it as solely "fit for chicken fodder." According to Deborah Andrews's (2017, 16) research, paradoxically, at the same time that the Spanish considered quinoa a "weed" among "crops," they also believed that "magical" qualities were embedded in it and that its ingestion could empower the "Indians" and threaten the conquest (Mujica et al. 2013, 11, quoted in Andrews 2017, 16).[5] The subsequent decline in quinoa production went hand in hand with what Andrews views as a form of "plant racism" and ignorance about "multispecies relations" among Indigenous Quechua people on the part of the Spaniards. For racist reasons, they sought to suppress the relationship between Indigenous people of the Andes, quinoa, and its qualities as a highly adaptable crop and a food with myriad valued properties (Andrews 2017, 16).

Few efforts took place before the second half of the twentieth century to make improvements to quinoa. Gradually, especially in lower valleys, maize and wheat came to substitute for quinoa. Because its kernels were larger, maize was far easier to harvest; it could be used immediately for food without lengthy processing; and it was the basis of chicha, which was fundamental to labor parties and religious rituals. In the case of wheat, its flour was used to bake bread, a European staple (Tapia Vargas 1976, 9, 31). At higher altitudes in the Cusco region where maize did not grow well, barley was grown, special kinds of which were sold to one of Cusco's breweries.

The boom in international demand for quinoa, which began in 2013, led the Peruvian government to incentivize farmers in particular regions to increase their cultivation of quinoa for purposes of export. Huanoquite was one of those regions. INIA, under the aegis of the Ministry of Agriculture (MINAGRI) to which it belonged, along with the Regional Government of Cusco, selected specific populations of farmers to cultivate new kinds of quinoa with the goal of marketing it internationally.

Lorenzo had eagerly signed up to become a part of the project, along with a few other men and women I had known for a long time. They were excited and nervous about the economic prospects that marketing quinoa offered. Some were taking the risk of replacing their barley, wheat, or maize fields with quinoa, but they were not at all sure what the outcome would be. In the past many households had intercropped quinoa with maize—they endearingly spoke of how quinoa had a special "kinship" with maize—and that "with maize,

4. The Expansion of Quinoa Production

FIGURE 4.2. Fields planted entirely in quinoa (Photo taken by John R. Cooper)

when you sow, the quinoa grows rapidly and beautifully. The maize protects the quinoa and even prevents weeds from growing around it." Now, farmers ventured to plant solely quinoa in those fields.

In the six years that followed (2013–2018), Huanoquiteños' experiment with quinoa turned out to be rocky, with a few wild successes and many frustrations. The effort to transform this Indigenous Andean product from peasant food to superfood serves as an important lens through which to understand how Huanoquiteños have engaged with changing state policies, agrarian politics and development projects over the years, and the entanglements of local and global dynamics in their lives.

Huanoquiteños have always experimented with crops and crop varieties, though not all of them took on the same degree of risk, especially because of differences in their economic standing and what they stood to lose if their tinkering did not have positive results. In addition, some of them operated with a broader and more diverse knowledge base than others, the result of their travels, curiosity, and years of experience farming. Two variables all too frequently ignored by government and parastatal agencies introducing new projects of one sort or another to Quechua communities were the noneconomic aspects of a project and an awareness that any project was but one among many different kinds of labor investments that were ongoing in agrarian households. Many innovations that Huanoquiteños embarked on independently tended to take

81

place slowly and incrementally. This was not true of the quinoa experiment. It was introduced rapidly and lasted a mere six years before funds were cut off and INIA and MINAGRI turned their attention to trying to encourage farmers in the region to cultivate more tarwi (*lupinus mutabilis*), another Indigenous crop. Despite decades of critical development knowledge that had accumulated demonstrating otherwise, agents also tended to assume that if a project were profitable, that would be what most mattered to people. I wondered if this would prove to be the case with the quinoa project. Before turning to the implementation and consequences of the quinoa growing experiment itself, it is important to understand the steps needed to grow and process quinoa.

Growing Quinoa

It makes sense that quinoa had been grown in small amounts in many Andean regions. It was hard to grow. I trekked to fields located at around 12,187 feet above sea level (3,713 msl.) to observe and participate in some of the activities entailed in cultivating it. Many farmers rented a tractor from the municipality at about sixty soles (twenty dollars) per hour to first turn over and aerate the earth. After breaking up the clods of dirt, they then used yokes of oxen to sow the field (each yoke of oxen also cost sixty soles), and finally, they would rake the dirt over the seeds by hand. This took place between October and November, at the very beginning of the rainy season. Once the quinoa began to grow, they mounded dirt around the stalk to better hold rainfall and support the stalk. They also had to weed it at least three times during the growing season, and farmers complained that the weeds were much worse than in the past because they were using fewer chemical pesticides, or none at all, so that their quinoa could eventually receive organic status. As soon as the seeds began to appear in the panicle, the birds (little finches called *ch'ayna*) swooped in for an attack. Farmers had many hypotheses about why some fields of quinoa were brutally and repeatedly attacked by birds while others were not. Some were convinced that intercropping maize and quinoa in furrows that were not straight had prevented the quinoa from being attacked as ruthlessly by birds because it was more hidden by the maize. Other farmers were sure that some of the quinoa varieties they were now growing—provided by INIA and the Cusco Regional Government—were sweeter because they had less saponin (the bitter outer hull) and were therefore far more attractive to the birds. Farmers spent a lot of time, energy, and fuel traveling to their fields, creating scarecrows, and setting off fireworks and bottle rockets to scare away the birds, none of which seemed to make much difference. The harvest took place between late May and June

4. The Expansion of Quinoa Production

and it was always difficult to figure out exactly when the quinoa was ready because the seeds were nestled in the panicle and not readily accessible. The rule of thumb was that they should be dry rather than moist. They harvested the quinoa by hand, and recruiting labor was a perennial problem.

Households needed labor at the same time and competed to gain access to it. In the past, better-off farmers could depend on luring workers by offering them wages, along with chicha, *trago* (pure-grain cane alcohol that is 90 percent proof), a substantial meal, and coca leaves to chew. However, since the 1990s, the pool of workers willing to work for wages had shrunk, partly because some had other sources of income, partly because some had migrated, and partly because many of them were engaged in reciprocal exchanges of labor with other households that they preferred to maintain. For example, each time a labor party was needed, the level of anxiety in Lorenzo and Margarita's household ratcheted up, reflected in whispers that grew more and more agitated and high-pitched as they discussed how many workers they needed, who they could invite, how much chicha they needed to prepare, and what Margarita should cook for the main meal. Women's labor was critical to the success of labor parties as they had to prepare chicha in copious amounts in advance, along with a meal that would be assessed and commented on, and they had to be at the ready to serve the meal in the field.[6] To make matters worse, because Margarita had been unwell for several years and had trouble walking, she always had to depend on a surrogate—a young girl, usually—to serve the meal. Given prevailing gender ideologies, it was unheard of for a man to perform that task, though a man could serve chicha and shots of liquor. Lorenzo, who almost always stuck to his counsel, brooded intensely, especially when workers did not show up. Without a word, he would abruptly get in his pickup and make the rounds. Usually, he successfully located those who had not shown up but had promised to participate, yet he was almost always short a worker or two who did not follow through with their commitment.

Harvesting a hectare of land required anywhere from twelve to fifteen workers who worked steadily and methodically, severing the long stalk of quinoa by hand with a finely sharpened scythe (*ichuna*).[7] After a day or two, the workers would return, and at yet another work party, create an extensive flat area by digging up the roots and sharp remains of the quinoa plants. They then bundled up the top-heavy, harvested stalks that lay in rows, slung the plastic cloth containing the stalks over one shoulder and carried them to a tarp where they spread them to dry. This looked easier than it was. The stalks were sharp, stiff, and unwieldy. When I enthusiastically volunteered to help in this task, I stupidly gave no thought to the fact that I was not wearing a long-sleeved shirt.

FIGURE 4.3. Margarita preparing quinoa beer (chicha) for the next day's labor party

The bloody scratches I inflicted on myself from the stalks took months to heal, and scars from them remain. It gave me insight into how harsh the labor entailed in harvesting quinoa was, and the toll it took on the body.

As we stacked and stacked, I ended up scratching my arms to bits, quinoa in every crevice of my clothes, and I stumbled, losing my balance as I tried to place the bunches of quinoa correctly in the plastic cloth and then tie the diagonal corners and throw it over my shoulder. Lorenzo admonished me immediately not to let the seeds of quinoa fall out and showed me how I should carry it. He did the same with one of the other workers as well, which made me feel a wee bit better as a novice. We were all grumbling about how far we had to walk to stack the quinoa since there was a tarp nearer to where we were working, but Lorenzo basically commanded us that we could not put it there because it would be much harder to thresh it—we'd have to dig up a space and get the thresher in there. Quinoa work was nasty even though the rewards could be a bit like rainbow gold or, in Europe and the United States, food to make healthy bodies.

FIGURE 4.4. Labor party harvesting quinoa

FIGURE 4.5. Carrying harvested quinoa and stacking it to dry
(Photo taken by John R. Cooper)

PART TWO. SOUP AND SUPERFOOD

FIGURE 4.6. Quinoa drying

Ascertaining when the quinoa was dry enough to thresh was critical. If the seeds were not dry enough once they were put in sacks, they could rot from too much moisture before a buyer was found. Farmers who cultivated quinoa on a small scale had been able to dry their seed in batches, using a sieve and spreading it out afterward. Once farmers determined that the seeds were dry enough on the stalk, they then had to rent a thresher and a mechanic to operate it. The mechanic/owner was paid according to the amount of quinoa harvested. The thresher was intended for wheat, not quinoa. It tended to clog and spew quinoa seed outside the funnel, which everyone then had to carefully gather up, an additional ongoing task. A woman or young girl was always charged with the awful and dusty work of holding the sack under the funnel. Although she would cover her head and shoulders with a plastic cape, she was exposed to fine dust and completely blanketed in it. At Lorenzo's harvest, once the quinoa was harvested, the sacks were hauled down in his pickup truck and stored in his shed until they were marketed.

Promises

INIA had first come to Huanoquite in late 2012 to establish demonstration plots of quinoa, selecting households that directly worked their land, after which forty households decided to participate in the QCA (Quinoa Cultivators

FIGURE 4.7. Threshing quinoa using a wheat thresher

FIGURE 4.8. Young girl sacking quinoa and trying to protect herself from the spewing dust

PART TWO. SOUP AND SUPERFOOD

Association), which was then formally established in 2013. The association grew out of a preexisting wheat association, and additional members were eager to join it, especially after Peru's first lady, Nadine Heredía Alarcón de Humala, visited the province of Paruro to promote quinoa cultivation. The project had the grand title "Project to Improve the Competitiveness of the Productive Commodity Chain of Quinoa and Kañiwa," and the slogan at INIA's headquarters was "Come, Grow with Us, and Take Advantage Today of the Benefits of the Agriculture of the Future." INIA and the Cusco Regional Government had selected 49 districts and 106 communities in 11 provinces for the project and Huanoquite was one of the districts. Together with the Regional Government of Cusco, INIA provided seed, *guano de isla* fertilizer (organic fertilizer from bird droppings on islands off the coast of Peru and from chickens), pesticides, pamphlets that explained how to grow and process quinoa, and cookbooks with recipes about how to prepare quinoa. INIA donated two threshers for quinoa cultivators in Huanoquite to use. The regional government also promised additional threshers and a mechanical processor called a *perladora* (pearler) or an *escarificadora* (scarifier) that would miraculously polish or scrape the quinoa seeds by means of friction to remove the saponin from their outer hull. The municipality also had five threshers and several tractors available for rent to households in the district.

I spoke with engineer Rigoberto Estrada, director of the project at INIA who oversaw the National Project for Agrarian Innovation of Andean Cultigens, and with engineer Adrian Wendell Olivera Ayme who directed the Project for the Improvement of the Competitiveness of Organic Andean Quinoa and Cañehua, of the Regional Government of Cusco. Estrada, who was very knowledgeable, explained that INIA was motivated to avoid the pitfalls of cultivating solely one kind of quinoa because Huanoquite (and other regions as well) boasted four production zones where different kinds of quinoa could be grown in accordance with altitude, tolerance of frost, and drought conditions, thus reducing risk. At the same time, INIA wanted to encourage farmers to selectively cultivate certain kinds of quinoa that could meet market demand, that did not suffer from pests so that farmers could reduce the use of chemical pesticides, and that did not get attacked by mildew. Both INIA and the Cusco Regional Government were focused on categorizing different kinds of quinoa for sale on the international market and achieving standardization and uniformity in the size and kind of quinoa grown (Estrada 2013, 30–31). Balancing these criteria was difficult. The goal of INIA, ultimately, was threefold and contradictory: to create a robust market for quinoa; to preserve multiple varieties; and to produce certified organic quinoa (which also involved steps of standardization and usually took approximately three years). Although the regional government and INIA both emphasized markets, the regional government was focused more on the export market than INIA, which believed that it was also important to stimulate local consumption of quinoa, preserve the varieties of quinoa, and guide farmers in their quest to achieve organic certification of their quinoa.

Quinoa cultivators encountered many headaches—from production to processing to marketing—that were not solely the result of budgetary constraints. They also were the result, as I show below, of a notable failure to recognize the value of women's labor and knowledge in making the production and marketing of quinoa possible, of a reliance on non-Indigenous Huanoquiteños as mediators in their relationships with INIA and the regional government, and of racism. This was especially true of the regional government's attitudes and practices. It had promised additional quinoa threshers and pearlers and technical trainers to provide guidance on how to use the machines. The machines did not arrive for several years. Engineers made an appearance once or twice to answer questions and demonstrate how to use the threshers, but after the pearler appeared, engineers never showed up to teach villagers how to use it. Women complained that the "experts" did not speak Quechua, and both men and women observed that when engineers did arrive, they almost never went to the fields where the quinoa was actually being cultivated. According to many of the women with whom I spoke, prior to the quinoa project, they had always helped in the fields, spreading fertilizer, weeding, harvesting, and winnowing, and processing, cooking, and marketing the quinoa they cultivated. In their words, "Igual, todo hacemos igual" (Equally, we do everything equally). They felt that the INIA or Región agents tended to ignore their input when it came to some quinoa tasks, such as cultivating or harvesting it.

Women had eagerly awaited the arrival of the pearler. They had been thrilled about having access to a machine that would make it worthwhile to scale up quinoa cultivation. They would be able to get a better market price for their quinoa, and the machine would decrease their own labor investment in processing and ridding it of saponin. The latter was a limiting factor for the consumption of quinoa, domestically, and for marketing it at scale for export. Japanese-designed rice pearlers had been adapted mechanically to extract 100 percent of the saponin from quinoa, whereas other internal agitation mechanisms combined with dryers could not get rid of all of it. Manual rinsing, using the current of a river or water in a bucket or sink, resulted in a loss of seed and took far more time—a minimum of ten minutes to rinse away the saponin of a small batch. The Japanese rice pearler took one minute to clean a pound of quinoa (Wood 1989, 54). This was what Huanoquiteños had been expecting. Women—hardly romantic about the marketing prospects of quinoa—had been at once excited about experimenting with scaling up quinoa, evaluating which quinoa varietals produced best for the market, and preparing what tasted good for their households. The reality was that six seasons passed (the end of the project itself) before an engineer finally arrived to teach growers how to use the pearler, and it turned out to be a huge disappointment. The pearler was capable of processing only very small amounts of quinoa to get rid of the saponin. Villagers had been led to expect a machine capable of doing much more. They were frustrated and angry at the regional government's lack of attention to this critical stage of quinoa processing and viewed it as a betrayal.

Another factor contributing to the challenges the QCA faced was their heavy reliance on non-Indigenous brokers in their quinoa production and marketing dealings. The majority of members of the association were comprised of Huanoquiteños—both men and women—but two of its officers were non-Indigenous even though they were from Huanoquite. Rolando Bonett Béjar, the president, was the principal mediator between the association, the regional government and prospective buyers of Huanoquite's quinoa. He claimed to cultivate his own fields but comported himself like a hacendado. He was, in fact, the son of what had been one of the most powerful families in Huanoquite, the Béjars, and his mother had owned more than 1,500 hectares in Huanoquite before the 1969 agrarian reform expropriated a good amount of it. The secretary, Juvenal Holgado, was the brother of a former parish priest in Huanoquite who had purchased a stunning estate belonging to one of the most notorious hacendados in Huanoquite. Holgado had inherited the land from his brother and had lived elsewhere in the Urubamba Valley for fifteen years before he returned to Huanoquite to assume ownership of his property. Unlike Bonett who was primarily a technocrat, Holgado had scholarly inclinations and had pursued his aspirations to become an ecological anthropologist. He was familiar with some of the classics on Andean ecology and agriculture, including works by John Murra and Enrique Mayer. Association members thought he might be able to offer them needed advice on how best to produce high-quality quinoa and expand its production.

Nonetheless, both Bonett and Holgado sought to distance themselves from "campesinos," and in my interview with Bonett, he was not shy about expressing his thinly veiled racism. He repeatedly spoke of Huanoquiteños in one breath as "no-good drinkers" and as the "source of future innovation and potential." He decried the "carelessness and irresponsibility" of Huanoquite's quinoa cultivators (which included several women) and concluded by pointing out that Huanoquite "had been the site of one association after another and all had

4. The Expansion of Quinoa Production

failed, that it was important not to give households something for nothing because they would just take and not care about investment in the project. Households needed to be responsible for investments to work" (Interview, June 7, 2019).

His attitude toward women was slightly more enlightened. He spoke of how important women were to the future of agriculture and why they should be targeted as quinoa growers. Embracing gender stereotypes, he emphasized how women were "much more detail-oriented and responsible about following through with sowing, weeding, harvesting and selecting seed." At the same time, though, he added that they had always been in the "frontlines" of agriculture, but that the assumption that they should remain in the kitchen had prevented their recognition. When I pushed him on this, he attributed these attitudes to the patriarchal behavior of Indigenous men rather than state or parastatal agents.

Bonett had appointed himself as a responsible expert with training in agronomy, a grasp of market principles, and networks that he could activate among wholesalers for purposes of marketing quinoa, but he had little interest in or respect for Huanoquiteños' knowledge or practices. He wanted me to see his spread of quinoa and maize fields, and in the conversation I had with him as we briskly walked to his fields, he repeatedly denigrated Huanoquiteños as "lazy, cunning, selfish traitors," but at the same time, without intending any irony, he characterized his own ambitions when he reflected that people only called themselves an organization or a community "to get resources from the municipality" and that the Regional Government of Cusco wanted to implement projects "because they fed the bureaucracy and created jobs for them [the bureaucracy]." Although these comments were directed at Huanoquiteños and at the regional government, they very much applied to Bonett himself. The QCA had been established by the Cusco Regional Government (and INIA), and Bonett made repeated demands for monies from the regional government and municipality to perpetuate his own position. His position and attitude were typical of many non-Indigenous brokers who mediated relationships between Indigenous inhabitants and the Cusco bureaucracy. Their purpose was supposedly to encourage development, but instead they disparaged the very populations they were intended to support.

Indigenous authorities of communities and of the district municipality also acted as brokers. One difference between them and brokers like Bonett was that negative sanctions could be more easily leveled against Indigenous authorities if they did not satisfactorily meet the demands of their communities when they represented them to other entities. However, even Indigenous

FIGURE 4.9. Rolando Bonett, President of the QCA and principal broker with wholesalers and the Regional government standing in his quinoa field

brokers had been found guilty of irresponsibility and acts of corruption, putting their personal ambition before the well-being of the community over the years. What mainly distinguished Indigenous and non-Indigenous brokers was that those resembling Bonett and Holgado behaved far more like patrons than brokers. Though members of the association were quietly critical of Bonett, they lacked the clout to force him to do his job better. They worried that if they tried to put pressure on him, they would lose access to the contacts he had to wholesalers and to agents at INIA and the regional government on which the QCA depended.[8] In short, mistrust underpinned the workings of the association since it was hard to know whether or not Bonett was being truthful about resources, visits from engineers, and the deals he was cutting with wholesalers for Huanoquite's quinoa, and he showed little respect for Huanoquiteños.

The Market

After the first lady of Peru, Nadine Heredia, was named as Special Ambassador for the International Year of Quinoa and charged with collaborating with the UN's "Scaling up Nutrition" program and efforts to "empower women" in 2013, the price of quinoa surged, quadrupling in 2014. Peru's president, Ollanta

4. The Expansion of Quinoa Production

Humala, also declared 2013 to be the "Year of Integrated Development" and of "Investment for Rural Development and Food Security" (Marapi 2013). Huanoquiteños who had begun to cultivate larger extensions of quinoa (up to several hectares) were overjoyed. The following year, however, quinoa production skyrocketed, the market became saturated, and the price then plummeted between September 2014 and August 2015. The precise impact this had on farmers is not known, but prices fell at least 40 percent and producer household incomes dropped about 5 percent. No doubt they would have dropped far more had households not continued to cultivate a diverse array of crops.

Samuel, one of the most respected farmers in Huanoquite, explained what had happened to him:

> We entered into commercialization. We were just at the point of marketing our quinoa—we were searching—there wasn't an automatic market. The first year (2014), there was a very high price for it at first, for two to three months. It was 1 kilo of quinoa for 9 or 10 soles.[9] We amassed all our quinoa together. We got organized and formed an association, we convinced the engineer and the other members of the association to sell our quinoa to one buyer. The engineer and Bonett selected buyers to bid on our harvest. There were three buyers coming to Huanoquite to bid. But then the price fell before they came. In 2015, we had 30 enormous sacks, a huge amount, each was 125 to 130 kilos. I had sown more than a hectare. The price fell to 2 or 1.80 a kilo, that's what it fell to, very rapidly. I just went ahead and stored mine. An arroba (12.5 kilos or almost 25 pounds) was only worth 16 to 20 soles. I stored mine. I put mine in 50 kilo bags. I stored it for two years. At the end of 2016, in almost 2017, I was able to sell it. I came out okay, more or less. I got 3.2 soles per kilo. Not great, not terrible.

It was mind-boggling for me to grasp all the calculations that farmers were making, sometimes on the fly, sometimes after pondering the situation for a long time. Samuel did what farmers who had grown enough good quality quinoa could afford to: He stored the best of it as seed. This was a wonderful property of quinoa. It could be stored for up to ten years. Hence, he was subsequently able to weather a loss by selling some of his quinoa as seed when demand for it increased a little.

Lorenzo did about as well as Samuel. His black quinoa purchase had not been a big success. The birds attacked it more than other kinds of quinoa, but it required less processing. He found that although wholesalers did not want to purchase it, Indigenous inhabitants liked it and thought it made a tasty juice. Even they agreed, though, that people were unfamiliar with black quinoa and then joked with me about the equivalence of blackness and excrement. The subtext of this equivalence, which I heard more than once from Huanoquiteños, was that some people pejoratively associated black quinoa with both Indigeneity/dark skin and with excrement. Margarita succeeded in selling most of the black quinoa in small amounts at a fairly good price at the Huancaro Agricultural Fair. The lion's share of Lorenzo's quinoa harvest was a kind of yellow quinoa called *quinoa amarilla marangani*; he reached a point when he decided to sell his eighteen *costales* (each was about 56 kilos or around 125 pounds) of quinoa for S./3,420 (about $1,140 or S./3.38 per kilo) and that was from only one of his fields. The figures INIA gave me for total production of quinoa between 2013 and 2017 was an average of 1,900 kilos of quinoa per hectare in Huanoquite. Some years, they had cultivated up to twenty-three hectares but in 2019 they only worked seven. Table 2 shows what one member of the QCA spent in 2018 to produce his quinoa, including his inputs and labor, and what he earned once he sold his quinoa.[10]

Another attractive feature of quinoa cultivation was that from a relatively small amount of seed, one could produce and harvest five times the amount of quinoa. Paulina, who had been a member of the Quinoa Association for four years, sowed four hectares of land in quinoa, using about 6 kilos of quinoa seed per hectare. From that, she harvested 120 kilos and set aside about 12 kilos for her family's domestic consumption. The rest she sold on the market.

Yet another positive feature of marketing quinoa that many cultivators commented on, especially women, was that it was easier than other agricultural products to sell to multiple market sectors. Households could sell some quinoa varieties directly to consumers in the Huancaro market and sell it for a higher price by breaking bulk; they could simultaneously market other varieties more in demand for export to wholesalers, some of whom came to Huanoquite, and sell still other kinds of quinoa in Huanoquite itself. This was exactly what Lorenzo and Margarita had done, retailing in small amounts their black quinoa while selling their yellow quinoa in bulk and retaining some of each kind for household use. It was also a way they could maintain cultivation of multiple landraces of quinoa and experiment with them, a subject to which I will return in the next chapter.

After their first success selling their quinoa harvest, growers decided, once again, to pool their harvest and market it cooperatively. They were crushed when their entire batch was rejected by a wholesaler in Arequipa. They were accused of having used chemical fertilizer and pesticides, although they insisted vehemently that they had not. Although they had not yet succeeded in obtaining formal organic certification, they had managed to negotiate a higher price for their quinoa, which they swore they had grown without using chemical

4. The Expansion of Quinoa Production

FIGURE 4.10. Flour from different kinds of quinoa and other grains being sold at the Huancaro Agricultural Fair

fertilizer or pesticides. Paulina, in fact, had worked with her cousin who was a civil engineer to concoct a local nonchemical pesticide for use in her family's fields. Initially intended for potatoes, it was so successful that farmers tried applying it to quinoa, and it worked. The pesticide was made from *tarwi*, a lupin, which also required processing because of its bitterness. To make the nonchemical pesticide, Paulina boiled the tarwi to create a juice and then mixed it with *rocoto* (hot pepper) seeds. It had to cool before it could be used. I also found that women had a heightened concern about using chemical fertilizer and pesticides because they felt it could damage the health of their children.

The association members took a terrible beating, selling their quinoa at a loss. The export brokers insisted the Huanoquiteños had used chemicals. Huanoquiteños insisted that they had not, but since the fields had been used in prior years for potatoes, they surmised that maybe traces of chemical inputs might have remained. Others insisted that the wholesalers had mixed their quinoa with batches that were not organic from farmers in other regions and thus had contaminated the entire crop. In any case, association members were angry and disappointed, and half of them pulled back from growing quinoa the following year.

PART TWO. SOUP AND SUPERFOOD

Marketing quinoa was not just a question of price. It was also a question of credit and of how parties involved in the project attributed value to different kinds of quinoa. INIA agents and quinoa growers themselves complained about the lack of credit available to them and their ability to make contacts with wholesalers who would buy up the quinoa. Rigoberto Estrada who headed the INIA project, softly remarked to me that "El Región," as the Cusco Regional Government was called, had not figured out "how to complete the chain from producer to buyer" (Interview, July 25, 2018). Growers were torn between selling their own harvest or pooling it to sell in bulk, and their lack of trust in Bonett exacerbated their indecision. In addition, some growers had produced better quality quinoa than others and did not want it all lumped together. Many growers could not gain access to credit that would allow them to expand production and mitigate the risk of pursuing organic production and finding a buyer for their harvest.

Finally, but not unimportantly, men and women were reluctant to view quinoa solely as a standardized and codified market commodity. One of the things they most appreciated about it was its multipurpose nature. They prized some kinds of quinoa as the very best and the most delicious, and they preferred it for household consumption, yet development agents viewed it pejoratively because it had more saponin, was harder to process for commercial purposes, and consumers in Europe and the United States did not like it as much as white or pink quinoa. Other kinds were hardier and less likely to succumb to weeds, birds, or drought, but again, they were not preferred by those who consumed it abroad. Those consumers wanted the sweeter quinoa that the birds also preferred. In short, cultivating quinoa could not be detached from the values and purposes associated with it, which were not necessarily economic.

They were also very concerned about quinoa exhausting their fields, something a worker had mentioned to me at the very first quinoa harvest I had attended. They were aware that growing quinoa had to take place carefully, in moderation, by letting the soil rest or by alternating quinoa cultivation with legumes that return nitrogen to the soil. And it also mattered what kind of quinoa was grown because some kinds exhausted the soil more than other kinds. They had to think hard about how cultivating quinoa could be balanced with ensuring the future fertility of their fields, and they also sought to take account of the whole array of products that they wanted to grow for domestic consumption and for the market.

The perspective of Huanoquite's cultivators contrasted with the narrow focus of El Región on the commercialization of quinoa as an end product. Even INIA had recognized that this was a poor path to take. INIA's ultimate goal

Table 2. Quinoa Inputs, Expenses, and Revenues of One Member of the QCA, 2018

Description	Unit Price	Unit Quantity	Total Value
EXPENSES			
Seed	20.00/kilo[1]	6 kg.	S/120.00
Fertilizer			
Guano de isla	50.00/sack	8 sacks	S/400.00
Nitrate	75.00/sack	4 sacks	S/300.00
Organic pesticides			S/203.00
Tractor rental	60.00/hr.	3 hrs.	S/185.00
Yokes, pair of oxen	60.00/yoke	2 pairs	S/120.00
LABOR PARTIES	20.00/worker/day	46 TOTAL	
Sowing	20.00/worker/day	10 workers/day	S/200.00
Hoeing	20.00/worker/day	8 workers/day	S/160.00
1st Weeding	20.00/worker/day	5 workers/day	S/100.00
2nd Weeding	20.00/worker/day	2 workers/day	S/40.00
3rd Weeding	20.00/worker/day	5 workers/day	S/100.00
Harvesting	20.00/worker/day	10 workers/day	S/200.00
Threshing	20.00/worker/day	6 workers/day	S/120.00
Food for workers[2]	6.76/worker	46 worker meals	S/310.96
Chicha for workers	10.40/container	16 containers	S/166.40
Coca for workers	10.40/lb.	1.25 lbs.	S/13.00
Alcohol for workers	4.16/liter	4.25 liters	S/17.68
Women's unremunerated labor[3]	20.00/worker/day	2 workers/3 days	S/120.00
Thresher Rental	30.00/sack	15 sacks	S/450.00
Sacks	3.64/sack	15 sacks	S/54.60
Transport[4]	6.24/sack	15 sacks	S/93.60
TOTAL DIRECT & INDIRECT COSTS			**S/3,474.24**
REVENUES			
GROSS REVENUES	5/kilo; 1 sack=130k.	15 sacks	**S/9,750.00**
Less expenses			-S/3,474.24
Harvest retained for home use[5]		3 sacks	-S/1,950.00
NET MARGIN ON SALES		NET 12 SACKS SOLD	S/4,325.76

1. All prices/values in Peruvian soles S/; Exchange rate in US dollars – S/3.00 = $1.00

2. Figures are estimated and based partly on data gathered by Regaño and Peña (2018), adjusted for rate of inflation between 2016, when their data on food, chicha, coca, and alcohol costs were gathered, and 2018, when these data were collected.

3. Entry refers to unremunerated labor of women who helped prepare chicha and food for labor parties. If figures for worker labor are used, this is estimated to be two women working over three days.

4. Total expenses do not include maintenance of pickup truck.

5. Three sacks of quinoa worth market value of approximately S/1,950.00 were set aside for household consumption. Rather than an outright expense, this could be viewed as an asset that strengthens household food sovereignty and autonomy.

was to concentrate on achieving organic production of five native crops: quinoa, kañiwa, kiwicha, tarwi, and *habas*. Tarwi also had a high protein content (twenty-six grams per cup) and returned nitrogen to the soil, revitalizing it, as did habas (broad beans).[11] In addition, INIA agents thought it was important to incorporate different modes of processing quinoa—what they called "transformation"—as a way of increasing the rate of return for households. Olivera Ayme had been working for a long time on the project, and he believed that by emphasizing transformation families could sell not just quinoa but also polished quinoa, quinoa leaves, and flours made from quinoa, as well as other value-added products, and thereby get a better return.

The organization of quinoa production in Bolivia was very different from that found in Peru, in part because of the flat terrain of the vast altiplano region and the organization of a high number of growers into cooperatives. Yet according to Ofstehage, similar sentiments and calculations prevailed among quinoa cultivators there. Many different kinds of growers in Bolivia, including communities, associations, and cooperatives, had sought to obtain what is known as "a denomination of origin" (CDO) for the quinoa that they marketed internationally.[12] Their hope was that these kinds of labels would serve as a mechanism to enhance a regional identity among cultivators, "a symbolic commons that links their identity, quinoa crop, and work" (Ofstehage 2011, 103). Instead Ofstehage found that the ways that quinoa growers in Bolivia attributed value to quinoa very much took account of the kinds of variables I have mentioned above—how different kinds of quinoa were selected and for what purposes, the care taken in growing and processing it, its relationship to other crops, and the embeddedness of human labor, sociability, and skill in the quinoa in question. Hence, CDOs did not result in upholding a single-branded crop but rather "added a politicized marketing movement to an already fragmented economic sector" (Ofstehage 2011, 104).

Given the range of variables farmers considered in a single community with respect to kinds of quinoa grown and how it was grown, processed, marketed, and consumed, Ofstehage concludes that Lorraine Aragon's (2011, 63) concept of a "split economy" fit better with understanding how quinoa cultivators attributed value to their quinoa. They "were not producing separate strands of quinoa for different economies but rather flexibly split their quinoa among fundamentally different ends" (Ofstehage 2011, 104). Some was for household consumption, some was for seed, some was for making chicha or preparing meals for labor parties or rituals, some might be saved to ensure its identity as a particular kind of quinoa or for future sale, given the vagaries of the market,

4. The Expansion of Quinoa Production

some was for wholesale to outsiders as a commodity on the market immediately, and some might be used for retail or trade. Farmers made distinctions among quinoa in terms of "the *method* of harvest and the *means* by which it circulated, not by inherent properties of the product" (Ofstehage 2011, 104). This was true in Huanoquite as well. The value of quinoa was embedded in who produced it, how it was produced and processed, and how it circulated in an economy that was not conceptualized as singular and globalized but rather comprised of differentiated circuits that overlapped and articulated with one another to constitute the fabric of an agrarian life that could be sustained.

While Huanoquiteños used scientific knowledge to improve their production, processing, and marketing of quinoa, their thinking and practices ran counter to the economistic thinking promoted by development agents and government personnel who prioritized economic capital, modernization, and economies of scale to the detriment of other kinds of capital and value. Huanoquite's farmers wanted to earn money, and they were open to trying out different kinds of quinoa, but they balanced those desires with taking into account food security in their calculations—that is, ensuring that the crops they grew would allow them to continue providing for their households and offer them resilience in the face of the changing and unpredictable environmental conditions they were increasingly disturbed by. More encompassing, as cultivators, they drew on a deep knowledge of what they needed to do and take account of to achieve balance and equilibrium among multiple natural, human, and other than human forces that constituted their universe. These forces were conduits and providers of life itself and Huanoquiteños paid attention to the state of each of their fields, their water supply, their relationships with their animals, plants, biomes, their neighbors, and so forth. A scientific, agroindustrial model of scaling up could, in fact, prove to be dangerous to their future well-being. Unlike the regional government, which was seeking to market quinoa at scale and thinking mostly about how it could achieve this with the greatest volume and/or profit margin, Huanoquite's quinoa cultivators, while united in desiring better economic returns for their quinoa production, varied among themselves as they assessed what kinds of quinoa they would grow, how they would do so, and why. Decisions about how to channel their social labor and cultural knowledge and how much personal sacrifice they would or could make to cultivate quinoa, and to what end, intervened in scaling up their cultivation of quinoa. Households, and the men and women within them, diverged in their assessments because quinoa was at once a part of "life and family and a cash crop" (Ofstehage 2011, 110).

Knowledge Exchange: Endings and Beginnings

In 2019 the experiment officially sponsored by INIA came to an end, a shock to cultivators who had not expected it to terminate so abruptly. When one thinks about the time it took them to shift the cultivation of their fields, introduce new seeds, convert to using only organic, nonchemical fertilizer and pesticides, and establish marketing networks, six years was a remarkably short project duration. INIA did not entirely abandon Huanoquite. Its presence in Huanoquite continued, but it shifted its focus to tarwi instead of quinoa. The Región, however, entirely ended its support for Huanoquite's quinoa project.

Nevertheless, Huanoquiteños continued to gather knowledge and information that would enhance their quinoa-growing efforts. Over the period of the project, INIA had encouraged cultivators to exchange information and knowledge about their experiences with quinoa cultivation with each other. That part of the project turned out to be more successful than they had imagined it would be. Every June they celebrated an International Day of Andean Grains at the Huancaro Agricultural Fair where quinoa producers exchanged their experiences, and they did the same in September when they had a meeting of quinoa producers, merchants, and businesses. They discussed seed varieties and their attributes and all aspects of quinoa production, processing, and marketing activities. The delight that cultivators felt when things went well for them was contagious. When I asked Samuel about why he continued to grow quinoa, he responded with a question: "Why have I vanquished everyone working quinoa? I like it, I like it more. Everything that I cultivate I dedicate myself to, I spend the whole day dedicated to it. I can't just leave things as they are. That's why the quinoa I cultivate, grows, it grows to a great height, up to five or six feet. I disappear in my field among the stalks. And when we train some of the growers, they disappear in the field, even some very tall women. I love Huanoquite. It's the best district in the province of Paruro, with lots of water and land. It's a beautiful place."

When Renato Quispe told me about how the association had gained access to black quinoa seeds and decided to grow it, he explained, "Because we are an association, we exchange a lot of information and experiences with other quinoa growers from other zones at the Huancaro Agricultural Fair. It is so interesting to exchange words, new varieties, cultivation practices—other provinces have now become interested in our varieties too." When I visited the Huancaro Fair, multiple banners hung above the vendors' stalls, advertising "Andean Crops: Let's Work Together" and "Production for the Cusco Region's Food Security: Quinua-Cañihua Project." These kinds of emergent networks have encouraged

4. The Expansion of Quinoa Production

FIGURE 4.11. The Huancaro Agricultural Fair

cultivators to continue experimenting with quinoa production. In addition to their desire for sufficient economic remuneration, they enjoyed having the opportunity to expand their knowledge base and to share their successes and failures with other growers.

One day I returned from the fields, sunbaked, parched, and exhausted, looking forward to retiring to my room to sip some tea and rest, only to find Josefina, a cultivator who had proved to be elusive, finally ready to talk to me. We sat at a table in the small store that she owned. The store had been shuttered because her husband had been the driver of a truck that was in a terrible truck accident at a dangerous hairpin uphill curve just before reaching Huanoquite. They were helping to pay the medical costs of the twenty-nine people who had been injured, and they could no longer afford to keep the store going. While talking to her, I asked if she thought it was worth her while to continue growing quinoa since it seemed like very hard work, given the returns and lack of support from the Región. She agreed that the Región had not done much, that it sometimes gave them a bit of organic pesticide, which hardly took care of the fields of all the cultivators, and sometimes they would just come and take photos. She thought that it was hard work going through all the steps to process quinoa, including drying it, before selling it. Yet she vehemently argued against my skepticism. She said she would continue to grow quinoa because the price

PART TWO. SOUP AND SUPERFOOD

of wheat and barley was low and "with quinoa, money always appeared." Another young cultivator, Lucio, also thought that growing potatoes was much harder work than quinoa—every stage of potato production required about twenty rather than eight to ten workers, and potatoes were far heavier to haul. And Hector, a third grower, said that potatoes "simply take more strength."

Since almost all of Huanoquiteños' agricultural production was destined for both household consumption and the market, and because the quinoa market was not stable, deciding when it was too costly or risky to grow quinoa or how much of one crop or one kind of quinoa rather than another that farmers would prefer to grow turned out to be a very subjective process of evaluation for households. The judgments they made were economic and pragmatic, but they also had to do with other considerations—social relationships, memories, the challenge, hardships, and risks of innovation, and the attributes of quinoa itself—that cultivators ruminated on and assessed. Economic well-being mattered but it was always intertwined with other kinds of well-being that could not be reduced to coin and profit, however much it appeared to simplify decision-making.

CHAPTER 5

Food Sovereignty, Food Security, and Sustainability

Despite some of their failures growing new varieties of quinoa, along with the lack of support from the Cusco Regional Government and the unstable market, most of Huanoquite's quinoa cultivators remained committed to growing it. While they were motivated by potential monetary returns from its sale, they also cared about its importance to the sustenance of their households, and in an age of tourism and globalization, they were intrigued by what it represented and projected to the world. In this chapter, I discuss how the surge in global interest in quinoa affected Huanoquiteños in terms of three intertwined dynamics: sustainability, food security, and food sovereignty. In the following chapter, I look at the meanings that consumers attributed to and associated with quinoa, and what might motivate the similarities and differences among them.

Quinoa Varieties

Before turning to these topics, it is important to raise a question that has frequently been asked but does not have a clear answer: Exactly how many varieties of quinoa actually *are* there in the Andes? Deborah Andrews (2017, 19), in one of the best discussions of this question, points out that *landraces* consist of "groupings of different types or varietals. There can be several subspecies names that make up the intermediate category of a race. Thus, while a *variety* or type name may be applied to a plant that demonstrates consistent, distinct characteristics, a host of varieties may apply to certain races or landraces and may be context dependent."[1] In an exhaustive comparison of how scientists, agronomists, and native farmers identified quinoa in the Andean highlands, Andrews found that it was almost impossible to dissociate terms for quinoa from context. They made broad distinctions between highland and lowland varieties; farmers distinguished quinoa in accordance with the specific ecological conditions in which it grew and its color and bitterness; duplication of names occurred depending on whether Quechua or Aymara speakers provided them; and government and NGO entities tended to only identify kinds that could be commercialized. In short, there were anywhere from between 24 to 131 landraces that grouped together up to three thousand varietals (Andrews 2017; Gamwell and Howland 2017). Andrews found that the list of landraces and the varietals within them was almost definitely subject to change over time because "local farmers added to scientific knowledge what the scientists did not." Their distinctions among quinoa took account of "local knowledge in a culturally laden environment," leading Andrews (2017, 21) to conclude that "the comprehensive list of quinoa names is surely only a small part of the evaluation of the biodiversity of the species and the folk classification system."

Andrews affirms the importance of establishing a systematic nomenclature but also persuasively argues that researchers should be aware that an extraordinary knowledge of cultural and environmental organization and racialized practices and values that inextricably link humans to quinoa (such as the polysemic qualities associated with black quinoa) are funneled into nomenclature. Human-plant-environmental contexts and interactions in the Andes have created a wide range of kinds of quinoa that are recognized, and great fluidity and dynamism accompanies designating a particular kind of quinoa as a variety. The many kinds of quinoa that can be successfully grown in differing conditions and the plant's versatile attributes underlie the tensions that have emerged in debates about its sustainability, its contributions to food sovereignty and food security, and what these terms actually mean in practice.

Imagining Quinoa

In their foreword to *Quinoa, the Supergrain*, a cookbook with quinoa recipes, Nicki Goldbeck and David Goldbeck stress the spiritual and pragmatic relationships mediated by quinoa. They underline how ancient the "grain" is and the cultural roles that it plays. Their narrative highlights the "personal saga" of the cookbook's author, Rebecca Wood, and suggests to readers that trying out her recipes will offer them "a culinary adventure." Cooking with quinoa will

5. Food Sovereignty, Food Security, and Sustainability

create relationships between them, "the ancient Incas," "modern-day Indians of Bolivia and Peru," and "contemporary 'quinoa pioneers' in the Rocky Mountains." At the end of their foreword, they offer practical advice for those who wish to eat well and nutritiously:

> Rely on historically selected foods, i.e., those foods our ancestors ate, eaten in similar proportions; reduce intake of food components which do not exist in nature and to which our bodies are unaccustomed; vary food selection to maximize the chance of receiving unknown, as well as known, nutrients; eat foods as close to their natural form as possible. In addition to its specific nutrient profile, quinoa fits all four of these criteria. (Goldbeck and Goldbeck 1989, 15)

In 1989, before quinoa was deemed a superfood, Wood had researched the cultural context in which it was grown and used. In her book, she noted that two Andean agronomists, Mario Tapia and Humberto Gondorillos, beginning in the 1960s, were already encouraging the cultivation of Indigenous crops such as quinoa as a good way to counter the effects of the Green Revolution with its narrow focus on high-yield grains and monocultivation (Wood 1989, 55). She observed that women dedicated considerable labor to processing quinoa. Quinoa, high in carbs, low in fat, rich in vitamins and minerals, according to Wood, could be used as an infusion, a diuretic, and an emetic; for the treatment of liver problems, urinary disorders, tuberculosis, cholera, appendicitis, cancer, motion sickness, and altitude sickness; as an external plaster for broken bones; and as an enhancer of mother's milk. Subsequent research has shown that between 16–20 percent of the seed's weight corresponds to proteins of high biological value, which contain all nine amino acids, including those that the body cannot synthesize itself and therefore must be supplied in the diet (Bojanic 2011, 8). Shirley MacLaine claimed that quinoa conveyed spiritual qualities that enhanced one's sensitivity during meditation (Wood 1989, 37), and both NASA and paratroopers in World War II relied on quinoa because of its nutritious value and portability as rations (Dobkin 2008, 31). In short, there were good reasons for the rest of the world to wake up to the powers of quinoa, and they did.

By the beginning of the twenty-first century, consumers in the West had recognized that quinoa "packs a lot of punch" and had also embraced quinoa because it could serve analogous functions to a grain but was gluten-free (Aubrey and Young 2013). In 2003 it was estimated that 36 products used quinoa as an ingredient; by 2007, there were 154 products; and in 2018 one review of data found more than 267 quinoa products (Dobkin 2008, 34; Mehdi and Abdelaziz

2018). Such is quinoa's value and stature that its seeds have now been included in the Svalbard Global Seed Vault, which is located on an island near Norway and preserves seeds from around the world in case of a regional or global catastrophe (Dobkin 2008, 34). Peru and Bolivia have also established germplasm banks of quinoa seed.[2]

The changing perceptions of quinoa from "a lowly Indian food" to one of high value has fueled its inclusion in seed vaults and germplasm banks. Yet quinoa was not a seed in danger of disappearing and therefore in need of rescue through germplasm banks. Rather, the desire to "preserve" quinoa varieties and germplasm took place because of the convergence of several forces: globalization and travel in the form of the circulation of people, capital, goods, and information worldwide; a growing concern on the part of people in the United States and Europe with ingesting healthy foods and beverages; and an increasing awareness and preoccupation with the impacts of climate change, now and into the future. Many countries and entities are now invested in preserving quinoa seed in germplasm banks and experimenting with new and existing quinoa varieties outside of the Andean region. In Peru, INIA runs eight germplasm banks in which approximately 6,302 quinoa accessions are conserved (Rojas et al. 2015, 59; Pinedo et al. 2020, 13). The establishment of these banks has not, however, addressed the rights and returns that quinoa farmers should receive from their investments over millennia that have resulted in adapting quinoa varietals to specific environments. Instead, the rhetoric and discourse surrounding the banks has been that they will serve as a significant mechanism for staving off world hunger and malnutrition (See McDonell 2015). Increasingly, the quinoa varieties that circulate within Peru are limited to those that are deemed commercially viable for export. However, their introduction to growers in differing regions has often been unsuccessful because they are not well adapted to local conditions. The ways that quinoa seeds are being viewed and protected globally has been of concern to quinoa farmers in Huanoquite and elsewhere and have underlain debates about what constitutes food security, and how and for whom quinoa should be grown.[3]

GMOs, Biopiracy, and Food Sovereignty

In part because of my presence and curiosity about quinoa, people I had known for a long time in Huanoquite shared with me their distress about a new development that they believed had taken place hand in hand with the popularity of quinoa globally: biopiracy—how researchers had been smuggling native quinoa seeds out of their communities in Huanoquite and taking them to Spain and the United States to establish their own domestic production of quinoa. That suspicion extended to me as well because of my curiosity about quinoa. Farmers were concerned about the future negative economic impact this might portend, but they were also upset that their painstaking work to establish multiple quinoa varieties, adapted to so many microecological niches, was being stolen and coopted without compensation.

In 2012 then-president Ollanta Humala had passed a ten-year ban on GMO seeds and foods, aimed at preserving Peru's biodiversity and supporting local farmers (INIA 2012). There was opposition to the ban because some claimed most foods were already genetically modified, but at the same time the ban provided some recognition that the impressive varieties of Indigenous cultigens, including quinoa, should be protected because they enhanced the prospects for resilience and food sovereignty for all Peruvians. Huanoquite's farmers, for example, were already aware that climatic patterns were increasingly unpredictable and their accessibility to multiple varieties of cultigens made a significant difference in their ability to bounce back from floods, plummeting temperatures, and droughts.

Many countries (among them, the United States, Canada, Portugal, Spain, Greece, and the Netherlands) have been trying to grow their own quinoa for a long time, often using seeds that originally came from Peru and Bolivia and then attempting to genetically modify them. In their article, "The Global Expansion of Quinoa," Didier Bazile, Sven-Erik Jacobsen (Founder of the Organic Quinoa Project in Peru in conjunction with INIA), and Alexis Verniau (2016) offer a succinct overview of the history of the exchange of quinoa germplasm and experimentation with it in different world regions. In 1980 only eight countries were experimenting with growing quinoa, but that number had increased to ninety-five countries by 2015 (Bazile, Jacobsen, and Verniau 2016, 1). This was not uncommon when an export resulted in high demand, but it was problematic that there was no unified international regulatory framework for importing quinoa germplasm.[4] As Bazile, Jacobsen, and Verniau (2016) note, the regulations were differently applied at local, national, and international levels, and for different purposes. In some cases, the regulations concerned genetic resources; in others, at issue were varieties and seeds, or agricultural by-products.

The Convention on Biological Diversity (CBD) became open to signatories in 1992. It regulates "bilateral access and benefit sharing" but does not apply internationally in a global market, and questions of benefit sharing between nations do not deal with the inequalities that have presented obstacles to benefit sharing *within* nations. Complicating matters further, 25 countries prior to the establishment of the CBD had already established their own collections of quinoa accessions outside the Andean countries, and when they developed new varieties from those sources, they were not required to acknowledge their country of origin. And while countries were not allowed to share their germplasm with other nations, this was true only of those countries that had ratified the agreement. Although the CBD has been ratified by 196 countries to date, the United States and a few other countries have not ratified it. The authors conclude that "for quinoa, there is no single existing legal framework providing a comprehensive coverage of all the issues related to the genetic resources and their sustainable management" (Bazile, Jacobsen, and Verniau 2016, 3–4). The CBD has some teeth to it, but its enforcement is limited by the deregulated international market, the multiplicity of diffuse investment flows, and the close ties between national governments, such as that of Peru, and global financial markets. Hence, the justifiable concerns of Huanoquite's quinoa growers about biopiracy.

Food Security and Sustainable Consumption

Sustainable consumption is an idea and practice intertwined with food sovereignty and food security issues. The international embrace of quinoa has incited competitive efforts to cultivate it outside of the Andean region and to ramp up its production within the Andean countries for purposes of export. While western and European-based consumers desired quinoa because of its nutritional properties, the global spike in demand for it raised concerns that Indigenous inhabitants in the Andes would no longer be able to afford to consume it (Blythman 2013; Jacobsen 2011; Kerssen 2015). The data are inconclusive—especially given the instability in market prices for quinoa, but further research should help to clarify if and why consumption patterns of quinoa among rural and urban populations have changed. For centuries, Huanoquiteños consumed only small amounts of quinoa on a daily or weekly basis. It may well be, for example, that they are consuming more of it because they are cultivating more of it. It may also be that because of the diminishing stigma attached to consuming quinoa, urban inhabitants may be consuming more of it in different forms (Tschopp 2018; Winkel et al. 2012; Walsh-Dilley 2013).[5]

At the same time that some international consumers of quinoa have become concerned that their own desire to pursue a healthier diet has had a negative impact on Indigenous consumers of quinoa in the Andes, others have taken a different position, arguing that the increased demand for quinoa could actually improve the welfare of Indigenous cultivators because even if they might not be able to consume as much quinoa as they had in the past, with their revenues

5. Food Sovereignty, Food Security, and Sustainability

from quinoa sales they could purchase lettuce and tomatoes for domestic consumption, adding more vegetables with healthy nutrients to their diet. While Huanoquiteños welcomed greater profits from the sale of their quinoa, women, who were in charge of their household gardens—amazing laboratories of experimentation—and who also were responsible for preparing meals, were not eager to take on the additional labor of boiling nonpotable water in order to wash raw vegetables for domestic consumption. There were good reasons for Huanoquiteños to prefer consuming hot soups! Nor was it clear that men or women much liked the taste of salads in the form of lettuce and tomatoes. As importantly, non-Andeans defined "health" in terms of the microproperties of foods—being gluten-free, providing fiber or certain proteins or vitamins—but were not thinking much of the health of Andean villagers in light of the assemblage of meanings and aesthetic considerations the latter valued in cooking and serving a meal, a subject on which I will expand in the next chapter. Alison Krögel (2010, 3) calls this kind of assemblage a "food landscape." The non-Andean association of foods with categories of healthful attributes observed a kind of segmented logic that did not coincide with the place of quinoa and other foods in Andean lives, even though people consuming imported quinoa

FIGURE 5.1. Brochure made by the Cusco Regional Government office describing the micronutrients of quinoa and how to prepare and commercialize it (Data source: Regional Government of Cusco, Division of Regional Economic Development)

outside of the Andes might find that the logic fit well with their life conditions and aesthetics.

Another result of the increase in quinoa production for export was the narrowing of varieties cultivated for purposes of satisfying a market that was being defined by consumers in other world regions. This had impacts on local food security. The UN FAO-sponsored World Food Summit in Rome in 2002 defined the attainment of food security as "the existence of physical and economic access to enough safe and nutritious foods to satisfy the requirements of an entire healthy and active population" (Krögel 2010, 211–212). In Huanoquite, quinoa was far from becoming a monoculture but there were indications that the rich biodiversity of quinoa varietals and landraces as a strategy that ensured flexible sustainability was diminishing. In addition, cultivation of quinoa, specifically for the market, was expanding into fields that had traditionally grown other crops, such as potatoes, barley, and wheat, and farmers were not allowing their fields to rest sufficiently to avoid soil exhaustion.

In her research on quinoa in Ecuador, Kristine Skarbø (2015, 96) found that the danger in the changing perception of quinoa from a relatively unknown crop for local consumption and marketing to a lucrative commodity also had a direct impact on food security and how it was defined. Greater *preservation* of varietals was taking place in germplasm banks but at the expense of possible "loss of experimentation with landraces" in real time. Indigenous quinoa cultivators and consumers have been less interested in western rationales for preserving germplasm in the form of ancient grains/seeds—for purposes of ensuring food security and health for the world—than in arriving at and maintaining quinoa varietals adapted to microecological zones and varying climatic conditions and in being able to savor kinds of quinoa that they prefer along with all the other foods from crops they grow. This is a dynamic undertaking because environmental and ecological conditions do not remain in a steady state. The preferences that Huanoquiteño quinoa cultivators expressed revealed the gap between how food security was viewed by the Cusco Regional Government, INIA, and MINAGRI. In my conversations with INIA personnel, I found that they respected and admired the agrobiodiversity represented by the many quinoa varieties but also felt that the cultivation of so many varieties resulted in agricultural inefficiency and poverty because it made for a less dynamic market even though it might be better for the environment (See also Shepherd 2000, 166). In short, Huanoquiteños and state and parastatal agents did not share the same understanding of what food security meant, and these differences in meaning were bound up with how they defined risk, profit, food, and sustainability.

5. Food Sovereignty, Food Security, and Sustainability

Disagreements about how to define food security and sustainability had abated because of two significant phenomena that have taken place too recently for me to assess their impact. The first is that, due to growing international and national recognition of climate change and its effects, the potential of agrodiversity and agroecology as a qualitatively different calculus of efficiency in and of itself is gaining greater respect from a range of policy makers, development agents, and NGOs. The ability to grow different kinds of quinoa successfully across a range of climatic conditions carries with it the potential to enhance and even ensure food security, not only for Indigenous growers but also for consumers in other parts of the globe. How this will impact economies of scale and the intense weight placed on market efficiency remains to be seen. The second phenomenon, which I address at greater length in the next chapter, has to do with how government agencies, in particular, are defining food security and its impact on the kinds of quinoa that are grown. Rather than solely focusing on particular kinds of quinoa as apt for export, especially organic quinoa, these agencies have begun to contemplate how tourists as well as some countries that import quinoa might welcome a broader range of quinoa and not be particularly concerned about whether or not it is organic. This could serve both the needs of agrodiversity and food security.

PROMPERÚ, the Commission for the Promotion of Peru for Export and Tourism, operates within MINCETUR, the Ministry of Foreign Trade and Tourism. In turn, MINCETUR has regional branch offices throughout the country. PROMPERÚ and—in a more decentralized fashion—any number of tourist operators, restauranteurs, and adventure guides have dedicated themselves to promoting Indigenous Quechua foodways and Peru itself, as a gastronomical mecca, to tourists. Beginning with the precipitous drop in the quinoa market in 2015, especially of organically grown quinoa, INIA and MINAGRI began reconsidering their focus on primarily producing organic quinoa for export. They realized that international consumers did not all necessarily demand the same standard from quinoa. While EU consumers generally placed a premium on organic quinoa, those in the United States (and other countries) did not. They began to encourage quinoa cultivators to grow both organic and nonorganic quinoa with specific qualities to encourage niche markets that, in turn, could stabilize the market and perpetuate the cultivation of more varieties of quinoa.

In Daniel Reichman's (2018) research on coffee in Brazil, he found that niche coffee production proved to be far more resilient than predicted, but as he explains, it thrived because it was incorporated into an agribusiness model of flexible, large-scale, industrialized production. This was a tall order, however, for small-scale producers like Huanoquite's cultivators of quinoa. They complained that although they wanted to successfully market their quinoa internationally and to tourists, the pressure to grow it organically created tremendous challenges for them because of the amount of time and risk it took to shift from nonorganic to organic farming and their need to invest energy, knowledge, and time to farm a highly diversified array of crops, not just quinoa. In reality, the goal of state agencies to create a national identity that equated Indigenous Quechua foodways with Peru as a gastronomical mecca masked many of the sacrifices that Huanoquiteños undertook to achieve both food security and sustainability.

The Domestic and Export Markets

In debating the consequences of quinoa's status as an export commodity for Indigenous cultivators, a growing chorus of researchers, as well as INIA, urged that the Peruvian government make greater investments in stimulating domestic consumption of quinoa, which was extremely low. Proposals included substituting quinoa for the rice and wheat used in school breakfasts and lunches that were subsidized by the state, a position echoed by the mayor of Huanoquite during the time I was doing my fieldwork there. In their study, Bellemare, Fajardo-Gonzalez, and Gitter (2018) found that roughly 30 percent of households consumed quinoa in Peru, a proportion that has been relatively constant since 2005. Granted this was an estimate, but it is revealing. One major obstacle to increasing domestic consumption was that some Indigenous inhabitants had internalized the negative, racialized status of quinoa as an "Indian" food and, until the recent celebration of Indigenous foodways in Peru, had been reluctant to have their children consume it instead of rice or wheat. This stance was reinforced by the cheap import price of wheat and rice and the unstable export price of quinoa. Food consumption and security thus existed in a complex political, economic, and sociocultural web.[6]

When I interviewed agronomists Estrada (INIA) and Olivera (Cusco Regional Government), Estrada noted that INIA had struggled with "habits of consumption." He explained that "campesinos were always looking for their rice and noodles from the city. They would sell their own products and buy these items" (Interview, July 24, 2018). The low status attributed to Indigenous foods extended to institutions of support, which distributed nonnative food products. He added optimistically that even if they cultivated quinoa in other regions like Europe, the United States, or Asia, Peru's market would always occupy a significant niche because the qualities of the soil, the altitude, and the lack of

5. Food Sovereignty, Food Security, and Sustainability

the use of chemicals made the taste of quinoa grown in the Andes distinctive. Estrada and Olivera, looking toward the future, believed that it was important to begin with problems surrounding the quinoa market. Olivera stressed that to promote domestic consumption, there was "a need to organize how the market worked so that growers were not over-exposed to intermediaries and exporters who arbitrarily determined the price" (Interview, July 30, 2018). Both Estrada and Olivera singled out as a key problem the lack of credit available to cultivators who usually had little to offer in the way of collateral. As far as local consumption went, Olivera thought that social welfare programs and school lunches needed to be improved by having the government buy and stimulate regional and local production of Indigenous crops for local consumption. This would also require the government to invest seriously in the stewardship of small family or peasant farming and in the value of Quechua cultural practices and knowledge.

The President of the QCA agreed that attitudes among both government institutions and inhabitants themselves needed to change and that it was "a disgrace that school children were given meat in cans and bananas from Argentina when they could be consuming quinoa instead, creating a dynamic national market" (Interview, July 19, 2018). In Huanoquite itself, a pilot program called "Siete Semillas" (Seven Seeds) had been established which emphasized incorporating five native crops (quinoa, maca, tarwi, kiwicha, and cañihua) into children's meals for school breakfasts and lunch. The state provided the food products so that they were ready to be cooked. It remains to be seen if this could become a more permanent arrangement.

Ironies abounded in the efforts to promote and celebrate quinoa as a miracle food. This was apparent in Renato's account to me of his wife's prowess in preparing quinoa. Renato Quispe, president of the community of Maska in Huanoquite and a member of the QCA, threw up his hands as he told me:

> My wife participates in cultivating quinoa. She also prepares quinoa milkshakes (*lacteos*), cakes (*torrejas*), soups (*pisq'e*), and puddings (*masamora*). Sometimes she sells it but mostly she makes it for us to eat and for contests. We have had contests in Huanoquite district. We had a gastronomic fair in our plaza on the 16th of June. My wife won a prize of rice and cooking oil for her quinoa preparations. That's because we sell the quinoa and consume rice and oil. It's true that quinoa is healthier than rice and noodles. In the past, we consumed more quinoa because there was no rice or noodles. We didn't sell the quinoa. And it's easier just to eat the rice and noodles because we don't have to process them. (Interview, July 12, 2018)

PART TWO. SOUP AND SUPERFOOD

The Right to Grow and Consume Quinoa

The Peruvian government's primary focus on quinoa as an export commodity, its lack of credit and price supports for a subsidized domestic quinoa market in the face of cheap imports of wheat, rice, and noodles, and the labor and time required by households, especially women, to process quinoa, created obstacles to stimulating the domestic market for quinoa. Food security meant different things to the Peruvian government, NGOs, Huanoquiteños, and international consumers of quinoa and quinoa products. These meanings were not diametrically opposed to one another. For Huanoquiteños, food security was entangled with questions of sustainability and food sovereignty. They viewed food security and sustainability in conjunction with the spirit and practice of the 2007 Nyéléni Declaration of Food Sovereignty, crafted at the World Forum for Food Sovereignty in Mali, from which I quote at length below. This definition of food sovereignty has been embraced by peasants across the globe in conjunction with major social movements and organizations, such as La Via Campesina:

> Our heritage as food producers is critical to the future of humanity. This is specially so in the case of women and Indigenous peoples who are historical creators of knowledge about food and agriculture and are devalued. But this heritage and our capacities to produce healthy, good, and abundant food are being threatened and undermined by neo-liberalism and global capitalism. Food sovereignty gives us the hope and power to preserve, recover, and build on our food-producing knowledge and capacity. Food sovereignty is the right of peoples to healthy and culturally appropriate food produced through ecologically sound and sustainable methods, and their right to define their own food and agriculture systems. It puts the aspirations and needs of those who produce, distribute, and consume food at the heart of food systems and policies rather than the demands of markets and corporations. It defends the interests and inclusion of the next generation. It offers a strategy to resist and dismantle the current corporate trade and food regime directions for food, farming, pastoral, and fisheries systems determined by local producers and users. Food sovereignty gives priority to local and national economies and markets and empowers peasant and family farmer-driven agriculture . . . and food production, distribution and consumption based on environmental, social, and economic sustainability. Food sovereignty promotes transparent trade that guarantees just incomes to all peoples as well as the rights of consumers to control their food and nutrition. It ensures that the rights to use and manage lands, territories, waters, seeds, livestock, and biodiversity are in the hands of those of us who produce food. Food sovereignty implies

5. Food Sovereignty, Food Security, and Sustainability

new social relations free of oppression and inequality between men and women, peoples, racial groups, social and economic classes and generations determined by local producers and users. (Nicholson 2013, 65)

Many (but not all) Huanoquiteños wanted to grow, consume, and market different kinds of quinoa tailored for different kinds of consumption; they depended on varietals that would thrive in a range of microecological zones even when climatic conditions were not optimal; and their preference was to market some quinoa for export without sacrificing the many other crops they grew for subsistence and the market.[7]

Existing stratification among households meant that better-off farmers could take advantage of the market and continue to farm their land, whereas poorer farmers had less of a cushion. While it was true that poorer households might be able to tolerate market volatility and its risks and insecurities better because they were not as dependent on money for their farming operations, if they did take a risk, they could lose their ability to feed their families, whereas better-off farmers were far more likely to be able to cobble together alternative sources of income (Van der Ploeg 2014; see also Stensrud 2019). Neither scenario was ideal. In the best of all possible worlds, all households would be able to continue farming their land and feeding their households. Achieving Indigenous food sovereignty may be an unrealistic goal but at the same time, whatever efforts are made to create viable alternatives must knit together global admiration around the world for Peruvian cuisine and crops with the benefit, well-being, and respect of those who grow, prepare, and consume Indigenous foods in places like Huanoquite. This would constitute a genuine practice of interculturality.

Until recently, the major focus of the Peruvian government and NGOs had been on stimulating quinoa cultivation as a successful export without paying much mind to how it might either jeopardize or enhance its consumption within Peru. These entities had begun to move away from a pure "developmentality" to one in which agrobiodiversity and conservation were playing more prominent roles (De la Cadena 2004, 278). Christopher Shepherd (2010, 644) found this to also be the case in his work on potatoes and concluded that:

we should not overemphasize choice and pluralism but look closely at both the particular range of choices and values made available to recipients of development and conservation through interventions. Institutions seek to control this range as they design and promote a particular kind of intervention based on a given set of values, beliefs, and knowledge. But as recipients consider their options and pursue their interests, they draw development actors into more and more complex interactions and political negotiating.

> ... [l]ocal knowledge and practice are not simply the counterpoint to institutional knowledge and the yardstick of local agency. "Local knowledge" itself becomes institutionalized and "known" in ways that may converge or diverge with other local knowledge-practices.

This admixture of local and institutional development knowledge and practices was in a nascent stage with respect to quinoa, and points of divergence existed between the conceptualization of well-being that Huanoquiteños held dear and those entertained by development agents. More convergence was nevertheless most apparent in the widely circulating knowledge among quinoa cultivators themselves across differing regions, such that what might have been viewed as "local" knowledge in the past had become far more extensive and diverse than has usually been understood. Convergence was also apparent in the myriad ways that cultivators modified directives of discipline and control that development agents had issued. They adjusted them in accordance with their own knowledge of what would work best, gauging the conditions of their environment, the dynamics of the market, and the needs of their households and communities.

The enthusiasm for quinoa and its properties among international consumers and nations as a key element of global food security has also brought about important shifts *within* Andean countries and among Indigenous growers concerning questions of food sovereignty and the ethics of rights to quinoa germplasm and varietals that Indigenous farmers have developed over millennia. With good reason, given the centuries of discrimination leveled against Indigenous foods and culture, including on the part of their own compatriots—Indigenous inhabitants viewed the celebratory international and national stance toward quinoa with some uneasiness and had begun to think harder about and to articulate more forcefully their own ideas about what constitutes food sovereignty and security.

CHAPTER 6

To Be Strong and Healthy

> Nature is replete with bountiful things that we can benefit from by living in harmony in the countryside among people, the community, society, and mother earth. (Author's translation.)
>
> —"Conociéndote Huanoquite Linda Tierra"
> Huanoquite Facebook page

The intertwined and contradictory meanings of sustainability, food security, and food sovereignty have contributed to the significations associated with, projected onto, and represented by quinoa. In this chapter, I discuss what quinoa meant to Huanoquiteños and how they have "ingested" the proliferation of meanings produced by Peruvian state agencies that have promoted Peruvian exports, agriculture, gastronomy, tourism, and Indigeneity. Quinoa has turned out to be a potent symbolic, political, and economic vehicle wielded by different entities to produce regional and national identities and establish a unique Peruvian brand in an explicitly instrumental fashion.[1] Frequently, those efforts have been dedicated to creating a national Peruvian identity that rests on the ancient wisdom and lifeways of Peru's Quechua inhabitants *and* their entrepreneurial spirit, both of which operate within a frame defined by the history of coloniality and modernity.

To ascertain how quinoa has been framed within this complex and dynamic symbolic, expressive, and sensory system, I pursued participant observation and extensive conversations with Huanoquiteños, consumers of quinoa in the United States, and purveyors of quinoa or quinoa products in Cusco's markets, as well as in restaurants and venues within and outside the United States. I also reviewed pamphlets, documents, and visuals produced by the two principal state agencies charged with popularizing quinoa as a nontraditional export commodity and as a global taste, PROMPERÚ (which operates under the umbrella of MINCETUR) and MINAGRI. Through a granular examination of their content, I was able to trace the themes they highlighted over time, the changes in their focus and emphasis, and the impacts of their approaches. The meanings that quinoa carried for promoters and consumers of quinoa exhibited some overlap, but marked differences among them became especially apparent when it came to how they understood Indigenous wisdom and lifeways, the assumptions that underpinned their understanding, and the instrumental purposes of their interest in quinoa.

Feeding

Anthropologists who have done research on cooking, serving, feeding, and eating in the Andean highlands (e.g., Allen 1982, 2002; Weismantel 1988; Krögel 2010; Corr 2010; and Sax 2011) have noted that no food stands outside a system. While the cultural norms may be arbitrary and their origins hard to decipher, they intervene powerfully in how meals are constructed. People take account of appropriate combinations of kinds of foods, their qualities, whether a food is central to or an accompaniment to a meal, the temperatures and texture of foods, the proper sequencing of a meal, and the condiments and beverages that are coupled with it. Class, race, gender, and ethnicity intervene significantly in which foods are selected for a meal and the way that a meal itself is conceptualized (Bourdieu 1987; Douglas 1972; Mintz 1986). In her review of literary and archival sources about Quechua foodways, for example, Krögel (2010) shows how food, cooking, and meals came to occupy a highly politicized place and concern, especially as the Spanish colonial regime tried to exercise control and discipline over Indigenous people's environments, their lives, and their bodies. Wielding food as a political and racialized weapon has continued to the present day, and quinoa is no exception.

Quechua households of the high Andes ideally have preferred to serve meals whose central component is a starchy staple with accompaniments, including additional starches (See Weismantel 1988, 91–92).[2] Over the centuries, they also have selectively incorporated foods, beverages, and condiments they value into their meals and rejected what they have not liked or found disgusting. Most of the time, they have slotted new foodstuffs or beverages into their preexisting templates of how food and meals should be prepared and sequenced. Tensions and occasional conflicts between the preferences of Indigenous inhabitants and their ideas of what constitutes a "good meal," and those of non-Indigenous people and development and NGO experts who do not necessarily respect Indigenous ideas and "affective maps" about food, have accompanied efforts of the latter to promote one rather than another foodstuff (see also García 2013, 518 on native notions of food sovereignty). Indigenous inhabitants were also not necessarily in agreement with each other about their food and meal preferences, depending on their views of high- and low-status foods and the introduction of new foods whose taste they preferred to what they had usually encountered.

Age, gender, migration or travel patterns, and stratification based on class and ethnic identification inflected how food was valued and consumed. García (2021), in her perceptive book on Peru's gastropolitics, documents the interactive dynamics and tensions between hegemonic discourses and practices promoted by state-led culinary projects and the counternarratives and projects taking place among Andean migrants in Lima and Indigenous food producers who have collaborated on state-led projects. My own analysis here complements García's insights by bringing into the mix the perspectives and experiences of Huanoquiteños, who were both cultivators and consumers of quinoa. I show how the associations they make with quinoa have undergone transformations in the context of their history of agrarian reform, development initiatives from the top-down and bottom-up, privatization, neoliberalism, and, most recently, the global embrace of quinoa as a food. Whereas quinoa's magical powers and its provenance as an Indigenous foodstuff had caused the Spaniards in the colonial period to marginalize it because they thought its powers could jeopardize the conquest, these same qualities were now being lauded as a positive force and a potential key to the food security of the world.

Along with considering the taste of various kinds of quinoa and its status as part of their meals, Huanoquiteños attributed meanings to quinoa in the context of its associations with gender relations, economic regimes, ritual and sacred power, social networks, and the environment they inhabited. While both men and women contributed to the labor of quinoa cultivation—three women were active members of the QCA in Huanoquite—it was women who processed, prepared, and served it, and they were among the first to talk about it with me as a delicious repast. They cared deeply about which kinds of quinoa were grown and into what kinds of food it was converted.

Rainbow Fields

In Huanoquite, men and women expressed discomfort about "mixing" kinds of quinoa. This stood in sharp contrast to what one might find in a grocery store in the United States, where pink, white, yellow, and black varieties of quinoa

PART TWO. SOUP AND SUPERFOOD

seed could be found mixed in a single see-through container. Importers of quinoa and chefs mixed quinoa varieties to maximize taste and visual appeal, and in some cases, to preserve biodiversity (Dobkin 2008). At the beginning of one of the very first brochures PROMPERÚ (2012, 108–113) launched to publicize quinoa were three photos, all of non-Indigenous women who ranged in height and skin- and hair color in order to project diversity. A second brochure included visuals that appeared with increasing frequency in subsequent publications: aesthetically pleasing varieties of bright pink, yellow, and red quinoa seeds mixed together, pictured side-by-side images of other kinds of seeds and grains in a range of earth colors. The text proclaimed quinoa as the "gold of the gods that was still captivating the world today" and celebrated that along with its nutritional value and versatility, it was "also becoming the star of the menu at the most exclusive restaurants on the planet." The brochures emphasized the desire to increase quinoa exports and expand the number of growers cultivating it and heralded it as "a key ingredient in state programs to prevent child malnutrition in different nations" (Gamarra 2013). As such, quinoa would "honor the memory of Andean communities which have preserved this food for more than eight centuries, a fitting recognition for a grain that fed the first pre-Colombian cultures and, despite the passing of years, is still part of the Peruvian diet." The conclusion of the brochure, entitled "Quinoa à la Carte," publicized the skills of renowned chefs around the world who have shown "how this grain can be successfully used in well-known Peruvian recipes, such as *cebiche, tamal, rocoto relleno, tacu tacu.*" The brochure continues, "Just imagine your favorite dish but with this product as the main ingredient. For example, quinoa balls with cheese sauce, stuffed quinoa with chicken, quinoa with pepper, quinoa stew with meat, quinoa with olives and fried fish, *quinoto* (risotto using quinoa instead of rice) with meat stew. . . . The limit is the imagination" (Gamarra 2013).

There are several notable aspects to how quinoa was being promoted. As has been amply documented, while Indigenous inhabitants have indeed continued growing many kinds of quinoa for millennia, only recently has their consumption of quinoa been correlated with "miraculously still being part of the Peruvian diet," and even by 2019, little had been done to improve underlying causes of child malnutrition in the countryside or poor urban areas. The kinds of meals made with quinoa mentioned above in the brochure were all Lima based and bore little or no resemblance to the meal or food preferences of Indigenous highland dwellers. The equation of quinoa and honoring Andean people with the Peruvian nation was a theme of these promotional brochures that became more and more pronounced with novel permutations in the years

6. To Be Strong and Healthy

FIGURE 6.1. Tricolored quinoa for sale in a US gourmet supermarket

between 2013 and 2021. Finally, as was true of most Indigenous inhabitants, Huanoquiteños did not view quinoa as the centerpiece of their meals, however delicious the recipes the brochure mentioned might be.

Because each kind of quinoa was distinguished by Huanoquiteños' knowledge of its taste, uses, processing, preparation, and the entire panoply of activities (including labor) that they invested in cultivating and harvesting it, these combined associations and values did not convert directly or simply into economic returns. When Ofstehage talked to farmers in Lipez, they too were openly anxious about aggregating and mixing quinoa from different sources. Ofstehage conjectured that this had less to do with the physical properties of quinoa itself but rather with the "social labor, cultural know-how, and personal sacrifices that materialize in their quinoa in Lipez" (Ofstehage 2011, 108).

In Huanoquite, I thought that farmers were trying not to mix different kinds of quinoa, mainly because of what the market (exporters) was demanding of them and this was partially true. However, after talking with "the feeders" themselves (the women), it became clear to me that they did not want to mix varieties either and carefully distinguished among them for different household uses. Thus, men and women shared similar feelings about the best kinds of quinoa for different purposes, especially for eating or drinking, but men, additionally, did not want to mix kinds of quinoa because they thought it could jeopardize what they could get for it on the export market, given higher demands for some, rather than other, kinds of quinoa.

I asked many Huanoquiteños about quinoa varieties, how they prepared them, and what their favorite dishes were. Their "lists" were always multivariate. Most interesting was that they rarely described in detail the varieties that they destined primarily for wholesale, or they described them in terms of what they knew international consumers appreciated—"Black quinoa has a higher amount of lysine" or "white quinoa has less saponin and is sweeter"—whereas they provided far more detail about the quinoa they used for domestic consumption or that they had adapted to microecological niches and which they planned to commercialize locally in agricultural fairs and markets. I provide below just a few of their descriptions to give the reader an idea of what they thought were some of the most important criteria:

> Black quinoa (*qollana*) is good for people. My wife has insisted that I feed all our children black quinoa, as a juice. People are not familiar with its qualities and maybe that is why it does not sell well. Black quinoa is excellent for flour, for milk, and it is good for cancer. (Personal communication, Milagros)
>
> We prefer yellow quinoa (*Amarillo marangani*) because it is much tastier. But it takes much more work to process the yellow quinoa because it is bitter and we still do it by hand. Sometimes I have to rinse it twenty or more times. (Personal communication, Paulina)
>
> We use quinoa as rice, as *p'esqe* (with milk and cheese), we make quinoa soups (*lawa*), quinoa chicha. For all of these dishes, yellow quinoa is tastier. We make chicha with corn, quinoa, and flour. [Note that people never used to make chicha with quinoa in Huanoquite but now they frequently do.] (Personal communication, Margarita)
>
> We like to eat maranganí and *blanca*. For breakfast, we clean and rinse it, we boil it, and we add milk to it and drink it hot. We like it in soups with lots of potatoes, *moraya* (freeze-dried potatoes), vegetables. It's very delicious. We make p'esqe with milk, cheese, eggs. And we make a main course (*segundito*) with it. We roast it like rice with a tiny bit of water in the frying pan and then put it in a pot. It substitutes for rice. You can add sautéed *lisas* (a kind of tuber) and stewed chicken to it. (Personal communication, Samuel)

There was overlap in how Huanoquiteños and Multiple Organics, one among many examples of companies marketing quinoa internationally, described quinoa and products made from it on its website. At the same time, as Multiple Organics' publicity materials, below, reflect, the exporters tended to

FIGURE 6.2. Boiled quinoa with corn on the cob and beef steak

FIGURE 6.3. P'esqe (milk, cheese, and quinoa soup), accompanied by a baked potato

concentrate on some attributes of quinoa that had never been articulated by Huanoquiteños, which in turn, circulated to international consumers.

> *Organic Quinoa flakes* offer a great alternative to wheat. Only 90 seconds cooking time, you can easily boost your nutrition while enjoying a hot bowl of quinoa flakes in the morning—no sodium or cholesterol, and great source of your daily fiber.
>
> *Organic Quinoa red*: The organic red quinoa has an earthier flavor than the white quinoa and, once cooked, turns a light reddish-brown color. This high in protein and amino acid-rich grain is loaded with nutrients and delicious. Cooked quinoa is fluffy and creamy, with a delicate crunch. Perfect added to your favorite stir-fry or tossed with sautéed veggies.
>
> *Organic Quinoa (Tri-Color)*: This high in protein and amino acid-rich grain is highly nutritious, delicious, and versatile. The texture of cooked quinoa is delicate, fluffy, and creamy, along with a slightly nutty flavor. It is great used in tabouli—a perfect wheat-free substitute for bulgar [*sic*] wheat. Also delicious added to soups, chilled and tossed with salad, or served warm as porridge along with fruits and nuts.[3]

Huanoquiteños and international consumers appreciated the taste and texture of quinoa and distinguished among different kinds. In addition, Huanoquiteños and international consumers, especially women, welcomed ways that could ease the hard work that went into food preparation. However, the latter placed a premium on the speed with which food could be processed and prepared, whereas Indigenous women thought more about the labor itself. There were other significant differences. Whatever kind of quinoa Multiple Organics promoted, it placed a premium on the value of specific nutrients (lowering cholesterol, substituting for wheat, providing protein), speed of preparation, and combining it with other foods that were considered healthy. Scientifically breaking down quinoa into its specific chemical elements as a way to publicize its nutritional value was very important to international consumers, as Kimura (2103) and McDonell (2015) have explained in their respective discussions of charismatic nutrients and miracle foods.

The most prevalent categories of quinoa preparations among Huanoquiteños were as soups, drinks—both hot and cold—and quinoa flour. As a soup, they served it as either a first course followed by an entrée of some kind of meat and starch, as a hearty breakfast before working in the fields, or less frequently, as a meal after people returned from work. They also specially prepared it (as indicated above) for ritual occasions as p'esque or roasted and combined it with stewed chicken and vegetables. They served it as a hot breakfast drink made

6. To Be Strong and Healthy

from quinoa flour and milk (for children), or from quinoa flour, broad beans, and alcohol (called *emolientes*, which were mainly for adults) and which vendors often sold from mobile food carts in urban areas; they also fermented it, often combined with maize, as chicha, and they occasionally made it into a pudding for their children.

Health and Well-Being

One day, Teodoro and Inés invited me to work with them at their maize harvest. After we worked for several hours, we took a break. Teodoro spread out a small woven cloth on which he carefully selected four ears of maize and placed them in the shape of a cross. He selected four more and placed them in a row above the cross. He picked up each ear, kissed it, and then blessed them with alcohol from a shot glass. He picked up a small clod of dirt, kissed it, and then stood up. He blessed the mountain spirits, *wacas*, and the earth, tossing the alcohol from his shot glass toward the sky. Inés and I then did the same, and afterwards we each drank a glass of chicha. Inés built a *watya*, an arched oven made of clods of earth, lit a fire with straw and bits of twigs, blew on it until it was burning well, and then placed corn, broad beans, and potatoes inside the earthen oven. Households traditionally made watyas for special occasions. After making the oven, Inés pounded down the clods of earth to permit the food to smolder and roast, and then after working for another hour, we took a break and she dug up the now roasted corn, beans, and potatoes, a filling and tasty meal we shared, accompanied by Huanoquite's homemade cheese and hot sauce.

Huanoquiteños, Indigenous and non-Indigenous alike, were preoccupied by what I call "cultures of well-being." In fact, Indigenous inhabitants throughout the Andes have always engaged in activities and rituals to ensure balance among natural, human, and animal forces, control over their territories, and protection of their resources. The combination of environmental precarity and tourism have now encouraged them to explicitly recognize and call attention to these practices as central to their identity and "well-being," culturally, politically, and economically. In Peru, Quechua speakers referred formally to this "well being" as *allin kawsachun* ("Let Us Live Well"); in Ecuador they referred to it as *sumaq kawsay*; in Bolivia, as *suma qamaña*; and, in Spanish, as *vivir bien*. Huanoquiteños' sense of well-being was undergirded by circuits of reciprocity and redistribution that involved consumption but also by acts of production, interaction, interconnection, replenishment, and sometimes excessive giving to ensure minimum returns and the sustainability of their lands and community. Their enhanced conscious attention to well-being had been partly catalyzed by

FIGURES 6.4 AND 6.5. Teodoro and his wife Inés blessing maize, Earth Mother (Pachamama), and Huanoquite's mountain spirits (apus) at their first maize harvest

the interest tourists showed in cultures of well-being, but Huanoquiteños were more concerned about the degradation of their environment due to activities like mining. They felt a growing uneasiness, even distress, as they increasingly found that cues that had served them well for centuries in ascertaining when they should sow or harvest their crops were no longer reliable. One such example was the appearance, size, and brightness of the Pleiades (*cabañuelas*), which they regularly observed each year for a week prior to June 24. Their observations had fairly accurately predicted the amount of rain that would come six months later and thereby had assisted them in timing when to sow their crops. According to many Huanoquiteños, their observations in June of the Pleiades no longer coordinated with the right time for them to plant. They had also come to recognize that their efforts to live in balance in their multidimensional environment had become of growing interest to many people around the world who were concerned about environmental destruction and climate change.

International consumers of quinoa also had embraced a culture of well-being in their daily activities and modes of consumption, especially those who were better off, but they were especially preoccupied with individualized regimes linked to consumption patterns, longevity, and health. They strived to consume products that were not highly processed and that benefited their mind and body, and given the increase in sedentary lifestyles, they sought to discipline their bodies through exercise routines and bodybuilding. The forces of neoliberal capitalism overwhelmingly shaped the attitudes and practices of international consumers even as they, like Huanoquiteños, were concerned about the state of the earth and were trying to change their habits.[4]

Quinoa, Gender, and the Body

Women's status in Andean agrarian communities depended greatly on how they fed others. Behind the success of labor parties for the different stages of quinoa production was women's work as feeders. They were key to ensuring the reproduction of the economic regime of their households. To that end, they activated social relationships among themselves and workers, and they also made claims on the labor of the workers. Even though wages in Huanoquite were frequently paid to workers, a work party would never go without an accompanying meal prepared by the female head of household (or a surrogate). When I went with Lorenzo to harvest his quinoa, Margarita, an excellent cook, had made stewed chicken and a side of roasted quinoa, complemented by a huge pile of hominy (*mote*) with hot sauce (*aji*) for the labor party. I was mercilessly criticized because I ate very little mote, while the workers ate enormous

FIGURE 6.6. Workers at quinoa harvest serving and sharing chicha made from quinoa and maize (Photo taken by John R. Cooper)

FIGURE 6.7. Workers chewing coca and making offerings at quinoa harvest

handfuls. Although I was not a member of the labor party, it was impossible for the workers to understand why I would not relish large, boiled kernels of maize. I did eat all my quinoa and stewed chicken, which allayed a bit of their criticism. After the workers ate their meal, Lorenzo offered them chicha made from quinoa and maize, coca, and small shots of alcohol. Huanoquiteños have always associated quinoa with strength; the same was true of mote, and it made sense that as the workers labored to produce and harvest quinoa, they would eat quinoa and mote to give themselves strength for the job (especially since maize and quinoa were frequently intercropped in the past).[5]

The Vitality of Quinoa

The equivalence of eating quinoa and providing strength to the body, including the brain, was not limited to men. Sydney Silverstein, one of my colleagues, generously shared in detail her own experiences of how inhabitants of Iquitos, a very different region of Peru located in the lowlands rather than the highlands, thought about quinoa (Personal communication, November 27, 2016). Quinoa was not generally viewed as an Amazonian seed, though some inhabitants were experimenting with cultivating it. Nevertheless, people in Iquitos consumed it, especially in the evenings, as a warm dessert drink or pudding (*mazamorra*). Much of what I recount below comes directly from Silverstein's notes on her experiences. When people there spoke of quinoa, they viewed it both as something that originated in the Andean highlands—that was coming from "outside"—and as a kind of "cultural patrimony" that Peruvians should be proud of and take advantage of. Silverstein, who was pregnant at the time, was urged to consume quinoa to give strength to her baby, and one of the household members with whom she stayed exclaimed to her, "That's what we all should be eating! Quinoa, *kiwicha*, those are god's gifts to Peruvians!"[6] Once she had her baby, Silverstein got in the habit of preparing large pots of quinoa pudding in the evenings for herself, including while she was breastfeeding, and then it became one of the first foods she fed directly to her baby. People commented, "That baby is developing fast. He's already very alert . . . Quinoa! Eating like that he's going to be very intelligent."

Silverstein also recounted to me another example in which an association between quinoa and intelligence was made. This was a case in which Michael, a young boy from the lowlands, very much wanted to attend a prestigious educational institute in Lima. His family made great sacrifices so that he could go, but he was poorly prepared by the local schools for what awaited him academically, and he quickly fell behind. At the same time, Michael made good friends with a boy from the highlands at the Institute. The latter happened to be a math whiz and tutored Michael, permitting him to catch up to the other students. While there were poor students from the highlands and lowlands attending the Institute, Michael's mother believed that all highland students had an advantage. As she put it to Sydney, "They grew up eating quinoa and Michael just eats plantains. How do you expect him to compete? Luckily that *serranito* (boy from the highlands) helped him out. He had real brain power! That's what you get when you eat those things. And look at us, eating *yuca* (manioc), *inguiri* (a kind of banana). How do we expect to keep up?" These kinds of Indigenous views of quinoa (and many other foods) reveal complex associations between food, gender, and the body, which also articulate valences (including strength and intelligence) associated with distinctive cultural and place-based practices and statuses. Hence, westerners and Indigenous inhabitants alike found quinoa to be a remarkable food source, but the attributes that its consumption signified diverged.

Women stood in the frontlines of determining the path(s) that the quinoa they cultivated took. When I asked agronomist Olivera (Cusco Regional Government) what women's roles were in the "Cultivos Andinos" initiative in Huanoquite, he explained, "We've supported them so that they can make products with a quinoa base. Every Friday, the Association of Women brings its products here to the Plaza Tupaq Amaru (in Cusco). They experiment with quinoa. Everyone knows about them. Women are important because while their husbands are working elsewhere, they are the ones working in the fields. It is women who are great fighters and work in the countryside" (Adrian Wendell Olivera, interview, July 30, 2018).

INIA gave women quinoa recipe books that showed them how they could prepare all sorts of new dishes, and they tried them from time to time. Most of the recipes were for snacks, desserts, and breads. MINAGRI and INIA distributed the recipe books to encourage women to create value-added products for purchase and possible export and to use as many parts of the plant as possible (Organización Internacional del Trabajo 2015, 9). Even the bitter outer hull of saponin that was once mainly viewed as a waste product turned out to have value because of its usefulness in fertilizers, pesticides, antiseptics, antibiotics, toothpastes, and for beer, detergents, cosmetics, and shampoos (Dobkin 2008, 34). Angeli et al. (2020, 16–17), outlined one interesting ongoing experiment with saponin, noting that,

> among the advances in developing novel molluscicides against the Golden Apple Snail (GAS) is using the quinoa husk. The GAS is considered to be

one of the most invasive species in the world and has threatened rice agriculture in many countries. The benefits of using the quinoa husk instead of a synthetic molluscicide are that it does not show any toxicity to fish that are included in rice production at the highest concentration tested. It was noted that the quinoa-based molluscicide killed 100% of the Golden Apple Snails in a laboratory setting, showing that it is effective at high doses without harming fish.

Huanoquiteños had long known about some of these uses—including its cleansing properties, the use of saponin as a pesticide that killed weeds, and using its stalks after the harvest for animal fodder—but they had not seriously thought about scaling up because of how much work it took to remove the saponin from their quinoa and because they had to prioritize many labor tasks. These variables were generally ignored by agents of development.

Many women I spoke with were excited about new quinoa preparations, but they rarely considered consuming the products themselves. I had the good fortune to meet Milagros, an unusual quinoa grower and member of the QCA. She was the daughter of a prominent hacendado family in Huanoquite and took care of her very elderly parents who had remained in Huanoquite. She had invited me to visit her, assuring me that her guard dog who protected her would be tied up. When I arrived, I was met by Lula, a huge ferocious but beautiful female German shepherd who had been tied with a heavy rope next to her adobe dog house. Milagros was in her brightly lit and spotless kitchen when I arrived. It was not so different from any other kitchen I had been welcomed into, except that it had bigger windows and a glass cabinet with china dishware. Milagros had not married and was totally committed to her farming.[7] She was able to take greater risks because she was better off than many farmers. Workers helped her in her fields, but she took genuine pleasure in working in the fields herself. She was proud of her immensely tall quinoa, and she also made cheese and yoghurt from her cows. She had tried out some of the INIA recipes and found that quinoa fried rice made from white, pink, and black quinoa was "very beautiful," and she loved quinoa for breakfast with fruit. She was among the women in Huanoquite who had been invited to the Universidad del Pacífico in Lima, where they had successfully sold their quinoa and exchanged many ideas, recipes, and practices with other growers. In addition to discovering foods prepared from quinoa that were good to eat, the women were experimenting with quinoa products that they could sell at the agricultural fair in Cusco. Whatever they made could be funneled into the reproduction of their households and savings for future unexpected expenses.

In comparing the general meanings non-Indigenous and Indigenous women associated with quinoa, I found that while Indigenous women did talk about health and nutrition in terms of strength (and intelligence, in the case of the women in Iquitos), they mostly appreciated how good quinoa tasted, and they were pleased when it grew successfully. This differed from talk associated with quinoa in the United States, as well as Peruvian restaurants catering to tourists in Cusco and Lima, which emphasized the "Indigenous," "native," or "ancient" nature of "healthy" and "organic" quinoa. Finally, as I discuss below, the food preparations of quinoa outside Indigenous contexts many times entailed mixing it with other superfoods, and in that respect, the focus was on how chewy or crunchy it was, in combination with the other foods.

Given women's influence—not only over how quinoa was grown and used but over many other food crops as well—it was understandable why PROMPERÚ, MINAGRI, and other NGOs saw them as important targets and images in their efforts to promote quinoa exports. In their promotional materials, women in native dress holding bags of quinoa or working in the fields appeared with increasing frequency in visuals from 2012 to 2021. MINAGRI celebrated them for being "fundamental guardians of biodiversity, for their labors transmitting and conserving traditional knowledge linked to the cultivation of quinoa, for their preservation of the diversity of quinoa varieties ... for feeding their families with nutritious quinoa and for jealously guarding their quinoa fields. It is they who are the guardians of this Andean grain which, in the twenty-first century, has become an important food to halt the malnutrition of the world. This is the immense significance of quinoa currently" (MINAGRI 2014).

Satisfaction: Feeding People, Feeding Places

The meanings Huanoquiteños associated with their foods emerged from their memories connected with it in some way, its associations with powerful places, and the entire ecosystemic and cosmological web in which their foodstuffs were produced. They felt that if they did not "feed" the sources that provided them with the ingredients for a particular food or beverage product, those sources would become depleted or turn away from them. Along with tending to human relationships, they understood water, mountain spirits, earth deities, and the particular places they interacted with to be sentient beings vital to creating a universe of well-being (Allen 2002). Marieka Sax (2011, 83–84), in her research on illness and well-being in the Peruvian Andes, found that "feeding accomplishes something in the world" and that agricultural and market-based

6. To Be Strong and Healthy

livelihood activities "are linked by an implicit understanding that feeding is a ritual and social act that drives household production onwards." This was readily seen in the importance that Huanoquiteños attributed to properly feeding labor parties, for example.

While quinoa was not the centerpiece of most meals, it *was* highlighted at ritual occasions—the Day of the Dead (Día de los Muertos), Semana Santa (the week known as Holy Week that precedes Easter), and the solstice. The Incas, in the past, had offered quinoa in receptacles of gold to their deities during the solstice (Tapia Vargas 1976, 10), and many Indigenous highland inhabitants prepared special dishes from quinoa during Holy Week. On the Day of the Dead at the beginning of November, the living consumed to excess, and the dead were fed enormous amounts accompanied by chicha so that they would remain satisfied and the earth would retain what it had consumed by fertilizing the soil.[8] In Huanoquite, bread dolls made from a kind of quinoa flour called *pasancalla* (and from wheat flour) were exchanged with extended families and they were also piled high on the graves of those who had died in the last three years.[9] During Semana Santa, they made quinoa in the form of p'esqe (cheese, milk, and quinoa soup), which many Huanoquiteños considered one of the most prized of the twelve plates of food (without any meat) that were prepared on Good Friday and the Thursday preceding Easter Sunday. Often, it was complemented by fish, preferably trout. During the week, at dawn, people went far up into the mountains to collect medicinal herbs that were considered especially potent at that time as well. Women catalyzed these circuits of feeding, nurturing, and consuming.

In a different vein, tourists and others who had either visited or heard about Peru—often through the promotional materials prepared by PROMPERÚ and MINCETUR and through chefs—spoke of its cuisine in terms of its ingredients, the wonders of Andean potatoes grown at dizzying altitudes and the existence of myriad kinds of rainbow-colored quinoa, and they were impressed by the breathtaking "landscapes" they had encountered, a kind of blur of highlands, lowlands, and Inca archaeological sites, perhaps. Indeed, each of these landscapes contained within it innumerable places. In contrast to the touristic scope which generally focused on landscape vistas, for Huanoquiteños it was the specific places and their characteristics and interconnections that were the basis for the productivity of their households. Men and women thought about how different ways of cultivating quinoa affected the health and fatigue of soil, the relationships between quinoa, other crops (such as maize, barley, and tarwi), and the intervention of human practices in these circuits through what they fed their crops, their goals of production, and the labor and forethought they invested in taking care of the many places where they cultivated crops and channeled water.

Sax (2011, 36) argues that westerners think in terms of *paisaje*, landscapes or the countryside, whereas Quechua people think in terms of *lugares*, "individualized places in which people have socialized and ritualized relationships." For Huanoquiteños, space could serve multiple purposes, but it was always differentiated by specific places and the interconnections among them. Folding multiple places into a single entity was alien. By erasing the specificity of places, it also diminished recognition and memories of the channeling of multiple kinds of energy-individuals-households-socialized labor-cultural knowledge that went into creating, producing, and disseminating quinoa and the concoctions that had become the cuisine that tourists consumed for many dollars.

The Popularization of Quinoa

When speaking of the taste of quinoa, consumers in the United States and Europe tended to describe it as fluffy, crunchy, chewy, and nutty, although several men I spoke with stated that they thought it had no taste at all! I visited restaurants in different price ranges that served quinoa in the United States, and even over a few years, it seemed to appear ever more frequently on menus in one form or other. One source reported that of all whole grains (but note that quinoa is actually a seed), quinoa led the way, appearing on 9 percent of all menus and an impressive 22 percent of fast casual menus. Between 2013 and 2017, the mention of quinoa on menus went up 350 percent and its use in restaurant dishes increased 33 percent, according to Mike Kostyo, senior publications manager for *Dataessential*, a food industry market research firm (Wolf 2017).[10] On one international journey I took, every airport lounge had quinoa, and in a single day I consumed three platters that included it. The chefs who prepared these dishes rarely had knowledge of the distinctive properties of different kinds of quinoa that were on the menu.[11] Quinoa clearly appealed to the cosmopolitan set, including me, who could travel and seek respite in airport lounges, but I also found it in less upscale settings such as workplace cafeterias, family restaurants, and salad bars.

People outside of the Andes have become familiar with quinoa, and they have also learned to imaginatively cook it in many different forms. Despite the remarkable variety of quinoa products, I was able to discern patterns in how it was used outside of Peru and in restaurants. In the restaurants I visited—outside Peru—quinoa was almost always "combined," often like a condiment, with

6. To Be Strong and Healthy

other "healthful" foods, such as beets, kale, spinach, cranberries, sushi, fish, or seaweed. It was also sprinkled on top of other foods. In addition to home baked goods, such as pancakes, muffins, bread, cakes, porridges, or cereal bars, I found it in tortilla chips, granola, pastas, pasta sauces, as a complement to salads, in instant soups, pilaf mixes, quinoa meat or rice substitutes, organic baby and pet food, ice cream, yoghurt, candy, vodka, beer, and skin and hair products, to give just a few examples (See also Bojanic 2011, 33; Montoya Restrepo, Alexandra Martínez Vianchá, and Peralta Ballestero 2005, 105). In general, Peruvians and non-Peruvians alike had come to view quinoa in highly positive ways, albeit differently from Huanoquiteños' appreciation of quinoa. The story of quinoa's ascendence on the world stage requires understanding global and historical forces at work that were taken up by the Peruvian state to promote it as a distinctively Peruvian brand. Chefs have played an outsized role in this positive view of quinoa, as the contributors to Matta and García's (2019) special journal issue on Peruvian gastro-politics have elaborated. Here I offer a brief exegesis of how state agencies have structured this embrace of quinoa.

"You Will Remember Peru." (2014)
"Peru: Dedicated to You, Dedicated to the World" (2016)
"Superfood Peru" (2017)

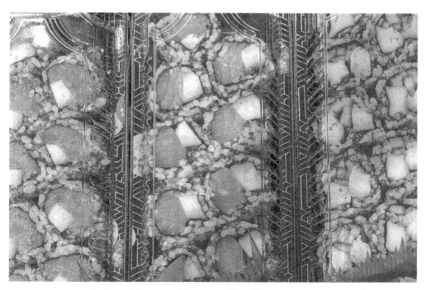

FIGURE 6.8. Sushi wrapped in quinoa for sale at gourmet supermarket in the United States

PROMPERÚ, charged with promoting and branding Peruvian products (among which were quinoa and other native cultivars) for export, used the above three slogans in their advertising campaigns and also circulated them in the form of full-length YouTube videos.[12] In a nonlinear, additive fashion, over time, PROMPERÚ's materials changed from primarily promoting quinoa as a tasty, vegetarian, and nonfatty food (PROMPERÚ 2012, 108–113), to advertising it as a "SuperA" ("Super Alimento"), a superfood with special appeal for gourmet supermarket clients (PROMPERÚ 2018a, 2018b). It then began to highlight quinoa's contributions to food security and safety and stressed the Peruvian state's efforts to acknowledge the contributions of quinoa growers by formalizing the traceability of quinoa's origin and quinoa's organic cultivation (INDECOPI and PROMPERÚ 2020). Most recently, Peru's promotional materials had introduced the concept of biocommerce as a way to support the goal of biodiversity (PROMPERÚ 2020a; PROMPERÚ 2020b).

In these materials geared to popularizing quinoa, four interrelated ideas wove in and out of the brochures, regardless of their principal themes: first, consuming quinoa was a way of consuming ancient wisdom; second, quinoa consumption was a constructive means of revindicating and valorizing the contributions of Indigenous Andean people to Peru as a nation *and* of integrating them into modernity and the Peruvian nation; third, quinoa was a component of Peru's gastronomical prowess as a nation; and fourth, buying and consuming quinoa was an excellent way to enhance the well-being of small- and medium-sized Indigenous cultivators.

It is no wonder that quinoa has been embraced as a magical food, given the success of these advertising campaigns. One powerful message the campaigns conveyed skillfully was the potency and value, not so much of reciprocity resulting from appreciating and consuming quinoa but of what I am calling transitivity, as reflected in the following statements:[13]

> Quinoa is more than just an Andean product: it is a metaphor for ancient wisdom converted into a promise for the future (Gamarra 2013, 4).
>
> Quinua: A Future Sown for Thousands of Years (MINAGRI 2014, 15).
>
> Quinoa has a millenarian history and culture provided by our ancestors who are giving it to the world . . . The entire nation speaks the same language with respect to this Andean grain . . . It is a national policy of work, integrated by a common objective (MINAGRI 2014, 38).
>
> Although it may seem incomprehensible, up until now there has been a lack of dialogue between wisdom and modernity which, now, thanks to initiatives of the FAO, MINGARI and AIQ [the International Year of Quinoa],

hundreds of thousands of farmers and enthusiastic cooks find themselves united by the same language: quinoa (MINAGRI 2014, 27).

This discursive or rhetorical strategy of purchasing and consuming quinoa as a project of creating abundance elides the history of brutality, colonialism, and civil war that has characterized life for Huanoquiteños and for many other Indigenous people of the Andes whose lives and lands were taken from them. Indeed, they have persevered for millennia but not necessarily in conditions of their own choosing. Their livelihood conditions have improved in some respects, but they have waged continuing struggles with policies that have promoted neoliberal entrepreneurialism and provided meager support for their communities in the way of health education and communication resources and infrastructure. Underlying these rhetorical, promotional statements was an economic, political, and affective extractive modality in which the "gift" of Indigenous knowledge, wisdom, health, and labor embedded in Indigenous quinoa would be converted into foreign exchange and economic growth, a celebration of a harmonious Peruvian nation, and the well-being of Peru's Indigenous population. Most damning perhaps was the persistent racism that characterized Peru's vision of modernity and celebration of quinoa as an export commodity.

One can nevertheless see why Huanoquiteños would find many of these slogans and assumptions appealing even as their reality of cultivating and marketing quinoa did not conform to these adulations and expectations. Florence Babb (2011), who began documenting the more prominent place that Indigenous women had begun to occupy for purposes of promoting tourism in Peru, found in her research that, quite suddenly, women had gone from being perceived and depicted as "more Indian" and more subject to racial discrimination and abuse than Indigenous men to being emblematic of the bright future of the Peruvian nation.[14] Although Huanoquiteños were aware that the place and meaning of quinoa in their daily practices and history did not coincide with the language of quinoa spoken by the FAO, PROMPERÚ, and MINAGRI, they were open to the growing appreciation of quinoa and Indigenous culture that tourists and international consumers expressed. Women in particular sought to manage these impressions for their own purposes. And both men and women were eager to find ways to make a better life for themselves, but they had to figure out how to do that in circumstances that were far from ideal and in which they had yet to experience moving beyond a modernity that had showed little respect for them and had managed to exclude them daily from the social fabric of national life and the centers of power. As international consumers of quinoa became more concerned about the ethical dimensions of quinoa cultivation and export in Peru, brochures and Expo Fairs in turn began paying greater lip service to the need to include Indigenous cultivators in their fairs. Yet even in 2020, in my review of PROMPERÚ's documentation of the major expo fairs they had sponsored, only one Quechua cultivator had been given a prominent role in promoting quinoa.[15]

Gastrotourism and the Celebration of Indigenous Foods

Huanoquiteños were mainly preoccupied with cultivating quinoa for domestic consumption and the export market. However, the increase in tourism within Peru, the beauty and possibilities of Huanoquiteños' agrarian landscape, and the existence of archaeological sites in the district of Huanoquite encouraged Huanoquiteños to think about how they could participate in the tourism economy. Peru's status as a top destination for gastronomic tourism had become well-known, especially because of its annual Mistura celebration, founded by Gastón Acurio, one of Peru's most famous chefs. Much has already been written about Gaston Acurio, the Mistura celebration, and the explosion of interest in Peru as a destination for exceptional food. Below, I highlight a few key aspects of gastronomic tourism in Peru that have specific relevance to the place of quinoa on the world stage and in rural communities, but I leave a much fuller discussion of the gastronomic boom to scholars who have dedicated themselves to extensive research on it.[16]

Mistura began in 2007 and lasted a decade before it came to an end, purportedly because of financial difficulties, in 2017. Sponsored by APEGA (the Peruvian Society of Gastronomy), up to four hundred thousand persons—Peruvians and foreign visitors—had annually attended it in Lima, though in 2017 those numbers had declined to about three hundred thousand. Acurio came from a relatively well-off background. While he was expected to become a lawyer, he followed his inclination and decided to study cooking at Le Cordon Bleu in Paris. When he returned to Peru, he began a French restaurant that failed. Because of his show, *Aventura Culinaria*, he then began to learn to cook Peruvian regional dishes that led him to create a unique Andean cuisine, now known as "Novoandino" ("New Andean" cuisine). Most tourists, prior to Peru's recognition as a gastronomical playground, had sought to make a beeline for Cusco, the heart of Inca culture and the main destination for those planning to travel to Machu Picchu. Acurio began to promote Andean cuisine in Lima to encourage tourists to stay longer there before making their way to Cusco. He succeeded, and his restaurants have received international acclaim. This

6. To Be Strong and Healthy

was his initial vision, but he subsequently embraced the idea that Novoandino cuisine could be wielded as a weapon to diminish class and racial differences and discrimination and enhance Peru's sense of proud nationhood that could then be projected to the world. His hopeful vision had great appeal to many Peruvians, given the painful (yet frequently hidden) wounds and scars from Peru's colonial past and its brutal civil war that had taken place, officially, between 1980 and 1992 (García 2015; Matta and García 2019).

María Elena García (2013, 508) has followed, analyzed, and critiqued Acurio's vision. In her article, she quotes Acurio's explanation of his philosophy, which Ernesto Cabellos (2009) includes in his documentary, *De Ollas y Sueños: Cooking Up Dreams*: "When I was a child, the word mestizo was pejorative; today it is our worth [*"nuestro valor"*]". By "mestizo," Acurio is referring to the mixing of Indigenous and Spanish culture and blood. García also discusses Acurio's feelings about Mistura, captured in a very interesting film Patricia Pérez made, entitled *Mistura: The Power of Food*:

> Perhaps Mistura is the fiesta we have been waiting for; where our emotional independence finally has arrived and, together, we can celebrate our ability to conquer the world. May the campesino be lauded much more than the chef that is featured in the famous magazine. May the most famous restaurant have a smaller clientele than the man on the street corner selling *anticuchos* (kabobs made from beef hearts or marinated chicken or steak). And may no one be bothered by the other, but instead may all help all, may all celebrate all, may all embrace all. From Peru we are helping to demonstrate that our cuisine contains weapons more powerful and, of course, less bloody, that can contribute to a world where justice and pleasure, ethics and aesthetics, always go hand in hand. The dreams of Mistura are large. History is just beginning (Qtd. in Pérez 2011).

When I heard Acurio speak in Lima at the annual meetings of the Latin American Studies Association in 2017, he emphasized the promotion of Peruvian cuisine because "it is a beautiful terrain of multiculturality." He also believed that the image of Peru could be changed and that the image could be exported; that by working "as a team" to accomplish these changes, Peru could simultaneously "reject the colonialist spirit" that had haunted it. He concluded that Peru was the only cuisine that had become global in reach in the last twenty years—what he called "a universal cuisine," which was now encountered in French restaurants (Acurio 2017; see also Acurio 2009).

Mistura was Peru's Disneyland. The skills of chefs on display, the staggering variety of foods that were being prepared, many of them Indigenous but combined with foods and food preparation techniques that hailed from across the world, and the star recognition granted particular "chefs"—men and women—who might have begun selling street food as urban migrants from rural villages created a celebratory atmosphere that for a brief time erased the fissures that characterized Peruvian social life on a daily basis. And as Mirko Lauer has pointed out, Acurio had a particular way of talking and a charisma that allowed him, as a kind of populist figure, to rhetorically bridge the very real and enduring economic gaps and racial divides among Peruvians (Matta 2019, 4).

Acurio and other chefs did try to purchase Indigenous ingredients directly from producers and to train Indigenous inhabitants in cooking schools, but serious obstacles tempered the success of their efforts. García points out that Mistura truly was not a celebration of Peru's variegated cultures; it was more about the monetary value (*valor*)—the same central concept used by Acurio— that such an event attracted. It was about "the marketability of Peruvianness." While it might appear that the huge influx of tourism and foreign exchange the festival generated was a good thing, the goal to unify Peruvians through "gastronomic revolution" and "gastronomic diplomacy" was thwarted for several reasons (2013, 508).

Most of the restaurants and events that highlighted "Novoandino cuisine" took place far from where native crops were grown and Indigenous food and culture were consumed and experienced by inhabitants. Acurio would frequently highlight the skills of a single potato farmer or street food vendor, but the bottom line was that this celebration remained superficial in its impact on the economic well-being of most rural dwellers, despite its best intentions, and it could not erase Peru's history that colored the present. In Pérez's film (2011), I saw a strange yet subtle example of the celebratory view of Andean farmers and a failure to grasp much about their actual lifeways. One cut showed a farmer working in his potato fields and eventually being asked to participate in Mistura. When Acurio introduced the farmer as a phenomenal producer of potatoes, Acurio stood at the farmer's side, waving several stalks of quinoa. Most people likely did not notice how jarring this was.

Mistura and other celebrations of Peruvian Novoandino gastronomy frequently had the consequence of exoticizing Quechua people, placing them "outside" of time even as their food products were innovatively and dynamically mixed "inside" time with any number of other ingredients in the spirit of fusion. Most starkly, these celebrations viewed being Quechua, being an Indigenous woman, and primordialism in general, as mechanisms to achieve modernization, nationalism, capitalization, and profit, even as it extracted culture and labor from Indigenous agrarian communities. The gastronomical revolution, in many ways, was analogous to the transitivity of the slogans prepared by PROMPERÚ and MINAGRI. Little returned to these communities, though much was taken from them. Jean Jackson (2019, 222–23), in a thoughtful book examining how multiculturalism was "managed" in Colombia, found that the celebration of "multicultural neoliberalism" ultimately served as a means to structure, channel, and manipulate global capitalism without changing racial hierarchies and economic inequalities; such celebrations often pitted Indigenous communities against one another, especially when they competed for scarce resources from NGOs and regional governments; and they successfully converted Indigenous communities into "a kind of local trademark of an ethnicity that 'sells.'" Jackson, noting the observations of anthropologist Carlos del Cairo that "good ethnicities are those that help produce capital," concludes that "although such patrimonialization makes vulnerable pueblos more visible, it hardly helps solve their grave problems" (2019, 228). These same dynamics were evident in the global gastronomical celebration of Quechua foods as integral and healing to the Peruvian nation.

Similarly, Lisa Markowitz (2019), reflecting on the celebratory discourse of the Andean gastronomical boom, queries whether the upheaval of the food pyramid, which is grounded in status and race, will correlate with a more substantial upheaval of social and political hierarchies and concludes that "Novoandina reprises old but persistent and formidable concerns." She notes that hurdles remain for Indigenous people to access the benefits of the revalorization of Andean foodways, in part because "Markets are not necessarily open; endowments of residence (rural vs. urban), knowledge, class status, and ethnicity structure access in mundane but ultimately powerful ways" (15).

Valuing Indigenous Food, Well-Being, and Livelihoods

Many Huanoquiteños were proud of the attention that their cultural practices, landscapes, and food commanded outside their communities, but they struggled to figure out how to manage the overwhelming emphasis on the market, which was the very context in which global tourism unfolded (Ypeij 2013). They tried out new ways of making quinoa, and they organized as associations in order to temper the harshness of market principles. While the celebration of Indigeneity and Indigenous foods, as well as a nostalgia for a Peru that no longer existed (García 2015; Hall 2019), has contributed to the gastronomic revolution, it has not yet substantially or sustainably improved the lives of Huanoquite's quinoa producers.

Although women were instrumentally of great importance to promoting Indigenous foodways, as I have noted above, their own quinoa recipes rarely made their way into cookbooks sold on the international market or into meals served with Indigenous foods in elite restaurants—what Clare Sammells (2019, 340) refers to as "haute traditional dishes." Sammells's research took place in Bolivia where a similar gastronomic boom has been underway. Making a distinction between culinary fields and gastronomic fields, she found that culinary fields still bore the weight of gender, class, and racial stratification, whereas gastronomic fields tended to appear to erase them (338–352). To put it another way, the symbolic capital of Indigeneity, native food stuffs, and the celebration of Peruvian multiculturalism could be skillfully converted into economic capital, but there remained a yawning gap between earnings reaped from tourists who attended such festivals and the economic returns, livelihood standards, and cultural valorization of quinoa cultivators in the Andean highlands.

Parallel experiments have begun as alternatives to Mistura, some catalyzed as a reaction to it. Huanoquiteños themselves are trying to develop tourism in their region and have been working to establish a regional agricultural fair in the district where they can prepare, serve, and sell their food; they welcomed knowledge exchanges about food products, seeds, and food preparation; and the pride, value, and curiosity that they were taking in their own food products and ritual practices were all changes worth noting (See García 2013).

Huanoquite was but one district among forty-nine others that was attempting to convert quinoa into a commodity for the international market. The government saw these efforts as mechanisms that obscured, smoothed over, and even reduced the long history of racial and class inequalities between Peru's Indigenous Quechua inhabitants and its mestizo populace, and the painful memories of Peru's civil war in which so many Indigenous lives had been lost. There was some room for hope and improvement in Indigenous economic well-being and the enhancement of women's power, but there was a need to uncover, probe, and reflect on what was not being sufficiently addressed by the discourse and practices surrounding quinoa as a superfood: food sovereignty for those who grow indigenous crops, such as quinoa, as well as for urban migrants; substantial transformations in living standards of Indigenous inhabitants; their incorporation and inclusion into mainstream decision-making (Kerssen 2015); and perhaps most important, protection of the territories and environments on which they depended for survival.

Amy Cox Hall (2019, 5–6) observes that the relationship between promoting Indigenous foods and nostalgia "evokes longings for an imagined past . . . that is comprised of emotional, affective and corporeal sensations . . . produced

6. To Be Strong and Healthy

through consumerism" and that the "construction of a collective, sensuous memory of Peru as a food nation from time immemorial . . . is foundational for nation-building." On the other hand, she also found—and this is reflected in my discussion of PROMPERÚ and MINAGRI's promotional materials as well—this same nostalgia for an invented past is not purely distorted and damaging romantic nation-stitching or -building but may also be invoked, rechanneled, and wielded to critique consequences of modernity, such as agroindustry, monocultivation, and environmental degradation (Hall 2019, 8).

Within Huanoquite, even as some farmers' livelihoods had improved, many others had been hard hit by market instabilities, their inability to access credit, and the growing unpredictability of environmental cues they had once been able to rely on. Still others were not producing any surplus; they struggled to use their harvests to reproduce their households. These conditions, which one readily sees in many Andean highland districts, reveal the flaws of a celebratory "globalization discourse." The creativity and liberation of the imagination, the freedom to explore, appreciate, and incorporate new ideas and practices because of globalization that permits for diffusion of material and knowledge resources that flow throughout the world may simultaneously produce or deepen inequalities between regions and within societies and classes, creating horizontal and vertical polarization (Friedman and Friedman 2013, 247, 248). This was, indeed, the case of the meanings and dreams of quinoa as it traversed the world. From its cultivation in Huanoquite's highland valleys and mountain fields to its consumption as a soup in dusky kitchens, fields or village schools, from its purchase and consumption at agricultural fairs, airport lounges, national gastronomical festivals, gourmet supermarkets, and five-star restaurants in Lima to its storage in germplasm banks and seed vaults, quinoa has become a powerful commodity and chameleon symbol, a vehicle to extract and accumulate energy, affect, and profits from Huanoquiteños as it wends its way across the international stage.

CHAPTER 7

Voracious Consumption

Huanoquiteños associated specific places of their landscape with economic, corporeal, and cosmological energy forces and fields that contributed, alternatively, to their well-being or to sickness and misfortune. For example, dangerous, negative beings or forces could emanate from "winds, pools of water, hillsides, and darkness of night." Such beings constituted "hungry, deindividualized spirits" that could sooner or later cause malingering illness and death to persons who encountered them (Sax 2011, 117). Sometimes, the beings could cause destruction to the polity at large (Seligmann 1987, 1999; Seligmann and Bunker 1994). These negative forces were almost always the result of human actions, whether deliberate or unwitting.

I could see at work the consequences of imbalances in Huanoquiteños' well-being even as they tried to provide for their families and communities into the future. As I have shown above, theirs was a pragmatic spirituality with instrumental and material qualities to it. Thus, they were attentive to the needs of their mountains, earth beings, and *wacas*, which took the shape of rock formations and water sources, feeding, appeasing, and pleading with them, and periodically providing them with abundant sacrifices in the form of spirits and food. At the same time, they paid attention to opportunities on the horizon, moving back and forth between Huanoquite and elsewhere, and many of them had a constantly running calculator by means of which they sought to determine what could work well for them. Even so, imbalances that were outside their immediate control but that directly impacted their lives and livelihoods loomed on the horizon.

This chapter discusses the imbalances Huanoquiteños were experiencing as a result of the mining concessions that had been established in their region. Concessions had already been staked throughout the province of Paruro, many of which were located in the district of Huanoquite and in neighboring districts and provinces, such as Ccapi and Chumbivilcas.[1] Most had not been activated. However, several concessions had been staked in proximity to natural water sources which came from a series of lakes that served the entire Huanoquite district as well as other provinces and districts that bordered Huanoquite, and Huanoquiteños had heard that they were about to develop them. The mines would not cause collateral damage but rather pollute Huanoquite's water sources, directly imperiling Huanoquiteños' agrarian livelihoods and jeopardizing their ability to sustain their communities, given their primary reliance on agriculture and herding. What had seemed far away but irritating suddenly became a proximate and dangerous threat to Huanoquiteños. They eventually decided to confront the mining concessions, drawing on their long history of resisting land incursions and their knowledge and experience of the workings of the state and corporations to organize. They took these steps knowing full well that, among communities that constituted the district of Huanoquite, they would also face conflicts, which were the result of the growing fragility of communities themselves and of the astute manipulation of legal tenets that regulated mining in Peru. They constituted "a motley crew" but nevertheless succeeded in mobilizing people—including a high number from neighboring provinces and districts. Their shared assumptions, history, networks, and experiences, and their memories of battles they had fought in the past, all fueled their decision to take action to rectify imbalances in their world.[2]

The Dilemmas of Extraction

Because mining companies offered potential services, jobs, and wealth in the form of foreign exchange, they were attractive to the Peruvian government and Peruvians living in both rural and urban areas. The huge copper mine, Las Bambas (owned by the Chinese mining company, MMG), had been the site of some of the most intense conflicts over mining and the transport of minerals in Peru. The mining operation was in the Apurímac Region, which bordered the district of Huanoquite, and ore from the mines was transported through the province of Paruro to which Huanoquite belonged (see chapter 2). In 2019 alone, 370 vehicles per day, 250 of which were of high weight (52.8 tons empty and 87 tons with cargo), thundered through 149 populated centers and 72 communities along the highway to and from the mines (Observatorio de Conflictos Minéros en el Perú (OCM) 2019, 53). Clashes at the mines, dating from prior to 2016, when the mines became operational, involved blockades of up to two months at a time and conflicts between police, soldiers, and over five thousand protesters had resulted in the deaths of three protesters and the arrests of twenty-five.[3] In addition to filing complaints about the dust, pollution, and environmental degradation caused by the road, especially where it was unpaved, communities argued that the mine had failed to respect them and their environmental demands and had not honored its commitments to local development. They were also seeking to have those who had been arrested in the conflicts pardoned (OCM 2019). The Cusco region was one of the country's principal producers of copper, along with molybdenum, gold, and silver. Ninety percent of Peru's copper mines were found there, the largest of which was Tintaya, in the province of Espinar, and the region was the site for about 50 percent of the national total of social conflicts that had erupted, in large part because of the impacts of mining on Indigenous communities (OCM 2019, 44).[4]

Legal tenets were supposed to protect Indigenous people and intervene in preventing land seizures for purposes of mining in Peru. ILO 169, a major component of Indigenous rights law established by the International Labor Organization, had been passed in 1989. Peru had ratified it in 1993 but nevertheless consistently failed to uphold it. ILO 169 required "free, prior, and informed consent" on the part of Indigenous peoples, peasants, and nations regarding management of their own territories.[5] The rationale was that since these peoples were the ancestral owners of their territory, they should be the ones to determine what happened to their territory, and therefore, any actions taken required their prior consultation. Nevertheless, before 2012 many claims or concessions had already been secretly made with mining concessionaires, and the state turned a blind eye to the requirement to consult peasant communities. In the seventeen years following the ratification of ILO 169, Peru failed to organize a single process of consultation (Ilizarbe 2019, 146). Indigenous inhabitants *were* occasionally consulted, but the strategic concept of "divide and rule," in which only those local authorities that companies thought were more aligned with state and multinational interests were consulted, was used. And all too often authorities were swayed by the resources and services they were proffered in exchange for acquiescing to mining concessions.

One key stumbling block was that ILO 169 required consultation with *Indigenous* communities, not *peasant* communities. Both the state and mining corporations used this to their advantage, reasoning that they did not have to consult with highland Andean peasant communities because they were not Indigenous and arguing that if prior consultation applied at all, it was only to Amazonian inhabitants. A study done in 2018 demonstrated that of more than 10,000 communities in the Andes, 6,160 were "comunidades campesinas" (peasant communities), or 61 percent of the total (Pajuelo Teves 2019, 45–46).[6] The majority of the 19 communities that comprised the district of Huanoquite, like many others throughout the Andean highlands, had obtained formal recognition after the 1969 agrarian reform as "Comunidades Campesinas."[7] The use of the term *indio* had been abandoned because it was considered derogatory, but in addition, the Peruvian state had decided to use the term *peasant* rather than *Indian* or *Indigenous community* as a deliberate mechanism to incorporate Quechua inhabitants into the nation as Peruvian citizens. Their assumption was that inhabitants of these communities would become part of the Peruvian nation but not as distinctively Indigenous citizens. This was quite an irony, given the recent celebratory status of Indigenous wisdom, livelihood and biodiversity practices, and foods that was being promoted by the Peruvian state.[8]

In 2011 then Peruvian president Ollanta Humala had also passed Law 29785, requiring that the tenets of ILO 169 be implemented so that that *all* Indigenous peoples (regardless of whether they were officially called Indigenous or peasant communities) would have the right and means to participate in decision-making about their lands and territory. Nevertheless, state agents preferred to reach compromise, avoiding conflict, and achieve reconciliation rather than honoring the rights of Indigenous self-determination. The issues around implementation of ILO 169 and Law 29785 regarding Indigenous participation in national decision-making processes, especially concerning their own lands and territory, resembled more general hierarchical judgments of inferiority in Peru that disparaged the validity of Indigenous legal and belief systems. Indigenous authorities and populations were considered *outside* the state and generally excluded from, not recognized, or disregarded in the public sphere of decision-making and valorization. As Ilizarbe (2019, 151–52) explains,

> The law of prior consultation and its implementation were part of this participatory wave in response to the increase of social conflicts and protests demanding direct participation in political decisions. The passage of the law was the result of violent confrontation between the state and indigenous communities defending their legitimate right to make decisions about their land. This struggle . . . also confronted different understandings of progress, justice, and democracy. Although the law seemed to emerge from the consensus about the need to rebuild the social and political pact, its implementation

> turned into an area of disagreement and dispute that revealed irreconcilable differences . . . Processes of consultation continue to reproduce mechanisms of control of indigenous representation by political and intellectual elites, ignoring the specificities of the social and politically constructed category "indigenous."

Indigenous inhabitants affected by mining operations had difficulty forming a united front of opposition to them. The power of communities to control what had been their corporate landholdings had been weakened by the passage of laws that had encouraged and authorized private land titling and a land market. The state was also canny in its appropriation of Indigenous rights discourse and rhetoric that could protect its interests and plans for development. (See Powęska 2017, 27–58 for similar state strategies in Bolivia.) The prospect of foreign exchange, infrastructural improvements, and employment were trade-offs that many Indigenous communities also willingly made in exchange for rerouting roads and privatizing, selling, or agreeing to changes in the uses of their existing agricultural lands (Salas Carreño 2016, 2017, 2019; Fitz-Henry 2019). Consequently, rather than outright resistance where the endgame might result in nothing for villagers, they too sought compromise in their negotiations and battles with the Peruvian state and mining companies. They had seen that if they did not negotiate, they might be excluded altogether from any resources or privileges the state and mining companies offered. On the other hand, even when they did negotiate, short of being willing to be displaced, they had seen that they might still suffer from environmental damages and not infrequently, takings of land or territory (with its own memories and history) that the mining operations would demand.

Although they did not share a unanimous stance concerning the incursions of mining concessions and operations in collaboration with the state, most Indigenous Quechua inhabitants regarded the state with some hostility and mistrust, not because they found it "alien," as Ilizarbe (2019, 153) suggests, but rather because they were all too familiar with the history of its actions, its failure to comply with its promises, and its single-minded focus on development. The failure of the state to take seriously Indigenous demands and the struggles of Indigenous communities to act collectively meant that efforts to implement prior consultation through dialogue were often unsuccessful, negotiations broke down, and another cycle of violent confrontation would transpire. This was the situation in Peru whereby the nature of dialogue between an exclusionary state promoting development and fractured populations of Indigenous communities had not resulted in a new social pact that "accommodate[d] difference and disagreement and [took] inequality into account" (Ilizarbe 2019, 154; see also Poole 2004).

The second legal tenet that intervened in whether mining could proceed without interference was whether resources in the area of operations could be designated as being of "intangible value." If resources received this legal designation because of their value to Peru's cultural and natural patrimony, the area would be deemed off-limits and in need of protection. The law offered possibilities, conundrums, and thorny problems. It was complex in its specific application to different kinds of resources and material culture but, in general, stated the following:

> Intangible zones are protected spaces of exceptional cultural and biological importance where no kind of extractive activity can take place due to their environmental value, not only for the region, but also for the county and the world. The declaration of an intangible zone includes the recognition, respect, and support of collective territorial rights, and domestic and daily use of natural resources for certain territory, which means guaranteeing the survival of the zone and the potential of the development of its social, economic, and cultural systems; that is, it means providing a way to protect ecosystems, recognizing at the same time, the role and forces of many native communities, which by means of their own cultures have protected and managed their environment.... Article 66 of the Political Constitution of Peru establishes that renewable and non-renewable resources are the patrimony of the nation.... The watercourses, banks, and shores of rivers, creeks, lakes, lagoons, and storage areas are intangible zones; their use for agricultural ends and human settlement are prohibited (Zonas Intangibles 2001).[9]

While designating specific areas as "intangible zones" could offer inhabitants some protection from the predations of extractive economies, the law could wreak havoc with existing territorial uses of those zones by Indigenous communities and exacerbate conflicts among them. Powęska (2017, 34) cautions, "Without denying that generally indigenous peoples have culturally specific understanding of and relations to their natural environment, and that there is a fundamental difference between their biocultural paradigm and the capitalist growth paradigm, I stress that the indigenous peoples should be themselves the only subjects defining their relations to land and environment, without imposing on them our visions and expectations." She adds that it is an essentialist, neocolonial position to assume that "indigenous peoples should enjoy the recognition of their substantial rights only because they are bearers of a culture worthy of being saved for the good of mankind." Citing several cases

PART TWO. SOUP AND SUPERFOOD

that had already taken place, she cautions that viewing Indigenous people as "Guardians of Nature" creates a risk that the state could forbid them to use lands or resources in ways that differ from the state's view of "traditional" use or could even refuse to recognize their status as Indigenous peoples because of their lack of supposed "sustainable" management of land (2017, 34).

In order to comprehend just how profoundly mining intervened in and threatened Huanoquiteños' quotidian agrarian activities, such as cultivating quinoa, the subject of this book, we do not need to exercise much imagination. Water and soil were the foundation of life in all its dimensions for most Huanoquiteños. Without it, most would not have been able to pursue other economic activities, and within their universe of pragmatic spirituality, they would be subject to distress, anxiety, and destruction as they were buffeted by the disequilibrium catalyzed by upheavals to their environment. In these circumstances, how did Huanoquiteños navigate their way through the thickets of the two legal tenets described above to confront the mining concessions near them and to figure out how to best sustain themselves and their families and not exhaust their resources, energy, and knowledge?

Narrative Accounts and the Power of Place

In Huanoquite, especially as dusk settled, dilemmas, discussion of the day's events, accounts of physical pain, gossip, and planning for the next day were shared around the table in the warm kitchen near the hearth after an evening meal. People generally did not converse while they ate because it showed disrespect and a lack of appreciation for the food that had been prepared. This was something I had to get used to, given that when I was growing up, conversation around the table during a meal was encouraged, even expected. Every so often, though, when people gathered in Huanoquite to eat together, they would share stories after a meal—telling of inexplicable, magical, and momentous events that they had either heard or directly witnessed.[10] Some of these accounts were very personal, while others, though people might not share them openly in public spaces, were known to most households and transmitted from generation to generation. In the course of being transmitted, they underwent modifications of content, often in accordance with ongoing preoccupations.

One evening, just after finishing our meal, Lorenzo began talking in a quiet, intense, and solemn voice about horses and lakes, wild geese, deer, and a stag with a bell. The television, with its very bad reception, was crackling in the background. In prior decades during my stays in Huanoquite, I had heard many stories about the lakes that were the focus of what Lorenzo was now telling us.

7. Voracious Consumption

Over two decades earlier, Stephen Bunker and I had done research on Huano-quite's extraordinarily complex irrigation system and the explanations that Huanoquiteños had offered for why a crucial part of it had been abandoned (Seligmann 1999; Seligmann and Bunker 1994). The lakes high above Huano-quite—known collectively as Qaranqa—were the source and protector of water that emerged over twenty-nine kilometers away and almost six hundred meters lower down to form the Qewar River, the primary source of irrigation water for Huanoquite. The lakes themselves were at an ethereal altitude, each over 4,200 msl., surrounded by high crags, tall grasses, and a stunning view of the Apurímac Valley. When we had asked why part of the canal system had been abandoned, we were told of a snake with golden braids or sometimes of a frog that had been killed by men as it led the water from the lake source to the ir-rigation ditches via underground canals. After the snake or frog was killed, the water that fed Huanoquite's irrigation ditches had begun to emerge from a source much farther down the hill from the opening to the ditch, so there was no longer any way of getting water to the existing irrigation canal that had been built at great cost of labor. In other instances, people told us that huge flapping ducks that guarded the lakes, the ditches, and the carved Inca thrones at the entrance to Huanoquite via the Inca road had been killed, after which the water returned to its source.

While these tales might sound odd, they conveyed the disruptions and tears in the fabric of people's lives brought about by the Spanish Invasion, ranging from the fragmentation of labor and land tenure regimes to a loss of political authority and power, all of which eroded the effective organization needed for irrigation management. They also conveyed cosmological imbalances and the loss of environmental control and knowledge that these dynamics created as ducks, snakes, frogs, Inca roads, thrones, and water sources for irrigation were perturbed, destroyed, or killed. Huanoquiteños' preoccupation with mining and the damage it could cause to their environment and water sources was al-ready evident when I had started my field research four decades earlier. Even then, two men from Chanca had told me about how the wrath of the mountain spirits had been unleashed in order to protect villagers, their earth, and their lake after an engineer became intent on exploring the area for minerals:

> A high peak was located in Chanca (an important community of Huano-quite), surrounded by lower ones. The peak was called Apu Mallmana and the lower peaks were its warriors. The area was famous for its gold, silver, and uranium. An engineer who was exploring the minerals there had a dream one night in which Apu Mallmana appeared to him. The Apu said, "The cost

PART TWO. SOUP AND SUPERFOOD

of taking my minerals will be very high, three million will die." The engineer paid no attention to the warning and continued working. His work went fine for a few days but then 300 workers were trapped by a landslide and died. The engineer hired more workers from outside, 500 of them, and they too were killed. One night, the engineer decided to visit the lake located on top of the Apu. He arrived and saw a golden bull in the lake. He resolved to return the next day and drain the lake by means of a dike so he could reach the golden bull. This he did, but the golden bull had disappeared. On his way down, he slipped and fell and died. The people of Chanca now know that their Apus can protect them and they can protect themselves. For this reason, they pay them great respect, unlike the engineer who did not heed the warnings of the Apu.

The narrative, which I recorded in 1984, called attention to the forces of greed, ignorance, colonialism (the golden bull), and extraction and the scarring of the earth itself, all of which incited the wrath of the mountain and water spirits in order to protect inhabitants from the destructive effects of these upheavals.

To return to our after-dinner conversation, Lorenzo again began to speak of the lakes of Qaranqa, a topic he had not addressed for many years. And as he talked, all of us gathered around the table began to chime in with our own additions or to ask questions to encourage Lorenzo to talk further about what he knew. Lorenzo mentioned specific place names in what he recounted to us. Most of them referred to outlying communities of Huanoquite, such as Tantarcalla, Huanca Huanca, Chanca, Arabito, and Cusipata, located high in the puna. Oqhupata, another village, was located at a pass, the highest point on both the Inca road and the modern road from Cusco to Huanoquite. The community of Qenqonay, which became a key actor in the mining conflicts, was closest to the lakes and was officially part of the district of Huanoquite. In addition, Lorenzo spoke of Chumbivilcas, Anta, and Chinchaypuquio (in the province of Anta), which also received waters from the same lakes. Although Huanoquiteños might appear to be closely linked to Cusco, they were just as closely (or even more) connected to and oriented toward the Apurímac Valley where the provinces of Chumbivilcas and Anta were located, and they considered many of the people living there as their "close neighbors." They maintained enduring environmental, social, and trading ties with all the communities Lorenzo mentioned. Finally, the waters from the Qaranqa lakes made their way from the high puna to Huanoquite and then proceeded further down, dividing into several branches to reach lower valley communities of Huanoquite, such as Llaspay and Chifia.[11] In short, the waters of the lake fed and unified a network of relationships that constituted a living, ecosystemic web. With that in mind, I reproduce below what Lorenzo shared with us:

Our [Lorenzo and his brother, Victor's] horses ran away when we were going over the pass toward Arábito. We reached the lake of Qaranqa right above Qenqonay. It is not huge, about the size of Totora [the lake at the entrance to Huanoquite proper] but not triangular like Totora, almost perfectly round. One bank of the lake is rock, and *rocoto* (a hot red pepper plant) grows on the rock. The rocoto guards a dog. A stag with an enormous bell around his huge neck visits the lake, along with his harem of females. A man in Huanca Huanca, who hunts deer, saw them there. The lake scares me. Victor saw a pair of *wallatas* [Andean goose, *chloephaga melanopetra*] and shot one of them. They went toward the middle of the lake. One had already been shot and was in the water. The other was flapping its wings to encourage the downed one to fly. Victor started toward the water. The ground began to shake. Everything turned black. A huge monster appeared with thunder and lightning, and we ran to take cover. We continued on our way back to Cusipata, where the man who sold us the horses lived. He did not have them but when we told him the story, he died of laughter. He knew all about the lake. He said we were foolish to have gotten so close to the lake. He lived only two and a half kilometers from it and knew everything about what had happened there. The horses, it turns out, had not gone back; they went from here to another site near Huanoquite, and we found them.

Anyone who gets near the lake bothers it. Everything becomes black with huge waves. One should never throw stones in it. If you must go by it, you should do so as tranquilly as possible. Otherwise, whirlpools will form. And if you drop a pebble in it, it will cause rain. From the lake comes all the water of Qeñaparo [a former, verdant landed estate]. Lakes, lakes, lakes. Above that lake are others that are enchanted. The ground is spongy and moves. The cattle or alpaca that approach the waters to drink drown because the ground sucks them in. It is the main source of all our water, and it goes all the way to Llaspay, Oqhupata, Tantarcalla, Huanca Huanca. It is the source, for us, for Anta, for Chumbivilcas, Chinchaypuquio.

The miners are bothering the lake. Last year, the village of Qenqonay decided to sell their land to the miners. All of Huanoquite, Anta, is concessioned. When we were finally told, Anta too, we went to Qenqonay in hundreds of trucks and cars. Thousands of us, armed only with sticks and picks, to stop the people of Qenqonay, to fight the sale of their land to their miners. If the miners upset the lake, it will rain and rain and rain, and the waters for our crops will be poisoned.

Margarita chimed in at this point, telling us,

> The mining enterprises have no fear. They can disappear an entire population. They want to do this, all for money, the municipalities, along with the regional government and private corporations. They've already done this in the Las Bambas mines. The mining companies gave them money for their land, and now everyone has a pickup truck. Working in the mines kills people. The machines injure people. If you work in the mines, it kills the body. We see the helicopters flying overhead to and from the Las Bambas mines every day. They are destroying the environment for our children, and then, what will they eat? The water is our life.

Some of the men who had been harvesting Lorenzo's quinoa similarly told me that the mines were contributing to climate change. They had seen pictures and videos of what had happened at other mining sites—Espinar, Tintaya, and Bagua—and how, afterwards, "all that was left was a desert." Bagua, located in the Amazon, was targeted for oil drilling and mining. In a massacre that took place in 2009 when Indigenous inhabitants blockaded a highway near the mines and six hundred miles north of Lima, twenty-three police officers, five Indigenous people, and five civilians were killed, and more than two hundred people were injured. Huanoquiteños were now much more easily able to obtain information about these mines and visual documentation of the damage caused by them because of their access to social media, as well as the radio on which they had long relied.

Several days earlier, again at dusk, I had hiked up to a field with two of Lorenzo and Margarita's grandchildren in order to collect *pasto* (fodder) for the household's guinea pigs and shift the irrigation aspersion sprinklers which were watering a steeply sloped maize field.[12] By the time we had finished moving the sprinklers on tall poles, it had become dark and windy, and a rainstorm threatened. It was then that the kids began to tell one story after another about *chukis*. They described them as "having huge eyes," and shouting, they told me that they went from "being very small to enormous." They were terrified of them and were adamant that "in the real world to come, dinosaurs, robots, and chukis will take over and rob everyone."

Although a Quechua word, *chuqui*, exists that refers to a sword or spear and is metaphorically associated with war and hurling multiple lances and thunder (see González Holguín 1952[1608]; Lira 1982), this probably is not a Quechua word at all. More likely, it refers to Chucky, a doll that was created from a horror film franchise called *Child's Play*. Chucky is portrayed as "a notorious serial killer whose spirit inhabits a 'Good Guy' doll and continuously tries to transfer his soul from the doll to a human body" and it was first seen in 1988 (Wikipedia, 2020). This

7. Voracious Consumption

FIGURES 7.1 AND 7.2. Lakes of Qaranqa, Huanoquite's principal water source and site where mining concessions are being developed

narrative is frightening and fascinating. Its pattern conforms to a structure often found in Quechua communities—one in which there are different spatiotemporal "ages" of the universe, and while each age is overturned by a cataclysmic upheaval of space and time (*pachakuti*), prior ages overlap with the present one. In the case of chuki—a doll with saturated blue eyes that appears somewhat half-crazed—the children appear to be suggesting that grotesque and frightening blue-eyed creatures, along with dinosaurs and robots (machines) will catalyze the upheaval.

FIGURE 7.3. High puna where mountain spirits (apus) surround the lakes of Qaranqa

The chuki resembles many cryptids in Quechua communities. Known in the Andes as *ñakaqs, pishtacos,* or *kharisiris,* these beings take the form of charismatic figures, usually foreigners and men (although there are some cases of women). Despite their humanlike appearance, however, they turn out to really be monstrous beings. In their narratives and stories, Huanoquiteños convey that in their encounters with villagers, ñakaqs suck the lifeblood or fat out of them like vampires, leaving them to die eventually. Although their existence cannot be substantiated, the forms they have taken over the years—as handsome foreigners, priests, industrialists, or soldiers—draw directly on the histories of traumatic and violent personas, events, and forces that have penetrated and threatened the fabric of Indigenous people's lives.[13] Weismantel (2001, 10–16) emphasizes that these beings are familiar but not real, estranged yet historical. Hence, the chuki and Lorenzo's stories about the perturbations to the wild lakes that feed Huanoquite. These beings exist within narratives but also leap out of them into people's lives, precisely because they have some grounding in reality. People have been known to label individuals as ñakaqs and then attempt to kill or exile them. This has been especially true if they have wealth that cannot be explained, if they have transgressed significant norms, or if an entire community is living in terror, not knowing who to trust, as was the case during Peru's civil war in the 1980s and 1990s. In Huanoquite, the current narratives of such figures—that have woven in and out of their history from time to time—allude to fear, anxiety, and reckless but deliberate actions and imbalances that are at once cosmic, economic, environmental, and political. Wreaking havoc, they are caused by the extractive intrusions and destructive demeanor and activities of miners and their machines, and more generally, of global neoliberalism as it reaches across the natural, human, and supernatural fabric of the universe that Huanoquiteños inhabit.

Confronting Qenqonay: Militancy in the Mining Corridor

The stories Lorenzo recounted above, complemented by Margarita's observations, and the commentaries of men in the fields and those of children resembled others unfolding throughout the Andes, though the particulars differed. They conveyed heightened concern among villagers about what was happening to their landscape and livelihoods. The villagers of Qenqonay, the nearest community to the lakes, had already negotiated with one mining concession to sell their lands, inciting the protests that Lorenzo described. The extensive area near the Qaranqa lakes was part of what was known as the "Southern Andean Highland Mining Corridor" which, as I mentioned above, had been the principal locus for social conflicts about mining in the country for some time (OCM 2019, 33).[14]

Huanoquiteños—who had a long history of political organizing—joined forces with communities from Anta, who were also known for their militancy, and confronted the inhabitants of Qenqonay who were planning to turn over their lands to the mining corporation. Hector, a young and ambitious man who had joined in the protest march, commented, "Rejecting the mines will destroy some jobs but we must look to the long-term future." People I spoke with, including Pablo, one of the leaders who had spearheaded the protest, recounted how five thousand people had gone to Qenqonay with picks and poles to demand that community members there not sell out to the mining concession.

Many argued that Qenqonay's inhabitants did not share the long history of resisting incursions on their land and territory that was more typical of other Huanoquiteños who had fought against landed estate owners because Qenqonay was a more recently established community. They even claimed that the villagers did not "really" belong to Huanoquite. In fact, many members of other communities of Huanoquite at lower altitudes *would* travel regularly to the environs of Qenqonay to purchase cattle, especially bulls, or to check on their sheep and cows, which they had arranged to be herded for part of the year with their Qenqonay compadres. It is more likely that, even though Qenqonay was a newer official community, the criticism leveled at them was because they had sold out to the miners. Regardless, the result was that lands in the Qenqonay region that once had been sparsely inhabited, thus protecting the powerful and enchanted Qaranqa lakes of Huanoquite, had now become vulnerable. Because of the protest, a split within Qenqonay took place, but uncertainty prevailed about what the future augured. Some of Qenqonay's inhabitants, despite the protests, sold their lands to the mining company and agreed to move to other lands offered to them, while others were persuaded to support the protests against the mines. The situation was dire as many mining concessions had already been established furtively in collaboration with the government. When I left, Huanoquiteños had filed a petition asking that a part of the area near the Qaranqa lakes be declared an intangible zone, to conserve the native trees (q'euña—Polylepis racemosa) and the water sources located there.[15]

This battle is likely to proceed into the future, with Huanoquiteños drawing on multiple weapons available to them to convey the urgency of protecting their environment and water sources. These weapons include lobbying for the content of a new general law of mining that might better protect their rights; demands that ILO 169 be properly enforced; telling the stories to people, both young and old, of the beneficial and destructive powers that ruled the earth via mountains, water fowl, and lakes that could suddenly become tidal waves; and direct engagement via blockades, strikes, and other kinds of collective resistance movements that might strengthen coalitions with people from other parts of Paruro, Anta, and Chumbivilcas. Huanoquiteños had to walk a fine line as they gauged whether it was best to make claims *in terms* of the state (drawing, especially, on existing legal tenets and their interpretation) or to make claims *against* the state, ones that could exert more pressure but could also end in a bloodbath with nothing gained.

There is no way to predict if Huanoquiteños, together with other Indigenous communities, will be able to strengthen their collective institutional structures and intercultural governance for political purposes of unification and resistance, but their ability to do so will be critical to them, whether it is for purposes of cultivating and exporting their quinoa, or more generally and dramatically, to combat climate change and to protect the lands and water on which they, their children, and all their crops and livestock depend. They will need to draw on all the weapons of the universe at their disposal to push back against the monsters of the lagoons and the chukis.

Conclusion

Pragmatic Spirituality and Quinoa Desires

Why and how did the relationships among mineral extraction, agriculture, "development," and more specifically, the cultivation and export of quinoa matter? The privatization of landholdings, the purchase and sale of land in a limited land market, and the many Huanoquiteños who maintained double (and even triple) residency, regularly moving between multiple living sites, challenged their identities as members of Indigenous communities (Pajuelo Téves 2019, 78). Amidst these kinds of pressures that encouraged individual action and decision-making, *institutionally*, Huanoquiteños sought to retain their identity as Indigenous communities with some autonomy about what happened to resources allocated to their communities, about *what* land meant, *how* it was bought and sold, and *to whom*. Part of that autonomy was their decision to pursue more militant undertakings, such as trying to unite in protest against entities like the mining concessions around Qenqonay that they concluded were threatening to their future.

Not long ago, one young Huanoquiteño, Marcelino, had what he thought was a brilliant idea: instead of cultivating or building houses on the flat lands of Tihuicte, he proposed that those lands be converted into a heliport for the mines. Marcelino was thinking in terms of revenues and possible employment for people in Huanoquite. His plan was discussed seriously and at length during a general assembly of Huanoquite's communities and then unanimously rejected, with the admonishment that Huanoquite's land should be used for

CONCLUSION

"the good of the community and for its agriculture" (Community Meeting, October 1, 2018).

The desires of Huanoquiteños to fortify and expand opportunities of their communities and the institutional presence of all sorts of exogenous entities and agents in the heart of indigenous communities created uneasy bedfellows, and they struggled with moral ambiguities in their decision-making. At the same time, they felt immense pressure to act collectively, even when they disagreed. One way this uneasiness manifested itself was in the form of chukis and the tremendous black waves and monsters of the lakes discussed in the last chapter. Many if not all Huanoquiteños believed that their future as an agrarian community depended on these lakes, whatever novel and constructive livelihood strategies emerged out of their pursuit of entrepreneurial endeavors, which promoted pride among Huanoquiteños. Huanoquiteños were enmeshed in clashing and contradictory forces. However, despite the predictions of social scientists and government officials—that development and modernization would eventually result in the disappearance and disintegration of highland communities—Huanoquite had survived and even thrived from time to time.

Returning to the story of quinoa—a small seed with outsized potential—it offers possibilities of different sorts, depending on who is contemplating it and what their desires are. For the consumer in Europe or the United States, it is a superfood, an excellent way to check off "good health" indicators, and it does not take long to prepare it, even in a remarkable variety of ways. For restaurants, the same is true, as quinoa on the menu attests to foods that are "organic" and "natural," and allows chefs a measure of playfulness and creativity in preparing it. For the Peruvian government, it means foreign exchange and a way to encourage tourism, multiculturalism, and prominence on the world stage, projecting itself as a nation that embraces the food practices and lifeways of its Indigenous people. Too often, however, Indigenous inhabitants themselves have become a commodity, experiencing manipulation and exhaustion as their culture and labor are extracted, distilled, highlighted, and broadcast, for purposes of increasing the value of quinoa and other indigenous foods. NGOs envision that quinoa cultivation on a grander scale could benefit growers, promote gender parity, and diminish malnutrition while contributing to global food security, and agronomists and scientists, in general, think that the preservation of quinoa landraces in germplasm banks might make a substantial difference to human survival in conditions of ecosystemic degradation and environmental unpredictability.

Within Peru lowland Indigenous inhabitants view quinoa as a source of intelligence and strength with significant nurturing qualities. As for Indigenous inhabitants of the Andean highlands, quinoa—and its byproducts such as saponin—travels in multiple directions simultaneously. It is good to eat and comforting; it energizes those who are served it at labor parties; it is adapted to many kinds of microenvironmental conditions; and it has given Indigenous women more recognition for their contributions to its production, processing, preparation, and marketing. Yet it is arduous to grow and process, it exhausts the soil, and it is an anxious challenge for growers to sell in quantity as a nontraditional export because of the instability of the market and their lack of access to credit. Even when the price is low, though, it has brought some growers additional income, given their initial investments of seed, labor, and food. Nevertheless, despite the enthusiasm that the Peruvian government has expressed for the viability of quinoa as a mechanism to improve the livelihoods of Indigenous Quechua people, it has not substantially changed their life circumstances for the better. Huanoquiteños openly voiced their desire to protect and deepen their agroecological knowledge and their concomitant wariness of techno-fetishism as a solution to the world's (and their own) food security. As I complete this book, COVID-19 has swept the world, making Huanoquiteños more aware than ever of the benefits of shorter supply chains and localized food production. Growing quinoa between tall stalks of maize that protect and hide it from pesky finches, or growing it in small amounts, remains what most farmers do.

FIGURE 8.1. Workers resting after a long day's work cutting quinoa
(Photo taken by John R. Cooper)

FIGURE 8.2. Carrying dried quinoa stalks to thresher

FIGURE 8.3. Paulina and Samuel, prominent quinoa growers in Huanoquite, at their maize harvest

Pragmatic Spirituality and Quinoa Desires

Whether it concerned their agrarian practices, approaches to infrastructural and development projects, or confronting mining operations, Huanoquiteños continued what they had always done—making choices that required them to move within worlds that had become fused and contradictory. This was, by now, a very old story, but a key difference was that they had become more knowledgeable about the ways of those worlds and, especially, the ways of the state at the same time that the world itself had become more cognizant of how potentially catastrophic the ecosystemic and environmental challenges they were facing were and, therefore, had begun attributing greater value to an idealized Indigenous way of being in the universe. Yet despite the growing interest the world demonstrated in Indigenous ways of being, Huanoquiteños rarely withdrew from the plurality of worlds in which they found themselves. From where they were situated, wielding their weapons of pragmatic spirituality, they understood that the universe itself was porous and historically constituted and that they had to remain engaged to counter the consequences of deep inequalities and systemic racism in Peru.

Quinoa will continue to make its way around the world, finding its place in the differing histories of prior economic, political, and cultural formations into which it is incorporated, and it will bring substantial economic returns to wholesale exporters, to restaurants that serve it, and to grocery stores that sell it. Globalization is hardly uniform, however. This volume has trained its eye on Huanoquite, one Andean highland district mostly inhabited by Quechua-speaking Indigenous peoples. Through ethnographic interpretation and analysis, it has argued that the story of transforming quinoa, a minor subsistence crop, into a nontraditional export commodity offers a surprisingly wide window onto the history of Andean highland agrarian lives and food politics. The problems Huanoquiteños have grappled with and their efforts to maintain multifocality—keeping in their line of vision the multiple valences and scales at which their lives unfold and, in some cases, depend upon—are not dissimilar to those encountered throughout the Andes. The story of quinoa highlights points of incommensurability in the Andean highlands between Indigenous and western perspectives, especially around politics, land, and social relationships, but also shows how problematic it is to romanticize Indigenous ontologies and epistemologies. Huanoquiteños live in a universe in which they move among specters of past regimes that inflect the present—and the way they envision temporality is not always linear. In their daily lives they regularly encounter the power and magnetism of neoliberal entrepreneurialism and the desire to nurture their autonomy and community sovereignty. These contradictions and tensions are constitutive of the pragmatic spirituality that structures their ways of being and acting in the world.

One advantage of engaging in long-term fieldwork is that it becomes possible to point to ruptures, continuities, and transformations that might not otherwise be as apparent. To unpack what quinoa means to Huanoquiteños requires being aware of the historical and current context in which it is grown, the history of human-environmental-cosmological relationships that circulate in the Andes and beyond, and the impact on Huanoquiteños of the worldwide demand for quinoa. For non-Andean parties interested in quinoa, its attraction lies in its versatility and aesthetic qualities, and they view communities in the Andes where it is cultivated as sites of refuge that may provide critical resources in the face of global climate change and food insecurity. For Indigenous Quechua cultivators, quinoa is one crop among others with distinctive attributes, and its cultivation is also one among many vibrant undertakings that they have embarked on to remain on their land, feed their households, and protect their territory for future generations to come.

The story of growing quinoa in Huanoquite is about much more than transforming seeds into rainbow fields of yellow, magenta, black, and white. It is a long tale that will continue of how Indigenous Quechua inhabitants have had to work hard at keeping the world in balance when it appears to be spinning out of control, whether because of the proximate tensions they have wrestled with, between staking individual and collective claims to resources in their communities, their marginalization in Peruvian society, the threats of pollution and water scarcity from the encroachment of mining operations, or because of the unpredictable effects of climate change. Because so many communities throughout the Andes face challenges and histories similar to those found in Huanoquite, opportunities have arisen for them to form coalitions and to mobilize in a more unified manner from time to time, even though these movements may be unstable and dispersed. In so doing, they have drawn on shared experiences and knowledge born of a long, sedimented history that is comprised of the Inca, colonial, and capitalist regimes of which they have been a part. The enduring strength of Andean highland dwellers has been to hone diversification, resilience, and their resolve and autonomy as they pursue their struggles to stay vigilant in the face of extractive forces, values, and relationships—affective, economic, political, and cultural—that consume their daily lives.

Notes

Introduction

1. Derived from the Spanish Catholic practice of establishing godparenthood for children at the time of their baptism, compadrazgo is a bond of fictive kinship, usually cemented ritually, in which co-mothers (comadres) and co-fathers (compadres) take on the responsibility of guiding their godchild. They may intervene in conflicts between their compadres as well. Sometimes the fictive kinship relationship is among equals, but just as frequently, compadres hold a higher status and may be able to provide resources to their godchildren that their parents cannot. Especially during the heyday of the reign of landed estates, these relationships spilled over into a patron-clientelism in which landed estate owners would treat their godchildren and fictive co-parents as servants in the house and fields and in exchange, offer them shelter in Cusco, education, loans, or even agricultural products or a sheep.

2. "Quinoa exports from Peru, 2013–2019 (in million kilograms)," *Statista Research Department*, Statista: The Statistics Portal for Market Data, Market Research, and Market Studies, www.statista.com, December 2020; "Quinoa exports from Peru, 2012–2019 (in million U.S. Dollars)," *Statista Research Department*, www.statista.com, November 2020; "Quinoa production share worldwide in 2019, by country," *Statista Research Department*, www.statista.com, May 2021. Interestingly, while Peru exported a little over 55 percent of its total production of quinoa in 2019, (49,500 million kilograms), almost 45 percent of its total production (40,275 million kilograms) was produced for domestic use, whether for seed, household consumption, trade, or regional markets within and beyond Peru.

3. This research would not have been possible without the support I received from

Notes to Introduction

the Wenner-Gren Foundation for Anthropological Research for my project, "Women and Quinoa Foodways: Making Soup and Superfood in the Peruvian Andean Highlands (Post-Doctoral Grant #9433)," which was conducted with IRB approval from George Mason University, Project #1072333–1.

4. "Población total al 30 de junio, por grupos quinquenales de edad, según departamento, provincial, y distrito, Cuadro 9"; III Censo de Comunidades Nativas y I Censo de Comunidades Campesinas, vol. 1, 425; *El III Censo Nacional de Comunidades Indígenas 2017, XII de Población, y VII de Vivienda. INEI (Instituto Nacional de Estadística e Informática)*. http://censo2017.inei.gob.pe/resultados-definitivos-de-las-comunidades-nativas-y-campesinas-2017/, December 2018.

5. The dynamics of internalized oppression have been well documented with respect to Indigenous language use—in this case, Quechua. Forces of conquest, colonialism, and other modes of domination have included the deliberate suppression and eradication of native languages, leading inhabitants to censor their use of their native language and to embrace the use of the dominant language for purposes of strategic political and economic mobility. The failure to transmit Indigenous languages through educational institutions often leads to its disappearance in subsequent generations (See, for example, Mannheim 1991, Durston and Mannheim 2018, and Huayhua 2010, 2014). Interestingly, in Huanoquite, Quechua was being more widely used than when I was there in prior decades, both publicly and privately. The reasons for this are beyond the scope of this volume, and further research is needed to understand why this is the case when the opposite has occurred in many other regions.

6. Laura Graham (2002) and Alison Brysk (1996) offer excellent overviews of the strategic deployment of Indigeneity for political and economic purposes in Latin America.

7. There are many articles and books that address, anthropologically, the relationships between food, culture, and food politics. Mary Weismantel (1988), María Elena García (2013, 2021), Raúl Matta and María Elena García (2019), Clare Sammells (2019), Lisa Markowitz (2019), and Eric Hirsch and Kyle Jones (2019) offer excellent perspectives on these topics in the Andes, and there are others that I also refer to in the course of the book, especially in chapters 3 and 6.

8. *Ex situ* accessions in genebanks differ partly from those found *in situ* where farmers live and experiment with quinoa varieties that are well adapted to their specific environmental conditions or even ease of harvesting or processing. Rojas et al.'s article (2015) offers an excellent account of the challenges of documenting and preserving quinoa varieties.

9. Belgian chemist and philosopher Isabelle Stengers (2010) has been at the forefront of arguing that it is necessary to recognize how people's conceptualization and understanding of the "cosmos" structure their political engagement (and vice versa) through technologies, practices, behaviors, and models they implemented in their daily lives. Stengers explains this as a "cosmopolitics" whose underpinnings may often be hidden but are very much at work in creating contradictions, conflicts, resistance, or imposition and domination.

Notes to Introduction and Chapter 1

10. See, for example, Bazile, Jacobsen, and Verniau 2016; Kerssen 2015; and Tschopp 2018. Many papers have also been published in scientific journals dedicated to the analysis of the genetic composition and varieties of quinoa, the conditions in which it grows, and the potential for commercializing it in different world regions.

In spite of the lack of more nuanced studies on quinoa, there have nevertheless been some fine anthropological studies on aspects of the place of quinoa in the lives of Indigenous growers in communities and cooperative associations in Peru, Bolivia, Ecuador, and Chile, including those of Bazile 2015; Laguna 2011; McDonell 2015; Ofstehage 2011; Tapia Vargas 1976; Walsh-Dilley 2013; and Zimmerer 1992.

11. The civil war between the Shining Path movement and military and paramilitary forces is discussed in greater detail in chapter 1.

12. It was especially heart-wrenching for me when the mother of a family I had known since my first trip to Huanoquite asked me to please give her any and all photos I had of her daughter as a young girl because she had recently died suddenly as a mature woman, at age thirty-three, leaving her mother bereft. When I returned the next year, I was glad that I could bring her four photos, including one of her daughter as an infant.

13. Maria-Luisa Achino-Loeb (2020) edited a special issue of the *Journal of Anthropological Research* in which anthropologists reflected on the silences in their field research— what they and their interlocutors did not grasp or talk about at different points in their research over time, as well as what they themselves or their interlocutors omitted or excluded in their accounts. Several contributors (Darnell 2020, 44–58; Lamphere 2020, 59–73, and Mitchell 2020, 74–89) discuss how long-term field research was very important to a fuller understanding of their prior and more recent findings (and omissions) and the ways that assumptions about knowledge and its production colored their praxis and the relationships they had with their interlocutors. Kathleen Fine-Dare (2020) also interweaves, throughout her volume *Urban Mountain Beings,* how longitudinal fieldwork affected her interpretations and the very act of arriving at valid ethnographic interpretations.

Chapter 1. Agrarian Reform, Revolution, and Reversals

1. Estimates vary, but about 0.1 percent of landholdings of 2,500 hectares or more (1 hectare is equivalent to 2.47 acres) made up 61 percent of Peru's arable land, while 83 percent of farms smaller than 5 hectares comprised only 5.7 percent of arable land (Klarén 2017, 28).

2. Burt 2007; Degregori 2012; Gorriti 1999; Palmer 1992; Poole and Rénique 1991; Rojas-Pérez 2017; Seligmann 2003; Starn 1999; and Stern 1998 offer excellent overviews and analyses of the causes and consequences of Peru's civil war.

3. The number killed or disappeared according to the CVR (the Truth and Reconciliation Commission of Peru [La Comisión de la Verdad y Reconciliación del Perú], 2001, 53) between 1980 and 2000, was 69,280. The CVR established that 79 percent of the victims had lived in rural areas, and 75 percent of the dead had spoken Quechua or another

Notes to Chapters 1 and 2

Indigenous language as their first language (CVR 2001, 160–62) Commissioners also determined that the PCP-Shining Path was responsible for 54 percent of the reported deaths (CVR 2001, 181). See "Chapter 1, Periods of Violence," "Truth Commission: Peru 01," Truth Commissions Digital Collection, United States Institute of Peace, July 13, 2001. https://www.usip.org/publications/2001/07/truth-commission-peru-01.

4. In looking through my archival notes on Huanoquite, records of conflicts over land boundaries have persisted for hundreds of years. Because land boundaries were "walked" and not formally surveyed, flexibility and error were always an issue. These conflicts over land boundaries have been exacerbated by contradictory land tenure regimes and macro-economic policies promoted by the Peruvian state. The result has been the creation of land tenure regimes that lack coherence, and the problematic fracturing of existing political entities. In addition, land boundaries have also always been a lightning rod—a way to channel any number of other kinds of disputes that arise between households and communities.

Chapter 2. The Power and Seduction of Infrastructure

1. Earlier road-building projects often deliberately took longer routes than necessary, even with the need to properly grade roads, because engineers were paid by the length of the road. I (Seligmann 1995) wrote extensively about the history of infrastructure in Huanoquite. Huanoquite had been an entrepôt, connected to Cusco via the Inca road and to regions far beyond in the Apurimac Valley, by trails and paths, because it had a valuable resource: salt mines. Caravans of llamas traveled back and forth to obtain salt and traded goods with Huanoquiteños. This was the case until modern dirt and asphalted road construction linked Huanoquite to Cusco directly and industrialized manufactured salt became available. Other regions similarly became connected to market towns and cities that bypassed Huanoquite. From a central node, Huanoquite became an end point, dramatically transforming its regional spatial orientations.

2. Many accidents have taken place on the road from Cusco to Huanoquite, especially along the portion that is unpaved and badly graded between Yaurisque and Huanoquite. In 2013, a truck accident took place, in which twenty-nine people were injured and one died. Several other fatalities have occurred since then.

3. Las Bambas is a joint venture between MMG, a subsidiary of Guoxin International Investment Co., and CITIC Metal Co.

4. Conociéndote Linda Tierra, Facebook, accessed April 2, 2020, https://www.facebook.com/huanoquite.tierralinda.

5. Especially during Peru's civil war in the 1980s and 1990s, conflicts and deepening polarization ensued between Huanoquiteños who considered themselves Catholics and a growing number who embraced evangelical faiths. These conflicts had subsided notably by 2013, and it appeared that Father Roy had tried to contribute to reducing tensions. Building the salon was an important step in this direction.

6. Conociéndote Linda Tierra, Facebook, accessed April 2, 2020, https://www.facebook.com/huanoquite.tierralinda.

Notes to Chapters 2 and 3

7. These same sentiments unfortunately helped to spread the virus as many Huanoquiteños, especially younger ones, returned home to Huanoquite where they felt more assured of having access to food and the comfort of family during the lockdown.

8. The distance between Yaurisque and Huanoquite was about twenty kilometers, taking close to forty-five minutes to travel. If the road were paved, it would end at the district capital but not where minerals could be mined, although as we will see, many minerals *are* found in the district of Huanoquite farther above the district capital in the high punas surrounding it. In fact, Las Bambas has encountered substantial resistance from villagers along the current road, and they have been lobbying to build an additional road that would go more directly to the mines via a different and shorter route altogether—one that, more or less, follows the ancient Inca road between Cusco and Huanoquite and then continues farther above to another district bordering Huanoquite called Ccapi, just beyond which are the Las Bambas mines as well as other concessions. To get there requires crossing the Apurimac River, and a new bridge, which replaced a spectacular yet dangerous swinging rope bridge, had already been built over the river. The first effort had ended in tragedy, and the bridge collapsed, causing the death of one of the engineers working on it.

Chapter 3. Contesting Development, Alternative Paths

1. Davies's (2019) edited volume offers one of the best and most up-to-date sources that provides a history of NGOs and the differences among their practices and assumptions. Bebbington (2004) also offers an incisive examination of NGOs, specifically in Latin America and the Andes, and Florence Babb (2018) and Sarah Radcliffe (2015), more generally, look at NGOs in the context of feminist issues and development practices.

2. See Kregg Hetherington (2020) discussion of similar attitudes and behaviors on the part of many government functionaries, even those who were well intentioned, in their efforts to expand soy monocropping in Paraguay over a ten-year period. One of the great strengths of long-term fieldwork, such as that conducted by Hetherington or my own work in Huanoquite, is that it becomes possible to gauge better the ambivalence of actors participating in these projects and to understand that, however innovative or promising the projects may seem, recipients integrate them into a *longue durée* assessment and have become accustomed to not viewing them as a panacea.

3. A comprehensive account of Cuna Más's work in Peru can be found in Josephson, Guerrero, and Coddington 2017.

4. "Promueven campana para combater la anemia y la desnutrición crónica." *La República*, July 12, 2019. https://larepublica.pe/sociedad/2019/07/12/promueven-campana-para -combatir-la-anemia-y-la-desnutricion-cronica/. According to the article, the statistics were obtained from Peru's Ministry of Health (MINSA). In a detailed booklet prepared by Estrada (INIA) to encourage cultivation of quinoa, he emphasized the need to improve domestic consumption because of the prevalence of anemia among children in the Cusco region, as much as the need to supply the international market for reasons of food insecurity (Estrada 2013, 5).

Notes to Chapters 3 and 4

5. I have painted the approach of these government- or NGO-sponsored initiatives with broad brush strokes. Each could be the subject of an in-depth analysis that would reveal differences among them. Nevertheless, in contrast to the NGO and government projects I have described thus far, those I discuss below entailed far greater involvement of Huanoquiteños, not only in getting them off the ground but also in following through and doing what they could to have them succeed.

6. García (2005) offers an interesting discussion of a similar process of reorientation of NGO practices, partly driven by community members themselves.

7. In the Huanoquite region, there were at least ten archaeological sites and relatively few people visited them, hence the former schoolteacher was attempting to establish the Huanoquite region as a tourist attraction.

8. Cornell leased the Vicos hacienda in northern Peru in 1952 to establish the Cornell-Peru Project (CPP), and a team of anthropologists from Cornell ran it in conjunction with campesinos who had worked on it. Its goal was to modernize the estate and how it was run, assimilate the Indigenous population into Peruvian society, integrate them into the market, and do research on what they were implementing. Not surprisingly, many of the practices they introduced took no account of preexisting relationships and history, land tenure practices, or local knowledge; yet the project was initially considered a model for international development. For further details on this project, see Dobyns, Doughty, and Lasswell's edited volume (1971), and for critiques of it, see Babb (2018) and Stein (2003).

Chapter 4. The Expansion of Quinoa Production

1. Cereal grains, such as oats, wheat, rice, corn, barley, rye, sorghum, and millet, are edible seeds of grasses that belong to the Poaceae family. In contrast, quinoa is harvested from a tall, leafy plant that is a relative of spinach, beets, and chard and belongs to the amaranth or goosefoot family (Amaranthaceae). It also has a hard hull that must be removed before it can be eaten. There are, however, similarities between quinoa and cereal grains in that quinoa is edible once the outer hull is removed so it is often popularly called a grain or pseudo-grain. "Quinoa," University of Wisconsin, Division of Extension, February 7, 2022, http://corn.agronomy.wisc.edu/Crops/Quinoa.aspx.

2. Professor Ralph Bolton (Pomona College) and Professor Jorge Flores Ochoa (UNSAAC) were responsible for crafting this ambitious, semester-long, tutorial program for students at both institutions, assisted by research assistants Carmen Rosa Araoz and Percy Paz Flores. The communities were located in the southern Andean highlands of Peru in the province of Canchis. In addition to cultural ecology projects, some of us undertook comparative cultural psychology and religious and ritual anthropology projects and produced documentary films. It was a remarkable introduction to Andean studies, which became a lifelong research interest for me. I remain indebted to the inhabitants of Santa Barbara for their tolerance of our naiveté and their willingness to share their life experiences with us despite our embarrassing insensitivity and blunders.

Notes to Chapters 4 and 5

3. The *altiplano* is a high Andean plateau located mainly in Bolivia but extending to part of Peru and has an average altitude of of 3,750 msl.

4. While many people translate "real" as royal, Ofstehage (2011, 105), in a personal communication with Pablo Laguna, a scholar who has done extensive research on quinoa in Bolivia, was told that the vernacular translation that farmers give of quinua real is "true" or "real" quinoa.

5. In her article, Andrews (2017, 16) includes a graphic depiction of a copper amulet, found in Argentina, of Pachamama (Mother Earth) holding out stalks of quinoa plants in her right and left hands. While the provenance is given, dating of the amulet, from a private collection, is not specified (Mintzer 1933).

6. Catherine Allen (2009, 30) makes the important point that chicha, a fermented beverage, whether made from maize or quinoa, was never prepared for household consumption alone because it was so labor-intensive and time-consuming. It required the cooperative labor of at least two, and often many more, women; and it was made in large quantities—for labor parties or special ritual occasions. Hence, it served to link multiple households to one another at the moment when it was served, and it brought women together from various households to make the chicha itself.

7. A hectare is equivalent to 2.4 acres. Most farmers make their calculations of inputs and outputs in terms of topus. Three topus equals a hectare; 2 kilos of quinoa seed are needed for each topu, hence 6 kilos of seed for a hectare; and 6 kilos of seed produces roughly, 1,950 kilos of quinoa.

8. Comparing the position, ideology, and functions of Indigenous and non-Indigenous brokers in Andean highland communities is a subject deserving of further research.

9. One US dollar was equivalent to a little less than three soles in 2014.

10. It was interesting to find out that the figures I had gathered with respect to this farmer's expenses growing quinoa and his gross revenue and net margin on sales approximated closely those reported by INIA for the cultivation of one hectare of quinoa, with a difference of only five hundred soles for expenses. Obviously, revenues varied somewhat in accordance with the quantity of quinoa put up for sale on the market and the price at the time (Estrada 2013, 33).

11. Luz Alexandra Martínez (2015) has written an excellent doctoral thesis on tarwi. Farmers have encountered similar issues in cultivating quinoa and tarwi, although tarwi has not become a major export crop as has quinoa.

12. A CDO or Certification of Denomination of Origin serves as a kind of intellectual property right that legally protects products based on the unique attributes of the geographic location in which they are produced, hence the kind of soil, quality, taste, and appearance may all figure in acquiring a CDO.

Chapter 5. Food Sovereignty, Food Security, and Sustainability

1. Urdanivia (2014, 42n3), for example, relies on Stephen Brush's (2004, 52–53) definition of landraces, "locally adopted varieties that are named, selected, and maintained

Notes to Chapter 5

by farmers in different regions . . . characterized by genetic and phenotypic variability within named types," and she alternates using the terms *landrace* and *variety*. Brush, like Andrews (2017), discusses the dynamic nature of landraces that emerge in the context of specific environmental conditions and more culturally grounded considerations that create complex challenges for those attempting to discern how to classify different varieties of a crop such as quinoa.

2. McDonell (2015, 80–81) offers an incisive account of national efforts in Bolivia to safeguard quinoa seeds in the Andes in germplasm banks at the same time that they have skirted the question of ownership of the germplasm itself. Growers there argue that ownership should be attributed to quinoa farmers, thus preventing "unauthorized use outside the Andes" and also protecting "the farmers (and others in the Andes) benefitting from the export boom against competition from other countries" (2015, 81).

3. Another extremely important variable outside the purview of this book that demands further investigation is whether the growing land market in rural areas of the Andes is creating control of agricultural production through purchase and lease by foreign corporations for consumption by their own countries, something that China has been pursuing astutely in Argentina and Brazil, for example (McMichael 2020). The ecological conditions of Huanoquite are such that this is highly unlikely, but in Puno, Arequipa, and Bolivia this might indeed affect the way that quinoa is grown and marketed in a global context.

4. It is beyond the subject of this volume to address many of the questions surrounding food security and food sovereignty, as well as control of biogenetic diversity, especially among small agricultural producers. Edited volumes prepared by Gerardo Otero, Gabriela Pechlaner, and Efe Can Gúrcan (2013), Marc Edelman et al. (2016), and Philip McMichael (2009) offer excellent analyses focusing on these themes and debates.

5. Bellemare, Fajardo-Gonzalez, and Gitter (2018, 167) analyzed results from research in which 220,000 rural households were surveyed in Peru between 2004 and 2013. Although this was near the beginning of the export boom of quinoa, they found that household consumption of quinoa had remained relatively constant. They also argued, using econometric measures, that welfare increased in regions with higher concentrations of quinoa consumers and that international trade of quinoa had not been harmful to household welfare in Peru (Bellemare, Fajardo-Gonzalez, and Gitter 2018, 167). At the same time, they also found that rather than put quinoa on the market, when prices fell, producers stored it, and thus it did make it more difficult for domestic consumers to find it. That is, although consumption was relatively steady, in their study, it did fall when quinoa prices fell (174). Between 2010 and 2013, quinoa consumption domestically only fell by 5 percent, nevertheless. The researchers argue that there has been a steady decline in quinoa consumption but that it is not in line with the quinoa price increase, indicating that the trend is not price-driven but likely due to a change in consumer preferences. They focused solely on economic measures and relied on an annual household survey administered by INEI (the National Institute of Statistics and Information) for each of eleven years in Peru in order to determine the varying price of quinoa for households that reported producing quinoa in relationship to household consumption patterns, which they equated with

household welfare. They conclude (175) that their findings "should assuage rich-country consumers' concerns about whether their growing demand for quinoa is having a negative influence on Andean households." Their study raises significant questions about the relationships between quinoa production, consumption, and household welfare, but more direct research is needed to ascertain shifts in welfare and distributional effects of rising quinoa prices on domestic producers and consumers, particularly in rural areas.

6. Among development agents and organizations, defining development in terms of the well-being of local populations has coexisted as a minority position in contrast to defining it in terms of gross domestic product or economic growth writ large. I had a chance to speak with Kevin Kinsella, who had been part of a nutrition planning contract with AID (Agency for International Development) in 1974. At that time, he had been hired to write a report for the Peruvian government about the prospects for encouraging the wider use of quinoa in the diets of poor people in urban centers. He proposed that quinoa flour substitute for wheat flour, especially since almost 100 percent of the latter was imported from Argentina and the United States, and Peru was spending about $1 billion per year on wheat imports. His argument was that the use of quinoa would substantially improve the diets of the urban poor and reduce foreign exchange spent on wheat imports by about 10 percent per year and that a price support program could be initiated for quinoa cultivators at high altitudes—like those of Huanoquite—to stabilize and guarantee their income from year to year. According to Kinsella, there had been some interest in the proposal, but it was eventually shelved and forgotten. Kinsella surmised that the individuals or groups holding the government-sanctioned wheat import license exerted pressure on the government to prevent the project from being pursued because of threats to his/their own business (Personal communication, January 15, 2020).

7. Excellent general discussion of the myriad conflicts surrounding Indigenous food sovereignty and regenerative agriculture can be found in Andrée et al.'s edited volume, *Globalization and Food Sovereignty: Global and Local Change in the New Politics of Food.* (See also Trauger 2014; and Grey and Patel 2015).

Chapter 6. To Be Strong and Healthy

1. The articles that comprise a special issue of *Anthropology of Food* 14 (2019), "The Gastro-Political Turn in Peru," edited by Raúl Matta and María Elena García, analyze how Peruvian food and cuisine became a recognized brand worldwide, among other themes. Cánepa (2013) also addresses how Indigeneity has been massaged through visual means as part of Peru's nation branding to promote and celebrate a multicultural Peru in the context of neoliberalism.

2. Scholars of food make an important distinction between diet and cuisine. Cuisine is a cultural system such that various starches, for example, could be slotted into a placeholder, and the meal itself could be more or less elaborated, depending on the availability of particular ingredients or the wealth of the household. Diet consists of what specific foods people eat, not necessarily how they relate systematically to one another. Quinoa is

Notes to Chapter 6

rarely a centerpiece of a meal except on particular ritual occasions, but with the growing attention to it, it is served more frequently as part of a meal—in soups, breads, or beer.

3. These descriptions are found at "Organic Quinoa," "Organic Quinoa (Flakes)," and "Organic Quinoa (Red)," Multiple Organics (website), accessed March 4, 2020, https://www.multipleorganics.com/products?start=30&id=54.

4. Climate change has created pressures for the implementation of less individualized practices of production and consumption, but it is harder for those with less economic resources to pursue such practices because they tend to be more expensive.

5. I cannot emphasize enough how important the reciprocal and proper offerings of food, chicha, alcohol, and coca for work at labor parties were to creating a deep sense of intimacy and social connectivity. The ambience that settled over people on the edge of a field as they ate, drank, and rested permitted intense and important conversations to ensue. In a very "private" group, matters of great public concern were frequently aired, and this had been the case since I had first started working in the Andes. Topics such as whether authorities were performing well or if mining operations should be protested were discussed, and unusual and inexplicable experiences were often shared. It was always a time for ruminating and reflecting, and for joking as well.

6. Kiwicha is in the same family as quinoa but has much tinier grains/seeds.

7. There were many women who farmed as single heads of household, but they were usually widows. Milagros was unusual because she had never married.

8. Similarly, Catherine Allen, in her close reading of Andean everyday activities, laid out the dynamics of the complete cycle of Andean feeding in which households "fed" their livestock to excess periodically on ritual occasions so that the dung/manure they produced would then nurture the living by becoming fertilizer for crops and satisfying the dead, who also had to be kept well-fed (Allen 2002).

9. The Day of the Dead (Día de los Muertos) follows Todos Santos (All Souls Day), a Catholic day of memorialization of those who have died. Many Indigenous inhabitants refer to The Day of the Dead as Todos Santos, but while it incorporates some aspects of the Catholic ritual, it has important differences, as specified here. The Catholic ritual usually involves a mass and a visit to the cemetery in order to clean the graves of loved ones.

10. It is beyond the scope of this book to systematically investigate restaurant use of quinoa outside of Peru, hence I have cited statistics from other sources that have looked at this as well as my anecdotal experiences with quinoa preparation and offerings in the United States, European Union, and New Zealand.

11. Chip Colwell, the editor in chief of *Sapiens*, the online publication of the Wenner-Gren Foundation, the organization that helped fund my research on quinoa, invited me to a restaurant that served quinoa in Washington, DC. We both ordered items with quinoa. We asked the server if he could find out from the chef the kinds of quinoa that had been used, but when he came back, he told us that the chef had no idea.

12. "Marca Perú: Campaña de Lanzamiento Internacional," streamed live on July 3, 2012. YouTube video, 3:06, https://www.youtube.com/watch?v=42AXjcP-B2U ; "Peru, Dedi-

Notes to Chapters 6 and 7

cated to the World," streamed live, July 20, 2016, YouTube video, 2:17, https://www.youtube.com/watch?v=tfLNvXYpzWU&t=71s; and "Superfoods Peru," streamed live, February 8, 2017, YouTube video, 2:32, https://www.youtube.com/watch?v=uca7sBDfOtQ. All of these videos were produced by Marca Perú, also referred to as PROMPERÚ.

13. Transitivity boils down to the following: a mathematical or logical relation between three elements such that if the relation holds between the first and second elements and between the second and third elements, it necessarily holds between the first and third elements. Mathematical equality is transitive, since if $x = y$ and $y = z$ then $x = z$, or it could be, as well, if $a > b$ and $b > c$, then $a > c$.

14. De la Cadena (1995) first argued that Indigenous Quechua women were doubly discriminated against as both Indigenous and female.

15. There are many examples that illustrate this persistent substratum of racism against Indigenous people that characterizes life in Peru. One of the most recent took place when then Prime Minister Guido Bellido, a member of newly elected President Pedro Castillo's government and an engineer originally from Cusco, addressed the parliament (of which he was also a member) in Quechua, causing an uproar from opposition members, who demanded that he speak Spanish since they could not understand him. While Quechua is one of Peru's official languages, it is not assumed to be part of Peru's daily social fabric or accorded a similar status as Spanish. In response to the uproar, Bellido noted, "What happened shows that our country still does not understand that there are pueblos (peoples or villages) that have their own deeply rooted culture, their own language," and that "this government is seeking tolerance" (Briceño 2021).

16. See especially the special issue of *Anthropology of Food* 14 (2019), "The Gastro-Political Turn in Peru," prepared by Raúl Matta and María Elena García, which includes excellent articles on this topic, García's earlier article on the topic (2013), her magisterial book on Peruvian gastropolitics (2021), and Patricia Pérez's (2011) film, *Mistura: The Power of Food*.

Chapter 7. Voracious Consumption

1. CooperAcción, "Paruro, Mapa de concesiones mineras en la provincia de Paruro, Cusco, al mes de noviembre del año 2016," https://cooperaccion.org.pe/mapas/paruro-noviembre-2016/.

2. Peter Linebaugh and Marcus Rediker (2000, 4, 27–28) have written a fine volume tracing the movements undertaken by sailors, slaves, pirates, workers, market women, and indentured servants as a "many-headed hydra," a "motley crew" which, nevertheless, managed to periodically engage in coordinated actions of resistance to burgeoning capitalist regimes on both sides of the Atlantic between the seventeenth and early nineteenth centuries. Their shared histories of brutal injustices, religious influences, circulation of knowledge, and their physical movements and settlement among colonies and imperial centers contributed to their capacity to coordinate despite the differences among them.

3. On August 28, 2021, seventeen workers died when the van taking them to the Las Bambas mine toppled off the road into a deep gorge. According to officials, the van took

Notes to Chapter 7

a different route because the usual one was being blockaded by protesters against the mines (Valdivia Romero 2021).

4. 2019 data show that about 48 percent of the entire mining construction portfolio of the country was concentrated in the south, which had received about 66.7 percent of the total amount invested in mining, an increase of 30 percent from the prior year (OCM 2019, 34). Mining investments in the region in the third quarter of 2019 reached $133 million (US), with mining concessions occupying 1,022,059 hectares—about 14.2 percent of the Cusco region. The provinces of Espinar, Chumbivilcas and Quispicanchis had the highest concentration of concessions (OCM 2019, 43).

5. "C169, Indigenous and Tribal Peoples Convention, 1989 (No. 169)." International Labor Organization, accessed February 10, 2021, https://www.ilo.org/dyn/normlex/en/f?p=NORMLEXPUB:12100:0::NO:12100:P12100_INSTRUMENT_ID:312314:NO.

6. There is a growing literature on what is called "the new rurality" in Peru that documents and debates the ways in which Andean highland Indigenous/Peasant Communities are changing and the consequences of those changes. Among the most useful authors I have reviewed are Egurén, Remy, and Oliart (2004); Remy (2013); Salas Carreño and Diez Hurtado (2017); Diez Hurtado and Ortiz (2013); Trivelli, Escobal, and Revesz (2009); and Burneo (2012).

7. A long history of the legal status of Andean Indigenous collective entities, such as *ayllus,* or communities, exists. Various statutes of Peruvian constitutions—in 1920, 1933, 1936, 1951, and 1970—determined not only how such entities should be defined but their legal rights, including corporate title to their lands, even when they were held in usufruct. Several of Huanoquite's communities had been recognized as "Indian Communities" in the 1920s but officially became "Peasant Communities" after the 1969 agrarian reform. With the reversals of the reform, community land had undergone varying degrees of privatization, as I explained in chapter 1. Pedro Germán Nuñez Palomino (1995) provides an excellent history of these complexities, which underlie the instability and fissures of contemporary highland communities.

8. It is crucial to understand that the positive invocation of Indigenous culture has a long history, beginning in the 1920s. Proponents of *Indigenismo* celebrated Quechua culture in an idealized and reified way but did little to improve the economic well-being or the political power of Quechua peoples. Indigenismo fostered the optimistic sentiment that folding the distinctive identities, economic practices, and sociopolitical organization of native inhabitants into aspirations for nation-building and development would result in a unique and strong people and nation. At the same time, the assumption, especially among intellectuals and politicians, that while Indigenous culture was something to be proud of, it could nevertheless be improved led to efforts to incorporate Indigenous peoples into class politics and integrate them into the western construct of the nation. Although the 1969 agrarian reform provided some positive economic and political benefits to Indigenous communities, the systemic discrimination against the latter has endured and become even more apparent in the context of neoliberalism coupled with the current rhetorical promotion of Quechua culture (see De la Cadena, 2000; Seligmann 2008).

176

Notes to Chapter 7

9. The laws that govern how areas are deemed "protected" are complex and divided into various categories. Good summaries can be found in Solano (2009) and "Zonas Intangibles" (2001). The complete law and modifications to it can be found at Ministerio de Energía y Minas (1997, 2001). I am grateful to Guillermo Salas Carreño (Personal communication, April 17, 2020), who suggested sources that clarify how areas are designated as "protected" and the dizzying bureaucratic complexity that surrounds the process of determining such status.

10. For genres of storytelling among Quechua peoples, see Catherine Allen (1982, 1983).

11. See maps 2 and 3 to locate these place names and to understand better the relationship between Huanoquite and neighboring districts and provinces.

12. Aspersion irrigation uses sprinklers and tubes to operate like natural rainfall over a limited area and wastes less water than gravity-fed irrigation.

13. Scholars have debated the significance, meanings, and behaviors associated with these beings. It is beyond the scope of this book to delve into these debates here, but should the reader seek to learn more about them, it would be worthwhile to consult the works of Catherine Allen (2002), Peter Gose (1994), Andrew Orta (2004), Nathan Wachtel (1994), and Mary Weismantel (2001).

14. In doing some archival research, I found that the same region that is now described as the "Southern Andean Mining Corridor" had been described in the past as the "Southern Andean Corridor of Poverty," drawing attention to the close articulation between poverty and extractive undertakings.

15. At this time, all mining activity has ceased, but that could quickly change. Just before this book went to press, Huanoquiteños told me that they were more worried than ever and were thinking about organizing again because they had seen helicopters flying overhead again "which cost plenty of money and they wouldn't do that for nothing." Again, they reiterated that the mines would be the end of Huanoquite because they would lose their water supply.

References

Achino-Loeb. 2020. "Silence/Salience, a Fluid Reality, and the Promise of Fieldwork: Introduction to the Special Issue." *Journal of Anthropological Research* 76, no. 1 (Spring): 1–6.

Acurio, Gastón. 2009. "Cooking is Combined with Moral Principles." Interview with Jeroen van der Zalm. *The Power of Culture.* http://www.krachtvancultuur.nl/en/current/2009/march/gaston-acurio.html.

———. 2017. "Gastronomía, Identidad Nacional y Desarrollo Sostenible." Paper presented at the Annual Meetings of the Latin American Studies Association. Lima, Peru.

Allen, Catherine. 1982. "Body and Soul in Quechua Thought." *Journal of Latin American Lore* 8 (2): 179–96.

———. 1983. "Of Bear-Men and He-Men: Bear Metaphors and Male Self Perception in a Peruvian Community." *Latin American Indian Literatures* no. 7: 38–51.

———. 2002. *The Hold Life Has: Coca and Cultural Identity in an Andean Community.* 2nd ed. Washington, DC: Smithsonian Institution Press, first published in 1988.

———. 2009. "'Let's Drink Together, My Dear!': Persistent Ceremonies in a Changing Community." In *Drink, Power, and Society in the Andes,* edited by Justin Jennings and Brenda Bowser, 28–48. Gainesville: University Press of Florida.

Andrée, Peter, Jeffrey Ayres, Michael J. Bosia, and Marie-Josée Massicotte. 2014a. "Introduction: Crisis and Contention in the New Politics of Food." In *Globalization and Food Sovereignty: Global and Local Change in the New Politics of Food,* edited by Peter Andrée, Jeffrey Ayres, Michael J. Bosia, and Marie-Josée Massicotte, 3–19. Toronto: University of Toronto Press.

———. 2014b. "Food Sovereignty and Globalization: Lines of Inquiry." In *Globalization and Food Sovereignty: Global and Local Change in the New Politics of Food,* edited by Peter

References

Andrée, Jeffrey Ayres, Michael J. Bosia, and Marie-Josée Massicotte, 23–52. Toronto: University of Toronto Press.

Andrée, Peter, Jeffrey Ayres, Michael J. Bosia, and Marie-Josée Massicotte, eds. 2014. *Globalization and Food Sovereignty: Global and Local Change in the New Politics of Food.* Toronto: University of Toronto Press.

Andrews, Deborah. 2017. "Race, Status, and Biodiversity: The Social Climbing of Quinoa." *Culture, Agriculture, Food and Environment* 39, no. 1 (June): 15–24.

Angeli, Viktória, Pedro Miguel Silva, Danilo Crispim Massuela, Muhammad Waleed Khan, Alicia Hamar, Forough Khajehei, Simone Graeff-Hönninger, and Cinzia Piatti. 2020. "Quinoa (*Chenopodium Quinoa* Willd.): An Overview of the Potentials of the 'Golden Grain' and Socio-Economic and Environmental Aspects of Its Cultivation and Marketization." *Foods* 9, no. 2: 216. https://doi.org/10.3390/foods9020216.

Aragon, Lorraine. 2011. "Where Commons Meet Commerce: Circulation and Sequestration Strategies in Indonesian Arts Economies." *Anthropology of Work Review* 32 (2): 63–76.

Aubrey, Allison, and Robin Young. 2013. "Busting the Quinoa Myth." *Here and Now.* Aired July 17, 2013, on National Public Radio, Washington, DC. https://www.wbur.org/hereandnow/2013/07/17/busting-quinoa-myth.

Babb, Florence. 2011. *The Tourism Encounter: Fashioning Latin American Nations and Histories.* Stanford: Stanford University Press.

———. 2018. *Women's Place in the Andes: Engaging Decolonial Feminist Anthropology.* Berkeley: University of California Press.

Baca Tupayachi, Epifanio. 1983. *Cuzco: Sistemas viales, articulación y desarrollo regional.* Cusco: Centro de Estudios Rurales "Bartolomé de Las Casas."

Bazile, Didier. 2015. *Le Quinoa: Les Enjeux d'une Conquete.* Paris: Editions Quae, Collection Essais.

Bazile, Didier, Sven-Erik Jacobsen, and Alexis Verniau. 2016, "The Global Expansion of Quinoa: Trends and Limits." *Frontiers in Plant Science* 7 (May): 1–7, article 622.

Bebbington, Anthony. 2004. "NGOs and Uneven Development: Geographies of Development Intervention." *Progress in Human Geography* 28 (6): 725–45.

Bellemare, Marc, Johanna Fajardo-Gonzalez, and Seth Gitter. 2018. "Foods and Fads: The Welfare Impacts of Rising Quinoa Prices: Evidence from Peru." *World Development* no. 112, 163–79.

Blythman, Joanna. 2013. "Can Vegans Stomach the Unpalatable Truth About Quinoa?" *The Guardian,* January 16, 2013. https://www.theguardian.com/commentisfree/2013/jan/16/vegans-stomach-unpalatable-truth-quinoa.

Bojanic, Alan. 2011. "Quinoa: An Ancient Crop to Contribute to World Food Security." In FAO, Regional Office for Latin America and the Caribbean. Rome, Italy. http://www.fao.org/3/aq287e/aq287e.pdf.

Bourdieu, Pierre. 1987. *Distinction: A Social Critique of the Judgment of Taste.* Translated by Richard Nice. Cambridge, MA: Harvard University Press.

Bourricaud, François. 1970. *Power and Society in Contemporary Peru.* Translated by Paul Stevenson. New York: Praeger.

References

Briceño, Franklin. 2021. "Quechua: eje de polémica entre gobierno y oposición en Perú." *San Diego Tribune* (Spanish version), August 26, 2021. https://www.sandiegounion tribune.com/en-espanol/noticias/story/2021-08-26.

Brush, Stephen. 2004. *Farmers' Bounty: Locating Crop Diversity in the Contemporary World.* New Haven: Yale University Press.

Brysk, Alison. 1996. "Turning Weakness into Strength: The Internationalization of Indian Rights." *Latin American Perspectives*, 23, no. 2 (Spring): 38–57.

Burneo, María Luisa. 2012. "Elementos para Volver a Pensar lo *Comunal*: Nuevas Formas de Acceso a la Tierra y Presión Sobre el Recurso en las Comunidades Campesinas de Colán y Catacaos." *Anthropológica* 31 (31): 15–41.

Burt, Jo-Marie. 2007. *Political Violence and the Authoritarian State in Peru: Silencing Civil Society.* New York: Palgrave Macmillan.

Caballero, José María. 1981. *Economía Agraria de la Sierra Peruana antes de la Reforma Agraria de 1969.* Lima: Instituto de Estudios Peruanos.

Caballero, José María, and Elena Alvarez. 1980. *Aspectos Cuantitativos de la Reforma Agraria (1969–1979).* Lima: Instituto de Estudios Peruanos.

Cabellos, Ernesto. 2009. *De Ollas y Sueños: Cooking Up Dreams.* Lima: Cuarango cine y Video.

Cánepa, Gisela. 2013. "Nation Branding: The Re-Foundation of Community, Citizenship and the State in the Context of Neoliberalism in Perú." *MedienJournal* 37 (3): 7–18.

Cant, Anna. 2021. *Land without Masters: Agrarian Reform and Political Change under Peru's Military Government.* Austin: University of Texas Press.

Carlos, Jonathan. 2018. "Qali Warma Articula Acciones para Identificar Nuevos Productos Regionales." *El Sol* (Cusco, Peru), July 17, 2018, 6.

Chao, Sophie. 2018. "In the Shadow of the Palm: Dispersed Ontologies among Marind, West Papua." *Cultural Anthropology* 33 (4): 621–49.

Collins, Jane. 1988. *Unseasonal Migration: The Effects of Labor Scarcity in Peru.* Princeton, NJ: Princeton University Press.

Conociéndote Huanoquite Linda Tierra. n.d. Facebook page. https://www.facebook .com/huanoquite.tierralinda. Accessed April 30, 2020.

CooperAcción. n.d. "Paruro, Mapa de concesiones mineras en la provincia de Paruro, Cusco, al mes de noviembre del año 2016." Accessed August 30, 2021. https://cooperaccion .org.pe/mapas/.

Corr, Rachel. 2010. *Ritual and Remembrance in the Ecuadorian Andes.* Tucson: University of Arizona Press.

Cotler, Julio. 2013. *Clases, Estado y Nación.* Lima: Instituto de Estudios Peruanos. First published in 1978.

Darnell, Regna. 2020. "Walking alongside Wisahketchak: Fieldwork, a Retrospective Exercise That Takes a Long Time." *Journal of Anthropological Research* 76, no. 1 (Spring): 44–58.

Davies, Thomas, ed. 2019. *Routledge Handbook of NGOs and International Relations.* London: Routledge.

References

Degregori, Carlos Ivan. 2012. *How Difficult It is To Be God: Shining Path's Politics of War in Peru, 1980–1999*. Translated by Joanna Drzewieniecki, Nancy Appelbaum, and Héctor Flores. Madison: University of Wisconsin Press.

De la Cadena, Marisol. 1995. "'Women Are More Indian': Ethnicity and Gender in a Community near Cuzco." In *Ethnicity, Markets, and Migration in the Andes: At the Crossroads of History and Anthropology*, edited by Brooke Larson, Olivia Harris, and Enrique Tandeter, 329–48. Durham, NC: Duke University Press.

———. 2000. *Indigenous Mestizos: The Politics of Race and Culture in Cuzco, Peru, 1919–1991*. Durham, NC: Duke University Press.

———. 2004. "Commentary on 'Agricultural Hybridity and the "Pathology" of Traditional Ways . . .' by Chris J. Shepherd: The Challenges of Translation Analysis for the Ethnography of Development." *Journal of Latin American Anthropology* 9 (2): 278–83.

———. 2010. "Indigenous Cosmopolitics in the Andes: Conceptual Reflections beyond 'Politics.'" *Cultural Anthropology* 25, no. 2 (May): 334–70.

———. 2015. *Earth Beings: Ecologies of Practice Across Andean Worlds*. Durham, NC: Duke University Press.

Diez Hurtado, Alejandro, and Santiago Ortiz. 2013. "Comunidades Campesinas: Nuevos Contextos, Nuevos Procesos." *Antropológica* 31 (31): 5–14.

Dobkin, Leah. 2008. "Quinoa Comeback." *Americas* 60, no. 5 (October): 28–37.

Dobyns, Henry, Doughty, Paul, and Harold Lasswell, eds. 1971. *Peasants, Power, and Applied Social Change: Vicos as a Model*. London: Sage.

Douglas, Mary. 1972. "Deciphering a Meal: Myth, Symbol, and Culture." *Daedalus* 101 (1): 61–81.

Durston, Alan, and Bruce Mannheim, eds. 2018. *Indigenous Languages, Politics, and Authority in Latin America: Historical and Ethnographic Perspectives*. South Bend, IN: University of Notre Dame Press.

Edelman, Marc. 2014. "Food Sovereignty: Forgotten Genealogies and Future Regulatory Challenges." *Journal of Peasant Studies* 41 (6): 959–78.

Edelman, Marc, and Angelique Haugerud, eds. 2005. *The Anthropology of Development and Globalization: From Classical Political Economy to Contemporary Neoliberalism*. Malden, MA: Blackwell.

Edelman, Marc, James C. Scott, Amita Baviskar, Saturnino M. Borras Jr., Eric Holt-Giménez, Deniz Kandiyoti, Tony Weis, and Wendy Wolford, eds. 2016. *Critical Perspectives on Food Sovereignty: Global Agrarian Transformations*. Vol. 2. London: Routledge.

Egurén, Fernando. 2004. "Las Políticas Agrarias en la Última Década: Una Evaluación." In *Perú: El Problema Agrario en Debate*, edited by María Isabel Remy, Fernando Egurén, and Patricia Oliart, 19–78. Lima: SEPIA (Seminario Permanente de Investigación Agraria) X.

Egurén, Fernando, María Isabel Remy, and Patricia Oliart, eds. 2004. *Perú: El Problema Agrario en Debate*. Lima: SEPIA (Seminario Permanente de Investigación Agraria) X.

Estrada Zúñiga, Rigoberto. 2013. *Cultivo de Quinua (Chenopodium Quinoa Willd.) en la Región Cusco*. Cusco: Programa Nacional de Innovación Agraria en Cultivos Andinos del Instituto Nacional de Inovación Agraria.

References

Fine-Dare, Kathleen S. 2020. *Urban Mountain Beings: History, Indigeneity, and Geographies of Time in Quito, Ecuador*. Lanham, MD: Lexington Books.

Fischer, Edward F., and Peter Benson. 2006. *Broccoli and Desire: Global Connections and Maya Struggles in Postwar Guatemala*. Stanford, CA: Stanford University Press.

Fitz-Henry, Erin. 2019. "Water Rights, Extractive Resources, and Petroleum Politics." In *The Andean World*, edited by Linda J. Seligmann and Kathleen S. Fine-Dare, 664–78. New York: Routledge.

Fraser, Nancy. 1992. "Rethinking the Public Sphere: A Contribution to the Critique of Actually Existing Democracy." In *Habermas and the Public Sphere*, edited by Craig Calhoun, 109–42. Cambridge, MA: MIT Press.

Friedman, Jonathan, and Kajsa Ekholm Friedman. 2013. "Globalization as a Discourse of Hegemonic Crisis: A Global Systemic Analysis." *American Ethnologist* 40, no. 2 (May): 244–57.

Gamarra, Luis Felipe. 2013. "Quinoa." PROMPERÚ. Accessed January 7, 2021. https://www.siicex.gob.pe/siicex/resources/sectoresproductivos/Folleto_quinua_Ingles.pdf.

Gamwell, Adam, and Corinna Howland. 2017. "Cooking Up an International Market for Quinoa." *Sapiens*. August 16, 2017. https://www.sapiens.org/culture/cooking-international-market-quinoa/.

García, María Elena. 2005. *Making Indigenous Citizens: Identities, Education, and Multicultural Development in Peru*. Stanford, CA: Stanford University Press.

———. 2013. "The Taste of Conquest: Colonialism, Cosmopolitics, and the Dark Side of Peru's Gastronomic Boom." *Journal of Latin American and Caribbean Anthropology* 18 (3): 505–24.

———. 2015. "Love, Death, Food, and Other Ghost Stories: Hauntings of Intimacy and Violence in Contemporary Peru." In *Economies of Death: Economic Logics of Killable Life and Grievable Death*, edited by Kathryn Gillespie and Patricia Lopez, 160–78. New York: Routledge.

———. 2021. *Gastropolitics and the Specter of Race: Stories of Capital, Culture, and Coloniality in Peru*. Berkeley: University of California Press.

Goldbeck, Nicki, and David Goldbeck. 1989. Foreword to *Quinoa, the Supergrain: Ancient Food for Today*, by Rebecca Wood, 15–16. Tokyo: Japan Publications.

Goldstein, Daniel M. 2012. *Outlawed: Between Security and Rights in a Bolivian City*. Durham, NC: Duke University Press.

González Holguín, Diego. (1608) 1952. *Vocabulario de la Lengua General de Todo el Perú Llamado Lengua Qquichua*. Lima: Instituto de Historia, Universidad Nacional de San Marcos.

Gorriti, Gustavo. 1999. *The Shining Path: A History of the Millenarian War in Peru*. Translated with an introduction by Robin Kirk. Chapel Hill: University of North Carolina Press. First published in Spanish in 1990.

Gose, Peter. 1994. *Deathly Waters and Hungry Mountains*. Toronto: University of Toronto Press.

———. 2011. Foreword to *An Ethnography of Feeding, Perception, and Place in the Peruvian Andes (Where Hungry Spirits Bring Illness and Wellbeing)* by Marieka Sax, i–xi. Lewiston, NY: Edwin Mellen Press.

References

Graham, Laura. 2002. "How Should an Indian Speak? Amazonian Indians and the Symbolic Politics of Language in the Global Public Sphere." In *Indigenous Movements, Self-Representation, and the State in Latin America,* edited by Kay B. Warren and Jean E. Jackson, 181–228. Austin: University of Texas Press.

Grey, Sam, and Raj Patel. 2015. "Food Sovereignty as Decolonization: Some Contributions from Indigenous Movements to Food System and Development Politics." *Agriculture and Human Values* no. 32: 431–44.

Guillet, David. 1979. *Agrarian Reform and Peasant Economy in Southern Peru.* Columbia: University of Missouri Press.

Habermas, Jürgen. 1989. *The Structural Transformation of the Public Sphere: An Inquiry into a Category of Bourgeois Society.* Translated by Thomas Burger, with assistance from Frederick Lawrence. Cambridge: Polity. First published in 1962.

Hale, Charles, and Lynn Stephen, eds. 1995. *Otros Saberes: Collaborative Research on Indigenous and Afro-descendent Cultural Politics.* Santa Fe, NM: School for Advanced Research.

Hall, Amy Cox. 2019. "Savoring Nostalgia: Food and the Past in Peru's 'La Casa de Don Cucho.'" *Anthropology of Food* no. 14: 1–22.

Harvey, Penny, and Hannah Knox. 2015. *Roads.* Ithaca, NY: Cornell University Press.

Hetherington, Kregg. 2020. *The Government of Beans: Regulating Life in the Age of Monocrops.* Durham, NC: Duke University Press.

Hirsch, Eric M. 2022. *Acts of Growth: Development and the Politics of Abundance in Peru.* Stanford, CA: Stanford University Press.

Hirsch, Eric M., and Kyle Jones. 2019. "Hip Hop and Guinea Pigs: Contextualizing the Urban Andes." In *The Andean World,* edited by Linda J. Seligmann and Kathleen S. Fine-Dare, 555–70. London: Routledge.

Huayhua, Margarita. 2010. "*Runama Kani Icha Alquchu?*: Everyday Discrimination in the Southern Andes." PhD diss., University of Michigan-Ann Arbor.

———. 2014. "Racism and Social Interaction in a Southern Peruvian *Combi.*" *Ethnic and Racial Studies* 37, no. 13 (December): 2399–417.

Ilizarbe, Carmen. 2019. "Intercultural Disagreement: Implementing the Right to Prior Consultation in Peru." *Latin American Perspectives* 46 (5): 143–57.

INDECOPI (National Institute for the Defense of Competition and the Protection of Intellectual Property) and PROMPERÚ. 2020. "Project on 'Intellectual property and gastronomic tourism in Peru and other developing countries: Promoting the development of gastronomic tourism through intellectual property': Scoping Study." https://www.wipo.int/export/sites/www/ip-development/en/agenda/pdf/scoping_study.pdf.

INEI (Instituto Nacional de Estadística e Informática). 2017. "Peru Census." http://censo2017.inei.gob.pe/resultados-definitivos-de-las-comunidades-nativas-y-campesinas-2017/.

———. 2009. "Censo de Población y Vivienda, 2007, Mapa de Desnutrición Crónica en Niños Menores de Cinco Años a Nivel Provincial y Distrital." https://www.exemplars.health/-/media/files/egh/resources/stunting/peru/part-2/map-of-chronic-malnutrition-in-children-under-five-at-the-provincial-and-district-levels-2007.pdf.

References

INIA (Instituto Nacional de Inovación Agraria). 2012. *Ley General de Semillas; Reglamento de la Ley General de Semillas.* Lima: Programa Nacional de Medios y Comunicación Técnica.

Jackson, Jean. 2019. *Managing Multiculturalism: Indigeneity and the Struggle for Rights in Colombia.* Stanford, CA: Stanford University Press.

Jacobsen, Sven-Erik. 2003. "The Worldwide Potential for Quinoa (*Chenopodium Quinoa* Willd.)." *Food Reviews International* 19 (1/2): 167–77.

———. 2011. "The Situation for Quinoa and Its Production in Southern Bolivia: From Economic Success to Environmental Disaster." *Journal of Agronomy and Crop Science* 197, no. 5 (May): 390–99.

Josephson, Kimberly, Gabriela Guerrero, and Catherine Coddington. 2017. *Supporting the Early Childhood Workforce at Scale: The Cuna Más Home Visiting Program in Peru.* Results for Development Institute. June 1, 2017. https://www.r4d.org/wp-content/uploads/Full-report-Cuna-Mas-country-study.pdf.

Kerssen, Tanya. 2015. "Food Sovereignty and the Quinoa Boom: Challenges to Sustainable Re-Peasantisation in the Southern Altiplano of Bolivia." *Third World Quarterly* 36 (3): 489–507.

Kimura, Aya Hirata. 2013. *Hidden Hunger: Gender and the Politics of Smarter Food.* Ithaca, NY: Cornell University Press.

Klarén, Peter. 2017. *Historical Dictionary of Peru.* Lanham, MD: Rowman and Littlefield.

Krögel, Alison. 2010. *Food, Power, and Resistance in the Andes: Exploring Quechua Verbal and Visual Narratives.* Lanham, MD: Lexington Books.

Laguna, Pablo. 2011. "Mallas y Flujos: Acción Colectiva, Cambio Social, Quinua y Desarrollo Regional Indígena en los Andes Bolivianos." PhD diss., Wageningen University, the Netherlands.

Lamphere, Louise. 2020. "Omissions and Silences in My Navajo Fieldwork: From Kinship Studies to Gendered Life Histories." *Journal of Anthropological Research* 76 (1): 59–73.

Larson, Brooke, and Olivia Harris, eds. 1995. *Ethnicity, Markets, and Migration in the Andes: At the Crossroads of History and Anthropology.* With Enrique Tandeter. Durham, NC: Duke University Press.

Lassiter, L. E. 2005. *The Chicago Guide to Collaborative Ethnography.* Chicago: University of Chicago Press.

Linebaugh, Peter, and Marcus Rediker. 2000. *The Many-Headed Hydra: Sailors, Slaves, Commoners, and the Hidden History of the Revolutionary Atlantic.* Boston: Beacon Press.

Lira, José A. 1982. *Diccionario Kkechuwa-Español.* 2nd ed. Bogota: SECAB/Instituto Internacional de Integración/Instituto Andino de Artes Populares.

Low, Setha, and Sally Merry. 2010. "Engaged Anthropology: Diversity and Dilemmas, An Introduction to Supplement 2." *Current Anthropology* 51, supplement 2 (October): S203–26.

Mannheim, Bruce. 1991. *The Language of the Inka Since the European Invasion.* Austin: University of Texas Press.

Marapi, Ricardo. 2013. "Radiografía de las Políticas de Seguridad Alimentaria." *La Revista Agraria* no. 152 (June): 12–13.

References

Markowitz, Lisa. 2019. "Making and Unmaking the Andean Food Pyramid: Agronomy, Animal Science, and Ideology." In *The Andean World*, edited by Linda J. Seligmann and Kathleen S. Fine-Dare, 205–18. London: Routledge.

Martínez, Luz Alexandra. 2015. "Seeds, Networks and Politics: Different Ontologies in Relation to Food Sovereignty in Ecuador." PhD diss., Wageningen University, the Netherlands.

Matos Mar, José, and José Manuel Mejía. 1980. *La Reforma Agraria en el Perú*. Lima: Instituto de Estudios Peruanos.

Matta, Raúl. 2019. "La Revolución Gastronómica Peruana: Una Celebración de lo Nacional." Entrevista a Mirko Lauer. *Anthropology of Food* no. 14. https://doi.org/10.4000/aof.9982.

Matta, Raúl, and María Elena García. 2019. "The Gastro-Political Turn in Peru." *Anthropology of Food* no. 14. https://doi.org/10.4000/aof.10061.

Mayer, Enrique. 2009. *Ugly Stories of the Peruvian Agrarian Reform*. Durham, NC: Duke University Press.

McDonell, Emma. 2015. "Miracle Foods: Quinoa, Curative Metaphors, and the Depoliticization of Global Hunger Politics." *Gastronomica: The Journal of Critical Food Studies* 15 (4): 70–85.

McMichael, Philip. 2009. "A Food Regime Geneology." *Journal of Peasant Studies* 36 (1): 139–69.

———. 2020. "Does China's 'Going Out' Strategy Prefigure a New Food Regime?" *Journal of Peasant Studies* 47 (1): 116–54.

Mehdi, Chergui, and Hirich Abdelaziz. 2018. "Analysis of International Market of Quinoa-Based Products." Poster at Conference presented at the Managing Water Scarcity in River Basins: Innovation and Sustainable Development. Agadir, Morocco, October 6, 2018. https://www.researchgate.net/publication/328568285_Analysis_of_International _Market_of_Quinoa_based_products.

MINAGRI (Ministerio de Agricultura y Riego). 2014. "Quinua: Un futuro sembrado hace miles de años. Memoria del Año Internacional de la Quinua en el Perú." https://www.midagri .gob.pe/portal/download/pdf/cquinua/libro_anho_internacional_de_la_quinua _2013.pdf.

———. 2015. "Titulación agraria en el Perú." http://minagri.gob.pe/portal/datero/69 -marco-legal/titulacion-y-creditos/409-titulacion-agraria-en-el-peru.

Ministerio de Energía y Minas, Peru. 1997. "Ley de Areas Naturales Protegidas, Ley No. 26834." https://www.minem.gob.pe/minem/archivos/file/DGGAE/DGGAE/ ARCHIVOS/legislacion/LEGISLACION%202017/normas%20ambientales%20 transversales/AREAS%20PROTEGIDAS/1.%20LEY%2026834.pdf.

———. 2001. "Reglamento de la Ley de Áreas Naturales Protegidos, Decreto Supremo No. 038–2001-AG." https://www.minem.gob.pe/minem/archivos/file/DGGAE/ ARCHIVOS/2_%20DS%20038–2001-AG.pdf.

Ministerio de Transportes y Comunicaciones. 2017. "Mapa Vial Cusco." July 2017. Lima: Dirección General de Caminos y Ferrocarriles, Dirección de Caminos.

References

Mintz, Sidney. 1986. *Sweetness and Power: The Place of Sugar in Modern History*. New York: Penguin.

Mintzer, Miguel J. 1933. "Las Quinoas su cultivo en la Argentina su importancia como planta alimenticia." *Boletin Mensual Ministerio Agricultura de la Nacion* 34 (1): 59–77.

Mitchell, William P. 2020. "Priming Ethnography: The Theoretical and Largely Unconscious Guides Structuring More Than Half a Century of Andean Research." *Journal of Anthropological Research* 76 (1): 74–89.

Montoya Restrepo, Luz Alexandra, Lucero Martínez Vianchá, and Johanna Peralta Ballestero. 2005. "Análisis de las Variables Estratégicas para la Conformación de una Cadena Productiva de la Quinua en Colombia." *Innovar, Revista de Ciencias Administrativas y Sociales* 25, no. 1 (June): 103–20.

Mujica, Ángel, Manuel Squilanda, Ernesto Chura, Enrique Ruiz, Alicia Leon, Sabino Cutipa, and Corina Ponce. 2013. *Organic Quinoa Production (Chenopodium quinoa)*. Puno, Peru: Universidad Nacional del Altiplano.

Multiple Organics. 2020. "Organic Quinoa, Organic Quinoa Flakes, Organic Quinoa (Red), Organic Quinoa (Tri-Color)." https://www.multipleorganics.com/products.

Nicholson, Paul. 2013. "La Via Campesina: The Revolt of the Peasants [Commentary]." *World Nutrition* 4 (2): 58–87.

Nuñez Palomino, Pedro Germán. 1995. *Law and Peasant Communities in Peru*. PhD diss., Wageningen University, the Netherlands.

OCM (Observatorio de Conflictos Minéros en el Perú). 2019. OCM, CooperAcción, Fedepaz, Grufides, January 1, 2019. http://conflictosmineros.org.pe/wp-content/uploads/2019/07/Revista-Informe-de-Conflictos-Mineros-24.pdf.

Ofstehage, Andrew. 2011. "Nusta Juira's Gift of Quinoa: Peasants, Trademarks, and Intermediaries in the Transformation of a Bolivian Commodity Economy." *Anthropology of Work Review* 32 (2): 103–14.

Organización Internacional del Trabajo. 2015. "Análisis de la cadena de valor en el sector de la quinua en Perú: aprovechando las ganancias de un mercado crediente a favor de los pobres." International Labor Organization. https://www.ilo.org/wcmsp5/groups/public/--ed_emp/--emp_ent/--ifp_seed/documents/publication/wcms_706800.pdf.

Orlove, Benjamin S. 1998. "Down to Earth: Race and Substance in the Andes." *Bulletin of Latin American Research* 17 (2): 207–22.

Orta, Andrew. 2004. *Catechizing Culture: Missionaries, Aymaras, and the "New Evangelization."* New York: Columbia University Press.

Otero, Gerardo, Gabriela Pechlaner, and Efe Can Gúrcan. 2013. "The Political Economy of 'Food Security': Uneven and Combined Dependency." *Rural Sociology* 78 (2): 263–89.

Pajuelo Teves, Ramón. 2019. *Trayectorias Comunales: Cambios y Continuidades en Comunidades Camepsinas e Indígenas del Sur Andino*. Lima: Grupo Propuesta Ciudadana.

Palmer, Scott, ed. 1992. *The Shining Path of Peru*. New York: St. Martin's.

Pérez, Patricia, dir. 2011. *Mistura: The Power of Food*. Lima: Chiwake Films.

References

Pilgrim, Sarah, and Jules Pretty. 2010. "Nature and Culture: An Introduction." In *Nature and Culture: Rebuilding Lost Connections*, edited by Sarah Pilgrim and Jules Pretty, 1–20. London: Taylor and Francis.

Pinedo-Taco, Rember, Gómez-Pando, Luz Rayda, and Alberto Julca-Otiniano. 2020. "Sostenabilidad ambiental de la producción de quinua (*Chenopodium quinoa* Willd.) en los valles interandinos del Perú." *Ciencia y Tecnología Agropecuaria* 21 (3): 1–17. DOI: https://doi.org/10.21930/rcta.vol21_num3_art:1309.

Poole, Deborah. 2004. "Between Threat and Guarantee: Justice and Community in the Margins of the Peruvian State." In *Anthropology in the Margins of the State*, edited by Veena Das and Deborah Poole, 35–66. Santa Fe, NM: School for Advanced Research.

Poole, Deborah, and Gerardo Rénique. 1991. "The New Chroniclers of Peru: U.S. Scholars and Their 'Shining Path' of Peasant Rebellion." *Bulletin of Latin American Research* 10 (2): 133–91.

Powęska, Radoslaw. 2017. "Indigenous Rights in the Era of 'Indigenous State': How Interethnic Conflicts and State Appropriation of Indigenous Agenda Hinder the Challenge to Extractivism in Bolivia. In *Natural Resource Development and Human Rights in Latin America: State and Non-State Actors in the Promotion and Opposition to Extractivism*, edited by Malayna Raftopoulos and Radoslaw Powęska, 27–58. London: School of Advanced Study, University of London.

PROMPERÚ. 2012. "Aprendiendo a exportar paso a paso (1era parte)." Lima: Departamento de Asesoría Empresarial y Capacitación, PROMPERÚ. pp. 108–13, February 2012.

———. 2018a. "SuperA Perú: Promoción de la exportación certificada de los súper alimentos quinua y castaña." May 15, 2018. https://www.mancomunidadregionaldelosandes.gob.pe/assets/ppt-proyecto-quinua.pdf.

———. 2018b. "Perú: mayor productor y exportador de quinua." August 5, 2018. https://peru.info/es-pe/gastronomia/noticias/2/12/peru--mayor-productor-y-exportador-de-quinua.

———. 2020a. "Informe de transferencia de gestión (19 de dic.-15 de julio 2020)." http://transparencia.mincetur.gob.pe/institucional/transferencia_gestion/PROMPERU/Informe_Transferencia_Gestion_PROMPERU_ReporteCumplimientoMisional.pdf.

———. 2020b. "Expo Perú Los Andes 2020 impulsa superalimentos y cafés peruanos en cuatro continentes." https://www.gob.pe/institucion/promperu/noticias/321412-expo-peru-los-andes-2020-impulsa-superalimentos-y-cafes-peruanos-en-cuatro-continentes.

Quijano, Anibal. 1980. *Dominación y Cultura: Lo Cholo y el Conflicto en el Perú*. Lima: Mosca Azul Editores.

Radcliffe, Sarah. 2015. *Dilemmas of Difference: Indigenous Women and the Limits of Postcolonial Development Policy*. Durham, NC: Duke University Press.

Rappaport, Joanne. 2017. "Rethinking the Meaning of Research in Collaborative Relationships." *Collaborative Anthropologies* no. 9: 1–31.

Regaño Florez, Johana, and Judy Valencia Peña. 2018. *Costos de Producción de la Quinua Orgánica—Caso Cooperativo de Productores de Granos Andinos Orgánicos, Huanoquite-Paruro-Periodo 2016*. Bachelor's thesis, Facultad de Ciencias Económicas, Administra-

References

tivas y Contables, Escuela Profesional de Contabilidad, Cusco, Universidad Andina del Cusco.

Reichman, Daniel. 2018. "Big Coffee in Brazil: Historical Origins and Implications for Anthropological Political Economy." *Journal of Latin American and Caribbean Anthropology* 23 (2): 241–61.

Remy, María Isabel. 2013. *Historia de las Comunidades Indígenas y Campesinas del Perú*. Lima: Instituto de Estudios Peruanos.

Rivera Andía, Juan Javier. 2019. "The Silent 'Cosmopolitics' of Artefacts: Spectral Extractivism, Ownership and 'Obedient' Things." In *Indigenous Life Projects and Extractivism: Approaches to Social Inequality and Difference*, edited by Juan Javier Rivera Andía and Cecilie Vindal Ødegaard, 165–193. London: Palgrave Macmillan.

Rivera Andía, Juan Javier, and Cecilie Vindal Ødegaard. 2019. "Introduction: Indigenous Peoples, Extractivism, and Turbulences in South America." In *Indigenous Life Projects and Extractivism: Ethnographies from South America*, edited by Juan Javier Rivera Andía and Cecilie Vindal Ødegaard, 1–50. London: Palgrave Macmillan.

Rojas, Wilfredo, Milton Pinto, Carolina Alanoca, Luz GómezPando, Pedro León-Lobos, Adriana Alercia, Stefano Diulgheroff, Stefano Padulosi, and Didier Bazile. 2015. "Quinoa Genetic Resources and *ex Situ* Conservation." In *State of the Art Report on Quinoa Around the World 2013*, edited by Daniel Bertero, Didier Bazile, and Carlos Nieto, 56–82. Rome: FAO; CIRAD.

Rojas-Pérez, Isaias. 2017. *Mourning Remains: State Atrocity, Exhumations, and Governing the Disappeared in Peru's Postwar Andes*. Stanford, CA: Stanford University Press, 2017.

Salas Carreño, Guillermo. 2016. "Places Are Kin: Cohabitation and Sociality in the Southern Peruvian Andes." *Anthropological Quarterly* 89 (3): 813–40.

———. 2017. "Mining and the Living Materiality of Mountains in Andean Society." *Journal of Material Culture* 22 (2): 133–50.

———. 2019. *Lugares Parientes: Comida, Cohabitación y Mundos Andinos*. Lima: Pontificia Universidad Católica del Perú.

Salas Carreño, Guillermo, and Alejandro Diez Hurtado. 2017. "Estado, Concesiones Mineras y Comuneros: Los Múltiples Conflictos alrededor de la Minería en las Inmediaciones del Santuario de Qoyllur Rit'i." *Colombia Internacional (Cusco)* no. 93: 65–91.

Sammells, Clare. 2019. "Reimagining Bolivian Cuisine: Haute Traditional Food and Its Discontents." *Food and Foodways* 27 (4): 338–52.

Sax, Marieka. 2011. *An Ethnography of Feeding, Perception, and Place in the Peruvian Andes (Where Hungry Spirits Bring Illness and Wellbeing)*. Lewiston, NY: Edwin Mellen.

Seligmann, Linda J. 1987. "The Chicken in Andean History and Myth: The Quechua Concept of *Wallpa*." *Ethnohistory* 34 (2):139–170.

———. 1989. "To Be in Between: The *Cholas* as Market Women." *Comparative Studies in Society and History* 31 (4): 694–721.

———. 1993. "The Burden of Visions amidst Reform: Peasant Relations to Law in the Peruvian Andes." *American Ethnologist* 20 (1): 25–51.

References

————. 1995. *Between Reform and Revolution: Political Struggles in the Peruvian Andes, 1969–1991*. Stanford, CA: Stanford University Press.

————. 1999. "Systems of Knowledge and Authority in the Huanoquite Landscape." *Journal of the Steward Anthropological Society (Special Issue, Studies Presented to Reiner Tom Zuidema on the Occasion of His Retirement)* 25 (2): 27–55.

————. 2003. "Civil War in Peru: Culture and Violence in Historical Perspective." In *The State, Identity and Violence: Political Disintegration in the Post-Cold War World*, edited by R. Brian Ferguson, 117–48. London and New York: Routledge.

————. 2008. "Agrarian Reform and Peasant Studies: The Peruvian Case." In *A Companion to Latin American Anthropology*, edited by Deborah Poole, 325–51. Oxford: Blackwell Publishing.

Seligmann, Linda J., and Stephen G. Bunker. 1994. "An Andean Irrigation System: Ecological Visions and Social Organization." In *Irrigation at High Altitudes: The Social Organization of Water Control Systems in the Andes*, edited by David Guillet and William Mitchell, 203–32. Washington, DC: American Anthropological Association.

Shepherd, Christopher J. 2000. "Mixing oil and water: agricultural development in the Andes." PhD diss., University of Melbourne.

————. 2010. "Mobilizing Local Knowledge and Asserting Culture: The Cultural Politics of In Situ Conservation of Agricultural Biodiversity." *Current Anthropology* 51 (5): 629–54.

Skarbø, Kristine. 2015. "From Lost Crop to Lucrative Commodity: Conservation Implications of the Quinoa Renaissance." *Human Organization* 74 (1): 86–99.

Solano, Pedro. 2009. *Legal Framework for Protected Areas: Peru*. IUCN (International Union for Conservation of Nature)-EPLP (Environmental Law Program of Peru), no. 81. https://www.iucn.org/downloads/peru_en.pdf.

Starn, Orin. 1999. *Nightwatch: The Politics of Protest in the Andes*. Durham, NC: Duke University Press.

Statista Research Department. 2018. "Quinoa Imports of the U.S., from 2013–2018." August 30, 2018. https://www-statista-com.mutex.gmu.edu/statistics/486411/us-quinoa-imports/.

————. 2019a. "U.S. Quinoa Import Value, by Country of Origin." November 28, 2019. https://www-statista-com.mutex.gmu.edu/statistics/520873/us-quinoa-import-value-by-country-of-origin/.

————. 2019b. "U.S. Quinoa Import Volume, 2018, by Country of Origin." November 28, 2019. https://www-statista-com.mutex.gmu.edu/statistics/520857/us-quinoa-import-volume-by-country-of-origin/.

Stein, William. 2003. *Deconstructing Development Discourse in Peru: A Meta-ethnography of the Modernity Project at Vicos*. Landman, MD: University Press of America.

Stengers, Isabelle. 2010. *Cosmopolitics I*. Translated by Robert Bononno. Minneapolis: University of Minnesota Press.

Stensrud, Astrid B. 2019. "Safe Milk and Risky Quinoa: The Lottery and Precarity of Farming in Peru." *Focaal, Journal of Global and Historical Anthropology* no. 83: 72–84.

References

Stern, Steve, ed. 1998. *Shining and Other Paths: War and Society in Peru, 1980–1995.* Durham, NC: Duke University Press.

Tapia Vargas, Gualberto. 1976. *La Quinua: Un Cultivo de los Andes Altos.* La Paz, Bolivia: Academia Nacional de Ciencias.

Trauger, Amy. 2014. "Toward a Political Geography of Food Sovereignty: Transforming Territory, Exchange and Power in the Liberal Sovereign State." *Journal of Peasant Studies* 41 (6): 113–52.

Trivelli, Carolina, Javier Escobal, and Bruno Revesz. 2009. *Desarrollo Rural en la Sierra: Aportes para el Debate.* Lima: CIPCA, Grade, IEP, and CIES.

Truth and Reconciliation Commission of Peru (Comisión de la Verdad y Reconciliación, CVR). 2001. "Introduction." https://www.usip.org/publications/2001/07/truth-commission-peru-01.

Tschopp, Maurice. 2018. "The Quinoa Boom and the Commoditisation Debate: Critical Reflections on the Re-Emergence of a Peasantry in the Southern Altiplano." *Alternautas (Re)Searching Development: The Abya Yala Chapter* (website). March 21, 2018. http://www.alternautas.net/blog/2018/3/21/the-quinoa-boom-and-the-commoditisation-debate-critical-reflections-on-the-re-emergence-of-a-peasantry-in-the-southern-altiplano.

University of Wisconsin, Division of Extension. 2022. "Quinoa" (website). February 7, 2022. http://corn.agronomy.wisc.edu/Crops/Quinoa.aspx.

Urdanivia, Claudia. 2014. "Andean Quinoa: Local Farmers in a Global Market." *Anthropology Now* 6 (2): 35–43.

Valdivia Romero, Melissa. 2021. "Apurímac: minibús de Las Bambas tomó ruta alterna por bloqueo de vía, volcó y dejó 17 muertos." *El Comercio* (website). August 28, 2021. https://elcomercio.pe/peru/.

Van der Ploeg, Jan D. 2014. "Peasant-Driven Agricultural Growth and Food Sovereignty." *Journal of Peasant Studies* 41 (6): 999–1030.

Wachtel, Nathan. 1994. *Gods and Vampires: Return to Chipaya.* Translated by Carol Volk. Chicago: University of Chicago Press.

Wade, Peter. 2010. *Race and Ethnicity in Latin America, 2nd ed.* New York: Pluto Press. First published in 1997.

Walsh-Dilley, Marygold. 2013. "Negotiating Hybridity in Highland Bolivia: Indigenous Moral Economy and the Expanding Market for Quinoa." *Journal of Peasant Studies* 40 (4): 659–82.

Weismantel, Mary. 1988. *Food, Gender, and Poverty in the Ecuadorian Andes.* Philadelphia: University of Pennsylvania Press.

———. 2001. *Cholas and Pishtacos: Stories of Race and Sex in the Andes.* Chicago: University of Chicago Press.

Wikipedia. 2020. "Chucky." https://en.wikipedia.org/wiki/Chucky_(character).

Winkel, Thierry, Daniel Bertero, Pierre Bommel, Jean Bourliaud, Marco Chevarría-Lazo, Geneviève Cortes, Pierre Gasselin, Sam Geerts, Richard Joffre, François Léger, B. Martinez Avisa, Serge Rambal, Gilles Rivière, Muriel Tichit, Jean-François Tourrand,

References

Anaïs. Vassas-Toral, Jean-Joinville Vacher, and Manuela Vieira Pak. 2012. "The Sustainability of Quinoa Production in Southern Bolivia: From Misrepresentations to Questionable Solutions. Comments on Jacobsen (2011)." *Journal of Agronomy and Crop Science* 198 (4): 314–19.

Wolf, Barney. 2017. "For Restaurants, Quinoa Is Just the Beginning." *QSR Magazine*, July 1, 2017. *Menu Innovations.* https://www.qsrmagazine.com/menu-innovations/restaurants-quinoa-just-beginning.

Wood, Rebecca Theurer. 1989. *Quinoa, The Super Grain: Ancient Food for Today.* Tokyo: Japan Publications (USA).

Yanacopulos, Helen. 2019. "International NGOs in Development Studies." Edited by Thomas Davies, 153–64. Oxford: Routledge.

Ypeij, Annelou. 2013. "Cholos, Incas y Fusionistas: El Nuevo Perú y la Globalización de lo Andino." *European Review of Latin American and Caribbean Studies* no. 94: 67–82.

Zimmerer, Karl. 1992. "The Loss and Maintenance of Native Crops in Mountain Agriculture." *GeoJournal* 27 (1): 61–72.

"Zonas Intangibles." 2001. https://www2.congreso.gob.pe/sicr/tradocestproc/clproley2001.nsf/pley/97C2E02DEF6C46B405256DEF0070175A?opendocument.

Index

Page numbers followed by an f indicate figures, t indicates tables, and m indicates maps.

Achino-Loeb, Maria-Luisa, 167n13
Acurio, Gaston, 138–140
Agency for International Development (AID), 173n6
agrarian reform (1969), 21–22, 31–35; cooperatives and, 32–36, 147, 176n7, 177n9; factors leading to, 31–32; landed estate owners and, 31–33, 90; uprisings and, 32
agrarian reform, reversals of, 34–42; land privatization and, 35–38; neoliberalism and, 38–42, 148; Peruvian civil war and, 34–35
agriculture, Huanoquite, 6; climate change and, 126–127; crop rotation in, 2, 36, 96, 98, 110; global market and, 141–143; kitchen gardens in, 68, 109; mining concessions and, 2, 145, 150; organic certification and, 82, 94–95, 98, 101, 112; production zones and, 10f, 36, 88; reversals of agrarian reform and, 35–38; scheduling of agricultural labor and, 41t. *See also* irrigation; labor par-

ties; new rurality; quinoa cultivation; women's labor
agrobiodiversity, 63, 111, 114–115; quinoa promotion and, 120, 132, 136, 147. *See also* food sovereignty; interculturality
Alarcón de Humala, Nadine Heredía, 4, 88, 92
Alarcón Urrutia, Richard Daniel, 49–50
Alexandra Martínez, Luz, 171n11
Allen, Catherine, 47, 171n6, 174n8
allin kawsachun ("Let Us Live Well"), 125. *See also* health of Huanoquiteños; reciprocity; well-being of Huanoquiteños
Alvarez, Elena, 31
Andean region geography. *See* geography of Andean region
Andrée, Peter, 14, 25
Andrews, Deborah, 15, 80, 103–104, 171n5, 172n1
Anta (province), 152–153, 157–158
Anthropology of Food (ed. Matta and García), 173n1
Aragon, Lorraine, 98
Aroni Peralta, Roy Wilson ("Father Roy"), 49–50, 168n5

Index

audit culture, 17, 62, 74

autonomy, 26–27; development and, 54–55, 62–64, 99; extraction and, 5, 148, 159, 164; moral discourses in, 12, 69–71, 160; pragmatic spirituality in, 17–19, 159–164; quinoa promotion and, 115–116, 137–138. *See also* cosmology

Aventura Culinaria (television show), 138

Babb, Florence, 73, 137, 169n1, 170n8

Las Bambas mines, 22, 48, 154, 168n3; politics and, 145–146, 169n8, 175n3

Bazile, Didier, 107

Belaunde Terry, Fernando, 34

Bellemare, Marc, 112, 172n5

Bellido, Guido, 175n15

Benson, Peter, 12

biopiracy, 106–108

Bojanic, Alan, 105, 135

Bolton, Ralph, 170n2

Bonett Béjar, Rolando, 90–93, 92*f*, 96, 113

borderland dwellers, 26, 52, 55, 163

Bourdieu, Pierre, 118

Bourricaud, François, 11

brokers, 5–6; export and, 95; Indigenous and non-Indigenous, 20, 90–92, 95, 171n8. *See also* Bonett Béjar, Rolando; landed estate owners

Brush, Stephen, 171n1

Brysk, Alison, 166n6

Bunker, Stephen, 58, 144, 151

Burneo, María Luisa, 38, 176n6

Burt, Jo-Marie, 167n2

Caballero, José María, 31

Cabellos, Ernesto, 139

del Cairo, Carlos, 141

Cánepa, Gisela, 173n1

Can Gúrcan, Efe, 172n4

Cant, Anna, 31

capitalism. *See* markets, global; neoliberalism

Castillo, Pedro, 175n15

Catholicism, 49–50, 165n1, 168n5, 174n9

Ccapi (province), 55, 145, 169n8

Certification of Denomination of Origin (CDO), 98, 171n12

Chao, Sophie, 18

chauffers' association in Huanoquite, 23, 48

chicha (beer), 80, 97n3, 122, 125, 128*f*, 133,

174n5; women's role in preparation of, 83, 84*f*, 171n6. *See also* labor parties

children's health. *See* health of Huanoquiteños

Chumbivilcas (province), 55, 145, 152–153, 158, 176n4

civil war. *See* Peruvian civil war (1980–1992)

colonialism, 6, 9, 31–32, 118–119, 151, 165n1; meanings associated with quinoa in, 80, 118, 171n5; quinoa production and, 79–80; road improvement and, 43–44, 168n1. *See also* Catholicism

Colwell, Chip, 174n11

Comedor Popular (development project), 59, 61

Commission for the Promotion of Peru for Export and Tourism (PROMPERÚ), 25–26, 111, 118, 174n12; promotional materials by, 120, 135–138, 143

Convention on Biological Diversity (CBD), 107–108

Cornell Vicos Project, 74, 170n8

corruption, 50–51, 68, 91–92, 146; brokers and, 92; land titling and, 39; patron-clientelism and, 50

cosmology, 24–25, 150–164; cryptids in, 154–157, 177n13; mines and mining concessions and, 151–154, 177n15; place meanings and, 133–134, 144, 150–153; power beings (*wacas*) in, 16–17, 125–126, 132, 144; pragmatic spirituality in, 17–19, 159–164; quinoa in, 119, 129, 132–134; sentient beings and, 16, 17–18, 132. *See also* autonomy; Huanoquite (district); quinoa, meanings associated with

cosmopolitics, 16–17, 33, 166n9. *See also* politics; pragmatic spirituality

Cotler, Julio, 11

COVID-19 pandemic, 53, 161, 169n7

credit, 37–38, 96, 114, 143, 161.

cryptids, 154–157, 177n13; *chuki*, 154–156; *pishtacos*, 156. *See also* cosmology

cultivator associations, 52, 88, 100–101, 130, 141. *See also* Quinoa Cultivators Association (QCA)

Cuna Más (development project), 59–60

Cusco, 12, 44, 138

Cusco, travel to. *See* roads and road improvement

Index

Cusco region. *See* geography of Andean region

Cusco Regional Government, 2, 47, 50–51, 109*f*; criticisms of, 55, 91–92, 96, 101, 154; quinoa boom and, 80, 82, 88–90, 99–100. *See also* development

Darnell, Regna, 167n13

Davies, Thomas, 169n1

decolonization, 73–74, 139, 149. *See also* colonialism; neoliberalism

Degregori, Carlos Ivan, 167n2

de la Cadena, Marisol, 11, 16–17, 115, 175n14

development, 11–12, 16, 56–74, 115–116; collective discourse and, 69–71; construction projects and, 52–53, 63; government programs, 59–63, 80, 112, 169n2, 170n5; grassroots initiatives, 23, 63–69, 73, 170n6; intangible zones and, 149–150; parastatal and NGO-led initiatives, 56–63. *See also* quinoa boom; quinoa marketing; quinoa promotion; women's labor, development and

disability activism, 69

Dobkin, Leah, 105, 108, 120, 130

Doughty, Paul, 170n8

Douglas, Mary, 118

Durston, Alan, 166n5

Edelman, Marc, 27, 59, 172n4

education, children's, 50, 59–62, 112–113. *See also* health of Huanoquiteños

Egurén, Fernando, 35, 37, 176n6

engaged anthropology, 71–74. *See also* fieldwork, long-term; research, shifts in

Enríques, Renato Quispe, 71

entrepreneurial ventures, Huanoquite, 23, 39, 48–49, 64–68. *See also* grassroots initiatives

Espinar (province), 146, 154, 176n4

Estrada, Rigoberto, 88, 96, 112–113, 169n4

extraction, 145–150, 152, 177n14; affective dimensions of, 5, 137, 164; autonomy and, 5, 148, 159, 164; ILO 169 and, 146–148; intangible zones and, 149–150, 177n9; production and, 6, 16; state rhetoric and, 11, 54–55, 137. *See also* mines and mining concessions

Fajardo-Gonzalez, Joanna, 112, 172n5

fieldwork, long-term, 6, 19–21, 164, 167n13, 169n2; migration and, 19; Peruvian civil war and, 19. *See also* engaged anthropology; research, shifts in

Fine-Dare, Kathleen, 72, 167n13

Fischer, Edward, 12

Flores Ochoa, Jorge, 170n2

Food and Agriculture Organization (FAO), 15, 110, 136–137

food culture, 109, 118–119, 174n5; aesthetics and, 25, 110, 139; Indigenous feeding and, 127–128, 132–134, 144, 174n8; politics and, 5–6, 13–14, 119, 133–138, 163, 166n7, 173n7; quinoa consumption in, 113, 121–125, 133; rituals in, 125, 126*f*, 133; tastes in, 15, 90, 109, 119–121, 124, 132, 134, 171n12. *See also* cosmology; labor parties; quinoa, meanings associated with; quinoa promotion

food landscapes, 109–110, 118–119, 132–134;

food security, 15, 132; global markets and, 24, 110–111, 114–116, 172n5; quinoa promotion and, 136, 169n4; sustainability and, 99, 108–112

food sovereignty, 24, 97n5, 114–116, 142, 172n3. *See also* agrobiodiversity; interculturality

food systems, 114, 118, 142, 173n2

Fraser, Nancy, 55

Fujimori, Alberto, 34, 47

Fund for Social Energy Inclusion (FISE), 59–60

García, María Elena, 57, 170n6, 173n1; on gastropolitics, 119, 135, 139–140, 175n16

gastronomic revolution, 111, 135, 138–143, 173n1

Gastropolitics and the Specter of Race: Stories of Capital, Culture, and Coloniality in Peru (García), 119, 175n16

gender, 74; development and, 11–12, 16, 55; food culture and, 13, 118–119; labor and, 83, 91, 127–129; quinoa promotion and, 130–132, 142, 160. *See also* sexism; women's labor; women's labor, development and; women's rights

geography of Andean region, 6, 32, 167n1, 171n3; precious metals in, 2, 55, 146, 151–152, 169n8; quinoa production and, 77, 82, 112–113; rivers and lakes in, 151–153

Index

germplasm banks, 15, 106, 110, 160, 166n8, 172n2. *See also* biopiracy; quinoa, kinds of

Gitter, Seth, 112, 172n5

globalization, 27, 99, 103, 143, 163; germplasm banks and, 106–107; local knowledge and, 14, 24–25; moral discourses and, 12; story-telling and, 26

global markets. *See* markets, global

Goldbeck, David, 104

Goldbeck, Nicki, 104

Goldstein, Daniel, 72

Gondorillos, Humberto, 105

Gorriti, Gustavo, 167n2

Gose, Peter, 19, 177n13

government programs, 59–63, 80, 112, 169n2, 170n5. *See also* development

Graham, Laura, 166n6

grassroots initiatives, 23, 62–69, 73, 131, 170n6; cheesemaking, 64–65, 131; fishfarming, 65–66; irrigation, 23, 68, 71; women and, 66–68. *See also* development; entrepreneurial ventures, Huanoquite; women's labor, development and

Guzman, Abimael, 35

Hale, Charles, 72

Hall, Amy Cox, 142–143

Harris, Olivia, 11

Harvey, Penny, 44, 54

Haugerud, Angelique, 27, 59

health, western conceptions of: microproperties of foods in, 60, 77, 105, 109, 124; miracle foods in, 14, 60–61, 113, 124; superfoods in, 14–15, 61, 104–105, 132, 160. *See also* quinoa consumption

health of Huanoquiteños: anemia and, 60–61; children's nutrition and, 60–61, 112–113, 120, 169n4; education and, 50, 59–62, 112–113; mothers and, 61; poverty and, 59, 61, 63, 110; protein and, 3, 14, 60, 98, 105, 109, 124; quinoa promotion and, 120, 132, 136–137. *See also allin kawsachun*; quinoa consumption; reciprocity; wellbeing of Huanoquiteños

Herrera Catari, Hugo, 39, 50–51

Hetherington, Kregg, 54, 169n2

Hirsch, Eric, 16, 166n7

Hold Life Has, The (Allen), 47

Holgado, Juvenal, 90–91

Huancaro Agricultural Fair, 94–95, 100, 101*f*; Huanoquite marketing and, 68, 78, 113, 131; road improvement and, 47–48, 51

Huanoquite (district), 6, 7*m*; communities of, 8*m*, 46*m*, 152; cultivator associations in, 52, 88, 100–101, 130, 141; digital communications in, 22, 48–49, 53, 73, 117; discourse of communities in, 69–71; diversity in, 57; generational relationships in, 20–21, 40, 53, 63; mobility of, 53–54, 61, 63–64, 70, 159; narrative culture in, 150–157, 177n10; Quechua language in, 6, 166n5, 177n10; rituals and festivals in, 125, 126*f*, 133, 174nn8–9; wealth disparity in, 39–40, 53, 90, 114–115, 143. *See also* autonomy; cosmology; labor parties

Huayhua, Margarita, 166n5

Humala, Ollanta, 92–93, 107

Ilizarbe, Carmen, 148–149

Indigeneity and non-Indigeneity, 9–11, 56–57. *See also* racism

Indigeneity and peasants, 11, 27, 32–33, 63, 146–147, 176nn6–7

indigenismo, 176n8

Indigenous Life Projects and Extractivism: Ethnographies from South America (Rivera Andía and Ødegaard), 56–57

INEI (National Institute of Statistics and Information), 172n5

infrastructure. *See* roads and road improvement

INIA. *See* National Institute of Agricultural Innovation

intangible zones, 149–150, 177n9. *See also* development; extraction

interculturality, 21, 115, 158. *See also* agrobiodiversity; food sovereignty

International Labor Organization Convention 169 (ILO 169), 146–148

International Monetary Fund (IMF), 13

International Year of Quinoa (AIQ), 4, 92–93, 136–137

Interoceanic Highway, 44

Index

irrigation, 6, 33, 58, 63, 154, 177n12; cosmology and, 26, 151–154; grassroots initiatives for, 23, 68, 71

Jackson, Jean, 141
Jacobsen, Sven-Erik, 107
Jones, Kyle, 166n7

kañiwa (native crop), 60, 88, 98
Kimura, Aya Hirata, 14–15, 60, 124
Kinsella, Kevin, 173n6
kiwicha (native crop), 60, 98, 113, 129, 174n6
Klarén, Peter, 167n1
Knox, Hannah, 44, 54
Krögel, Alison, 109, 118

labor parties, 83–86, 125; exchange practices in in, 66, 83, 97t, 171n9, 174n5; women and, 25, 83, 97n3, 127–129, 171n6. *See also* chicha (beer); women's labor
Lamphere, Louise, 167n13
landed estate owners (hacendados), 6, 17, 71; agrarian reform and, 31–33, 90; Catholicism and, 49, 165n1; road improvement and, 43–44
land tenure, 19, 24, 32, 35, 72f; colonialism and, 151, 168n4; land titling and, 22, 33–40 *passim*, 148, 176n7; memory and changes in, 40; neoliberalism and, 22, 36–37, 39, 170n8; in usufruct, 33, 176n7. *See also* agrarian reform (1969); agrarian reform, reversals of
Larson, Brooke, 11
Lassiter, Luke, 72
Lasswell, Harold, 170n8
Lauer, Mirko, 140
Law 29785 (on Indigenous state participation), 147
Law of Agrarian Development, 34
legal status of Huanoquiteños, 38–39, 168n4; agrarian reform and, 33–35, 147, 176n7, 177n9; biopiracy and, 106–108; mining concessions and, 146–150; neoliberalism and, 38–42, 146–149. *See also* Peasant Communities
Linebaugh, Peter, 175n2
Low, Setha, 72

machinery, industrial, 35, 51–52; quinoa production and, 67, 86–90, 87f
Mannheim, Bruce, 166n5
markets, global, 5, 15; food security and, 24, 110–111, 114–116, 172n5; Indigenous consumption of quinoa and, 108–113, 114, 127; organic certification and, 88, 111–112, 136; quinoa boom and, 92–94, 98, 112–113, 143, 172n5; wholesalers and, 51. *See also* neoliberalism; quinoa boom
markets, local. *see* Huancaro Agricultural Fair; quinoa marketing
Markowitz, Lisa, 141, 166n7
Maska (community), 36
Matos Mar, José, 31
Matta, Raúl, 135, 166n7, 173n1, 175n16
Mayer, Enrique, 31, 90
McDonell, Emma, 60–61, 172n2
McMichael, Philip, 172n4
Mejía, José Manuel, 31
Merry, Sally, 72
mestizo identity, 139, 142
mines and mining concessions, 4, 16, 26, 145–158, 177nn14–15; agriculture and, 2, 145, 150; cosmology and, 151–154, 177n15; environmental degradation and, 127; legal backing, 34–35, 145–150; road improvement and, 48, 175n3; scope of, 176n4. *See also* extraction; neoliberalism
Ministry of Agriculture and Irrigation (MINAGRI), 80, 118, 132, 136–137, 143
Ministry of Foreign Trade and Tourism (MINCETUR), 111, 118, 133. *See also* Commission for the Promotion of Peru for Export and Tourism (PROMPERÚ)
Mintz, Sidney, 118
Mistura celebration, 138–140, 142
Mistura: The Power of Food (Pérez), 139, 175n16
Mitchell, William, 167n13
mobility, 52–53, 61, 63–64, 70, 159
Morales Bermúdez, Francisco, 34
Murra, John, 90

National Institute of Agricultural Innovation (INIA), 80, 86–89, 92, 96–98, 100; on agrobiodiversity, 110

Index

National Institute of Statistics and Information (INEI), 172n5

National University of San Antonio Abad of Cusco (UNSAAC), 77, 170n2

Nature and Culture (Pilgrim and Pretty), 24–25

neoliberalism, 5, 13–14, 16, 24, 176n8, 177n14; decentralization and, 35, 39, 47; legal status of Huanoquiteños and, 38–42, 146–149; quinoa promotion and, 136–137, 140–143; road improvement and, 44–45, 47, 53–55. *See also* agrarian reform, reversals of; markets, global

new rurality, 176n6. *See also* agriculture, Huanoquite

nongovernmental organizations (NGOs), 56–63, 132. *See also* development

non-Indigenous brokers, 20, 90–92, 95, 171n8. *See also* landed estate owners

Nuñez Palomino, Pedro Germán, 176n7

Nyéléni Declaration of Food Sovereignty (2007), 114–115. *See also* food sovereignty

Ødegaard, Cecilie, 56–57

Ofstehage, Andrew, 79, 98–99, 121, 171n4

Olivera Ayme, Adrian Wendell, 88, 98, 112–113, 130

De Ollas y Sueños: Cooking Up Dreams (Cabellos), 139

organic certification: agriculture and, 82, 94–95, 98, 101, 112; global markets and, 88, 111–112, 136

Orlove, Benjamin, 44–45

Orta, Andrew, 177n13

Otero, Gerardo, 172n4

pachakuti (cataclysmic upheaval), 155

Pachamama Raymi (NGO), 59, 68

Palmer, David, 167n2

Palomino, Nunez, 34

patron-clientelism, 50–51, 92, 165n1

Paz Flores, Percy, 170n2

Peasant Communities, 33–35, 38, 146–147, 176n7, 177n9

peasants and Indigeneity, 11, 27, 32–33, 63, 114–115, 146–147, 176nn6–7

Pechlaner, Gabriela, 172n4

Pérez, Patricia, 139, 175n16

Peru's Ministry of Health (MINSA), 169n4

Peruvian civil war (1980–1992), 19–20, 139, 142, 168n5; cosmology and, 156–157; reversals of agrarian reform and, 34–35

Peruvian Society of Gastronomy (APEGA), 138

Peruvian state. *See* development; extraction; neoliberalism; politics; state power

p'esqe (quinoa and cheese soup), 122–124, 133

Pilgrim, Sarah, 24–25

plant racism, 80, 104, 119, 171n6. *See also* racism

politics, 2, 37, 158; borderlands knowledge and, 26, 52, 55, 113; community meetings and, 69–72, 159; mines and mining concessions and, 145–150, 169n8; non-Indigenous brokers and, 90–92; progressive corporativism and, 54–55; role of narratives in, 151–157. *See also* cosmopolitics

Poole, Deborah, 149, 167n2

Powęska, Radoslaw, 148–150

pragmatic spirituality, 16–19, 26, 144, 150, 159, 163–164. *See also* cosmopolitics

Pretty, Jules, 24–25

Programa Juntos (development project), 59, 61–62

progressive corporatism, 54–55

PROMPERÚ. *See* Commission for the Promotion of Peru for Export and Tourism

protein, 3, 14, 60, 98, 105, 109, 124. *See also* health, western conceptions of; health of Huanoquiteños

Qali Warma (development project), 59, 61

Qaranqa (lakes), 151

QCA. *See* Quinoa Cultivators Association

Qenqonay (village), 152–153, 157–158

Quechua (language), use of, 6, 10, 166n5, 167n3, 175n15

Quijano, Anibal, 11

quinoa, kinds of, 77, 95*f*; black quinoa, 79, 93–94, 100, 122; germplasm banks and, 15, 106, 110, 160, 166n8, 172n2; mixing in, 95, 120–122; saponin and, 82, 96, 122; varieties and landraces and, 15, 103–104, 110, 171n1; in western consumption, 119–121, 174nn10–11; yellow quinoa, 94, 122

198

Index

quinoa, meanings associated with, 12–13, 106; cosmology and, 119, 129, 132–134; gastronomic revolution and, 111, 132, 138–143, 173n1; magical properties, 79–80, 119, 136, 171nn4–5; origin narratives and, 79, 171nn4–5; in Peruvian state campaigns, 120, 135–137, 142–143; racism and, 79, 106, 112; Spanish colonial, 80, 118, 171n5; strength and intelligence, 129–130, 132, 136, 160–161; western superfood, 14–15, 61, 104–105, 113, 132, 160. *See also* food culture; health, western conceptions of; health of Huanoquiteños; quinoa consumption; well-being of Huanoquiteños

Quinoa, the Supergrain (Wood), 104–105

quinoa boom (2013–2018), 3, 80–82, 86–90, 99–100; global markets and, 92–94, 98, 112–113, 143; Indigenous consumption and, 108–113, 172n5. *See also* quinoa marketing

quinoa consumption, 80, 120–133, 133n2; charismatic nutrients and, 14, 124; food security and, 24, 108–112; poverty and, 59, 61, 63, 110; preparation methods and, 121, 124–125, 131, 133–135, 140; quinoa boom and, 108–113, 172; rituals and, 124–125, 126f, 133; western consumption and, 120–125; women's preparation of, 25, 109, 113, 119, 124, 131, 161. *See also* chicha (beer); health, western conceptions of; health of Huanoquiteños; labor parties; quinoa, meanings associated with; well-being of Huanoquiteños

quinoa cultivation, 77–86, 89, 96, 119, 130, 171n7; cultivation, 77–82, 89, 96, 119, 130, 171n7; geography of Andean region and, 77, 82, 112–113; harvesting in, 83–84, 85f; Incas and, 79–80; Indigenous knowledge exchange and, 100, 142; intercropping in, 80–81, 129, 161; organic certification and, 82, 94–95, 98, 101, 112; pesticides and, 95, 101; processing in, 67, 78, 86–90, 87f, 98; revenue and expenses in, 97t; storage in, 93; technology in, 67, 86–90, 87f. *See also* agriculture, Huanoquite; germplasm banks

Quinoa Cultivators Association (QCA), 16, 37, 39, 52; collaboration among, 52,

94–96, 100, 131; quinoa boom and, 86–90, 92. *See also* Bonett Béjar, Rolando

quinoa defined, 3, 77, 170n1

quinoa marketing, 92–99; food security and, 108–112; global markets and, 3, 92–94, 98, 112–113, 143, 172n5; Huancaro Agricultural Fair and, 78, 94, 95f, 100, 131; Indigenous knowledge exchange and, 100, 142; split economy and, 9, 98–99, 165n2. *See also* quinoa boom

quinoa promotion, 4, 14–15, 102, 119–121; agrobiodiversity and, 120, 132, 136, 147; gastronomic revolution and, 111, 135, 138–143, 173n1; Indigenous representation in, 13, 132, 173n1, 176n8; nationalism and, 120, 142–143; Peruvian state campaigns, 120, 135–137, 169n4; women and, 120, 124, 130, 132, 142. *See also* Commission for the Promotion of Peru for Export and Tourism (PROMPERÚ); National Institute of Agricultural Innovation (INIA)

Quispe Enríques, Renato, 71, 100

Quispicanchis (province), 176n4

racism, 21, 32, 34, 57, 89, 118; autonomy and, 27, 55, 64, 163; development and, 12, 14, 60, 74; gastronomic revolution and, 139–140; meanings associated with quinoa and, 24, 79, 104, 106, 112; non-Indigenous Peruvians and, 10, 30, 45, 89–91, 175n15; quinoa promotion and, 137, 141–142; sexism and, 137, 141, 174n14. *See also* plant racism

Radcliffe, Sarah, 169n1

Rappaport, Joanne, 72

reciprocity, 71, 125, 136; reciprocal relationships and, 16–18, 40, 83, 174n5. *See also* health of Huanoquiteños; well-being of Huanoquiteños

Rediker, Marcus, 175n2

El Región. *See* Cusco Regional Government

Reichman, Daniel, 111

Rénique, Gerardo, 167n2

representation of Indigenous culture, 13, 132, 173n1, 176n8

research, shifts in, 19, 27, 72–73, 167n13. *See also* engaged anthropology; fieldwork, long-term

Index

reversals of agrarian reform. *See* agrarian reform, reversals of

Rivera Andía, Juan Javier, 56–57, 60

roads and road improvement, 43–55, 46*m*; colonialism and, 43–44, 168n1; Huanoquiteños' response to, 22–23, 48–52; Inca road, 22, 43–44, 55, 151–152, 168n1, 169n8; infrastructure and, 22, 52; mining concessions and, 48, 53–54, 146, 148, 169n8; mobility and, 53–54; neoliberalism and, 44–45, 47, 53–55, 137; networking and, 52; road accidents and fatalities, 22, 101, 168n2, 169n8, 175n3; tourism and, 48–49. *See also* mines and mining concessions; mobility; tourism

Rojas, Wilfredo, 15

Rojas-Pérez, Isaias, 167n2

Rosa Araoz, Carmen, 170n2

Salas Carreño, Guillermo, 177n9

Sammells, Clare, 142, 166n7

Sapiens (ed. Colwell), 174n11

saponin, 161; kinds of quinoa and, 82, 96, 122; removal of, 67, 88–90; uses for, 78, 130–131

Sax, Marieka, 132, 134

Seligmann, Linda, 11, 31–32, 58, 144, 151, 167n2, 168n1, 176n8

sexism: development and, 59, 61–62; disregard of women's labor, 13, 59, 72, 73–74, 89; racism and, 137, 141, 174n14. *See also* women's labor, development and

Shepherd, Christopher, 63, 115–116

Shining Path movement, 35, 47, 59, 168n3

Siete Semillas (government program), 113

Silverstein, Sydney, 129–130

Skarbø, Kristine, 110

social welfare programs. *See* development

Solano, Pedro, 177n9

Starn, Orin, 167n2

state power, 48, 54–55, 148. *See also* audit culture

Stein, William, 170n8

Stengers, Isabelle, 166n9

Stensrud, Astrid, 115

Stephen, Lynn, 72

Stern, Steve, 167n2

story-telling, 150–154

superfood, quinoa as, 14–15, 61, 104–105, 132, 160

sustainability, 99, 108, 110–112, 114

Tapia, Mario, 105

tarwi (native crop), 82, 95, 98, 100, 113, 133, 171n12

Tihuicte (cooperative), 33, 35–36, 65, 159

tourism, 5, 16, 133–134; archaeology and, 48–49, 133, 138, 170n6; gastronomic revolution and, 26, 111, 135, 138–143, 173n1; Huanoquiteños' participation in, 10, 48–49, 69, 138, 142, 170n7; Indigenous images and, 13; women's rights and, 73–74, 137, 142. *See also* Commission for the Promotion of Peru for Export and Tourism (PROMPERÚ); National Institute of Agricultural Innovation (INIA); women's rights

Truth and Reconciliation Commission of Peru (CVR), 168n3

UNSAAC (National University of San Antonio Abad of Cusco), 77, 170n2

Urban Mountain Beings (Fine-Dare), 167n13

Urdanivia, Claudia, 171n1

Van der Ploeg, Jan, 115

Vaso de Leche (development project), 59–60, 64

Velasco Alvarado, Juan, 32, 34

Verniau, Alexis, 107

Via Campesina, 114

Wachtel, Nathan, 177n13

Wade, Peter, 11

Weismantel, Mary, 118, 156, 166n7, 177n13

well-being of Huanoquiteños, 5–6; development and, 24–25, 56, 115–116, 173n6; economic and non-economic forces and, 102, 142; environmental conditions and, 99, 125, 127; food sovereignty and, 115–116; imbalances in, 144; non-Indigenous cultures of well-being and, 125, 127, 141; reciprocal relationships in cosmos and, 16–19, 125, 126*f*, 132; women and, 13. *See also* cosmology; health of Huanoquiteños

Wenner-Gren Foundation, 174n11

women's labor, 13, 66–68, 174n7; chicha preparation by, 171n6; disregard of, 13, 59, 72, 73–74, 89; equality, in cultivation tasks, 89, 119, 130; food preparation, 25, 109, 119, 124, 131; labor parties, 25, 83, 97t, 127, 171n6; quinoa promotion by, 137, 142

women's labor, development and: disregard of, 89–91; mistreatment, 86; reliance on, 14, 25, 61–62, 130, 132; surveillance of, 68. *See also* development

women's rights, 60, 69, 91; Peruvian tourism and, 73–74, 137, 142

Wood, Rebecca, 104–105

World Bank, 13

Zonas Intangibles (law), 149–150, 158, 177n9. *See also* development; extraction

LINDA J. SELIGMANN is Professor Emerita of Anthropology at George Mason University. Her books include *Broken Links, Enduring Ties: American Adoption across Race, Class, and Nation; Between Reform and Revolution: Political Struggles in the Peruvian Andes;* and *Peruvian Street Lives: Culture, Power, and Economy among Market Women of Cuzco.*

INTERPRETATIONS OF CULTURE IN THE NEW MILLENNIUM

Peruvian Street Lives: Culture, Power, and Economy among Market Women of Cuzco
  Linda J. Seligmann
The Napo Runa of Amazonian Ecuador *Michael Uzendoski*
Made-from-Bone: Trickster Myths, Music, and History from the Amazon
  Jonathan D. Hill
Ritual Encounters: Otavalan Modern and Mythic Community *Michelle Wibbelsman*
Finding Cholita *Billie Jean Isbell*
East African Hip Hop: Youth Culture and Globalization *Mwenda Ntarangwi*
Sarajevo: A Bosnian Kaleidoscope *Fran Markowitz*
Becoming Mapuche: Person and Ritual in Indigenous Chile *Magnus Course*
Kings for Three Days: The Play of Race and Gender in an Afro-Ecuadorian Festival
  Jean Muteba Rahier
Maya Market Women: Power and Tradition in San Juan Chamelco, Guatemala
  S. Ashley Kistler
Victims and Warriors: Violence, History, and Memory in Amazonia *Casey High*
Embodied Protests: Emotions and Women's Health in Bolivia *Maria Tapias*
Street Life under a Roof: Youth Homelessness in South Africa *Emily Margaretten*
Reinventing Chinese Tradition: The Cultural Politics of Late Socialism *Ka-ming Wu*
Cape Verde, Let's Go: Creole Rappers and Citizenship in Portugal *Derek Pardue*
The Street Is My Pulpit: Hip Hop and Christianity in Kenya *Mwenda Ntarangwi*
Cultural Heritage in Mali in the Neoliberal Era *Rosa De Jorio*
Somalis Abroad: Clan and Everyday Life in Finland *Stephanie R. Bjork*
Hierarchies of Care: Girls, Motherhood, and Inequality in Peru *Krista E. Van Vleet*
Remaking Muslim Lives: Everyday Islam in Postwar Bosnia and Herzegovina
  David Henig
Quinoa: Food Politics and Agrarian Life in the Andean Highlands *Linda J. Seligmann*

The University of Illinois Press
is a founding member of the
Association of University Presses.

University of Illinois Press
1325 South Oak Street
Champaign, IL 61820-6903
www.press.uillinois.edu